Happy Birthday to Gertrude .

    + Many More .

        Love.

           Marian + Sid -

12/18/49

No Cause For Alarm

NO CAUSE FOR ALARM

VIRGINIA COWLES

"We are now come, or coming fast, to a time when Labour laws will be made by Labour... Personally I can discern no cause for alarm in this prospect..."

Extract from a letter written by Lord Randolph Churchill to Arnold White in 1892.

HARPER & BROTHERS
NEW YORK

To My Tory Father

So MANY people have helped me in collecting material for this book it is not possible to name them all. But I particularly wish to thank Mrs. Margaret Cole and Professor Denis Brogan for reading large portions of the manuscript and making many valuble suggestions. I also wish to thank my husband, Aidan Crawley, who has helped me most of all.

V. C.

CONTENTS

Contents

Introduction

TO FOREIGNERS Britain often appears as a land of curious and baffling contradiction. It is a land where the King reigns but has no power; where trade union leaders can become knights and Old Etonians can become Labor ministers; where the constitution is strictly observed but remains unwritten; where money makes a gentleman but a gentleman is often ashamed of making money; where it is possible for democracy to flourish under an oligarchy and a class system to exist under socialism.

The key that unlocks these paradoxes is a further paradox: it is a sense of order. No country places such emphasis on historical continuity as Britain, and as a result new ideas are never allowed to wipe out old institutions but are gently grafted on to them.

The many changes taking place today therefore can be understood only against the background which has given rise to them. But the extent of these changes should not be underestimated. As a famous Englishman wrote:

> The Labour community is carrying on at the present day a very significant and instructive struggle. It has emancipated itself very largely from the mere mechanism of party politics; it realizes that it now possesses political power to such an extent as to make it independent of either party in the state; and the struggle which it is now carrying on is less against Capital, less one of wages or division of profits, but rather one for the practical utilization in its own interest of the great political power it has acquired. The Labour interest is now seeking to do what the landed interest and the manufacturing capitalist interest did for themselves when each in turn commanded the disposition of State policy. Our land laws were framed by the landed interest

for the advantage of the landed interest, and foreign policy was directed by that interest to the same end. Political power passed very considerably from the landed interest to the manufacturing capitalist interest, and our whole fiscal system was shaped by this latter power to its own advantage, foreign policy being also made to coincide. We are now come, or coming fast, to a time when Labour laws will be made by the Labour interest for the advantage of Labour. . . . Personally I can discern no cause for alarm in this prospect. . . .*

That the present struggle was foreseen nearly sixty years ago, by Winston Churchill's father, is some indication that in Britain change is a growth rather than a cataclysm. In writing this book, therefore, I have humbly attempted to analyze the present experiment in social democracy without removing it from its context.

The importance of this experiment should not be underrated, for, as the English know, it is impossible to turn the clock back. No matter which party wins the next General Election the present trend is bound to continue. And if Britain succeeds in uniting Europe in the next twenty-five years, the pattern which she is now seeking for herself may become the design for Western civilization.

London, March, 1949   VIRGINIA COWLES

* Extract from a letter written by Lord Randolph Churchill to Arnold White in 1892, as quoted in Winston Churchill, *Lord Randolph Churchill* (1906). Reprinted by permission of Winston Churchill.

No Cause For Alarm

CHAPTER 1

The English Scene, 1949

Oh! What a snug little Island,
A right little, tight little Island!
—THOMAS DIBDIN, 1800

BEFORE the war Britain was as fascinating as the pictures in a child's storybook. When you thought of England you thought of the scarlet tunics of the guards at Buckingham Palace; the bright doublets of the Beefeaters at the Tower of London; the top-hatted bank messengers hurrying through the narrow streets of the City; the flowing gowns and the gray frock coats at Ascot.

Although there were nearly two million unemployed out of a working population of sixteen million and the distressed areas were gray desolate patches of poverty, visitors did not usually go so far afield. To them England meant pubs and tea and thatched cottages, historic monuments, country houses, hunt breakfasts, debutantes with ostrich feathers in their hair, civil servants in pin-striped trousers, nurses pushing babies in prams with coronets on them.

As a nation she was prosperous. Her flag flew at the far

1

corners of the earth and her ships sailed all the seas. She wore proudly the independence of a thousand years and her parliamentary government and her system of justice were the envy of the world. She wielded great power and assumed great responsibility. Her prestige was unequaled; she was the Elder Statesman of Western civilization.

Then came the war and with a wave of the wand the color disappeared; the country lay beneath the gray-green of camouflage. Country houses were turned into schools and hospitals, motor cars came off the roads, parks were fenced in for antiaircraft batteries. Seventy-five percent of Britain's industrial power was converted to war production as the whole might of the nation was thrown into the struggle.

Life for civilians settled into a hard, monotonous routine. Food was severely rationed and consumers' goods were cut to bare necessities; even the beaches of the summer resorts were empty stretches hemmed in by barbed wire and marked by red letters saying: "Danger—Mines." There were few pleasures, and at night families waited anxiously behind darkened windows for the boom of Big Ben which announced the evening news; they listened in silence and when it ended there was comfort in the solemn, familiar strains of "God Save the King."

After six long years of sacrifice the floodlights were turned on Buckingham Palace. The struggle was over. On that warm summer evening thousands flocked across the Mall to cheer the King and Queen. And as the Queen stood on the balcony dressed in a white gown, the diamonds in her tiara sparkling in the light, it seemed as though she had stepped out of splendor England had left behind to greet the new day that had come.

That new day has fashioned a Britain that is a strange mixture of peace and war. The nation still faces peril and is still fighting, but this time for its economic survival. Stripped by two world conflicts of the foreign investments that once tipped the balance toward prosperity, Britain must now produce a volume of goods 60 percent greater than ever before in order to provide her fifty million people with an adequate standard of life. She is galvanized to a purpose almost as intense as during the war. Workers seeking new employment are directed to essential industries, and unmarried women between eighteen and forty who want work must register at the Labor Exchange where they are told what jobs are most urgent. Priority in housing is given to miners and agricultural laborers, and the public is urged to put its money in the bank while British goods flow across the seas, marked "Export Only."

No country has ever been more thoroughly grounded in economics. Industrial targets are front-page news, politicians hammer home the slogan that more from each is more for all; hoardings in all the big cities cry out: "Jobs . . . The danger to full employment is not producing too much but too little— and too dear." Last Christmas when records were broken by coal miners, wool makers, and cotton weavers the *Daily Express* ran a banner headline saying: THANK YOU, EVERYBODY.

And yet, in spite of the austerity that frowns down like a severe schoolmaster, many familiar scenes are returning. While the Ministry of Food advertises new ways to dish up the national diet of cod and herring, Parliament opens in customary splendor with peeresses in diamonds and full evening dress at ten o'clock in the morning; while thousands still live in overcrowded conditions the Derby and the Grand National draw the largest throngs in history; while the cupboard shelves remain bare, and food, fuel, and gasoline are severely rationed, the seaside resorts have an unprecedented holiday boom. Scarlet uniforms are back again and flowers are growing in the parks; houses are being repainted, luxury hotels are filled with men and women in evening dress, and the King and Queen drive through London in a golden coach; the Lord Mayor holds his show again, country houses are occupied, and the fashionable world flocks to Ascot and Wimbledon and Lord's.

But is the old England returning? Beneath the struggle for recovery in which the nation is united there is another struggle in which the nation is divided. Values are being revised; new institutions are transplanting old ones; wealth and power are changing hands.

The internal conflict is slow and persistent and revolves inside the effort for recovery like a wheel within a wheel. It is co-ordinated so closely with the national effort that if Britain succeeds in re-establishing herself, and one day leads a united Europe of 250 million people, it may well be that she will again give the democratic world a new pattern of society. Britain is not groping for the past. Vigor runs through her veins and adventure is in the air; history is being made.

If you were English and you had a wife and two children to support, and a job that paid you the equivalent of $6,000 a year, what sort of life would you lead? British taxes are the highest in the world, with a standard rate of nine shillings in the pound or 45 cents out of every dollar. Added to this, surtax begins on $8,000 incomes, rising gradually until at $20,000 the total tax payable is $2.70 out of every $4.00.* However, on your $6,000-a-year salary you would have allowances for marriage, children, and earned income; you would pay $1,500 and have $86.55 a week to spend.

Your luxuries would depend almost entirely on whether or not you were living in a house which you had rented before or during the war. In 1939 a small unfurnished house within an hour of London would have cost no more than $6.00 or $8.00 a week, and since rents on unfurnished houses are controlled you would not be paying more today. But if you had married since the war, housing would be your most difficult problem. Luck seems to play an important part. Some people have found suburban houses ranging from $8.00 to $18.00 a week; others have had to pay $24.00 a week, which is a high rent for England. In London houses rent for $40 or $50 and large, comfortable flats in a fashionable area are sometimes as high as $100. The house that you might find for $16 a week would probably have three or four bedrooms, two sitting rooms, a dining room, kitchenette and bath, a garden and perhaps a garage. It would

---

* Anyone with an income of over $80,000 a year pays a tax of 19/6 in the pound; surtax levels the highest incomes to about $20,000 a year.

not have central heating, and electric fires and an electric stove would average over the year about $4.00 a week. Your wife would find that her food bills averaged $4.00 per head per week, and if she wanted someone to come in every day to clean it would cost $6.00, or if she had a resident cook $12. You would be able to get a two-course lunch every day in London of meat and two vegetables and a dessert for 60 cents, and your train fare for the week would come to $1.50, but this would be charged against income tax. If you owned a car your garage bill would average about $2.50. A deduction from your salary each week of 98 cents would entitle you to benefits including sickness, old age, and unemployment besides giving all members of your family the right to free medical care and free dentistry; it would also enable you to draw $1.00 a week for your second child.

These expenses would come to $47 a week. You would have $39 left for telephone, incidentals, clothes, and amusements. Luxuries are expensive. Cigarettes cost 70 cents a pack and are in short supply; whisky and gin are $6.00 a bottle. On the other hand, the best seats at an evening performance at a London theater cost only $3.00. And you would find that you and your family would be able to spend a two-weeks holiday at the sea at a good boardinghouse for $100. You would undoubtedly consider it a hardship that you were allowed only six gallons of gasoline a month for your car (English cars run about thirty miles to the gallon) and that you had to eke out a coal and coke ration of a ton and a half for the six winter months. Although clothes rationing has been lifted, your wife would complain loudly about the prices.

Her greatest worry, however, would be food. On each of her four ration books she would be allowed only 20 cents' worth of meat a week, only half a pound of sugar, fourteen ounces of butter and margarine, one-half pint of milk a day for the adults and one pint for the children. You would have a roast once a week of your combined meat rations, eat what was left the following day, and the rest of the week exist on fish. Occasionally you might be lucky enough to buy a chicken or a duck (poultry and game are unrationed) at the controlled price of about 60 cents per pound.

Your major worries of housing and food would be less acute outside the London area. If your job were in Bristol, Edinburgh, or any of the big cities, you would have little difficulty in finding a comfortable house for half what you paid in the London area. You would probably have a large enough garden to grow your own vegetables, which would cut down your food bills, and if you lived in a country village within commuting distance of a city you would be able to raise your own chickens and ducks and you could kill a pig every six months. Food would cease to be a major worry.

However, English people who remember what the equivalent of $6,000 a year brought them before the war find life very hard. In 1938 their taxes were only $881. They fed not adequately but well on $4.00 per week per head. Cigarettes were 25 cents a package; whisky $2.50. They could rent a good house or a large flat in London for $12 a week. They could have a cook and a nurse for wages of $6.00 each; someone would come in and clean for 20 cents an hour.

Life was agreeable and easy, and the people earning anything from $4,000 to $8,000 a year were often described as the backbone of England. They were the middle classes: the civil servants, professors, shop proprietors, journalists, army and naval officers, editors, doctors, junior ministers of the Crown. And these are the people most discontented in England today—who feel the taxation most and who have had to reduce their standard of living the most.

On the other hand, many sections of the working and lower middle classes are better off than before the war. First of all there is less unemployment in the whole of Britain than in the state of New York alone. Secondly, there is national insurance which, for a dollar a week, insures all wage earners against unemployment, sickness, and old age. Thirdly, there is a free medical service. Fourthly, although many workers are still living in overcrowded conditions, three out of every four houses which are being built are for rent, not for sale, which puts them within the reach of the lowest incomes. Houses ranging from two to four bedrooms, with sitting room, bath, and kitchenette equipped with a refrigerator, cost from $4.00 to $7.00 a week, or about one-fifth of a worker's weekly income. Houses are allotted by local councils from a waiting list on a basis of strict priority. What workingmen complain of most is the price of beer, which has been doubled since prewar days, and the exorbitant tax on cigarettes, which was deliberately slapped on by the Chancellor of the Exchequer to cut down tobacco consumption because of the dollar shortage.

But what about the pleasures of life? For me, England has still the same magic it always had. First of all, it has London, and as Dr. Johnson once said: "Sir, the happiness of London is not to be conceived but by those who have been in it." London lacks the beauty of Rome and the grace of Paris, but it has a quality of sheer fabulousness which stems from the fact that its history is not a dead, detached thing but part of the very blood that flows through its arteries; its King still lives in Buckingham Palace; its great men are still buried in Westminster Abbey; its barristers still eat dinners at the Inns of Court; its politicians still walk across Westminster Hall where Parliament first met six and a half centuries ago. Even the yard where M.P.'s park their cars has been a yard for a long, long time; it was named "New Palace Yard" in 1098 to distinguish it from the one that already existed.

Like all things English, London is a city of superb contradictions with narrow, twisting Elizabethan streets suddenly leading into spacious Georgian squares, with hideous Victorian mansions giving way to elegant Regency terraces. You cannot master directions by method but only by memory for the streets run higgledy-piggledy, this way and that, from the City to the Strand, from Bloomsbury where the writers live to the Isle of Dogs where the dockers live, from Soho with its foreign restaurants to Mayfair with its smart shops, from Kew famous for its gardens to Chelsea famous for its artists and custards and china and buns. Even the statues of its famous men seem to have been placed by a hand indifferent to order, with Oliver Cromwell standing in front of the Parliament he tried to destroy, and on a pinnacle high above all the other great men except Nelson, that legendary figure who was defeated in the Napoleonic war —"The grand old Duke of York, Who had ten thousand men, Who marched them up to the top of the hill, And marched them down again."

Despite the mediocre food in the restaurants and thin ale in the pubs, despite yawning craters and shabby house fronts, you can still see the best acting in the world at the Old Vic, or sample English humor at its most English at the Palladium; you can journey along the Thames on river ferries or travel an hour and a half from London for a day's punting on the Isis or the Cam; you can browse through the National Galleries or inspect the Crown jewels at the Tower of London or watch the greyhound racing at Wembley or stroll through the parks and listen to the Hyde Park orators; you can go to the Chelsea Arts Ball and the Aldershot Tattoo; you can watch the King on his birthday taking the salute at the trooping of the colors; you can line the streets for the Lord Mayor's Show, or line the riverbank for the Oxford-Cambridge boat race.

You can go fox hunting in the winter, fishing in the summer, and shooting from August to February; in any country area you can enjoy point-to-points, pubs, garden fetes, cricket, and bicycle trips along unspoiled roads; you can enjoy quaint houses, pretty gardens, and old churches and visit famous castles open to the public; and above all, you can enjoy the superb beauty of the countryside when spring turns the soft, rain-washed landscape into a world of bright and vigorous color.

In the summer you can spend a high-brow holiday at the Edinburgh Festival or a low-brow one at Blackpool; you can visit the Lake District or a Butlin camp, go to Cowes for the regatta or to Stratford-on-Avon for the Shakespeare plays. You can make an excursion to Ireland, the Isle of Wight, or the Channel Islands.

Yet what distinguishes life in Britain and makes it attractive to me is not its variety but its atmosphere—the fact that it has all the intimacy of a small nation but none of the provincialism. Whereas in America hundreds of areas are cut off by distance from the culture and advantages of the large cities, in Britain the whole nation shares the same events.

First of all, the newspapers are national, not local, and there is only one radio network, the B.B.C. Although newspaper opinions differ sharply, the same emphasis is placed on events whether foreign or domestic. Secondly, whatever people's political opinions, they are bound together by the activities of the royal family, which are given great publicity. Thirdly, the houses and the culture of the aristocracy are spread evenly throughout the land.

These are strong links but they are only the beginning. London plays are reproduced by repertory companies in many of the big cities, and cricket and football teams tour all parts of the country. And when the Grand National and the Derby are run, people arrive in special trains and charabancs from every part of Ireland, Scotland, Wales, and England. No one lives so far away that he cannot aspire to a trip to London or Edinburgh and even M.P.'s whose constituencies are farthest away can visit them several times a month.

These common threads produce an intimacy that runs right through English life. You see it reflected in London theaters, where people sit in their seats drinking tea and eating sugar buns even when the curtain has gone up; you see it at the opening of Mills Brothers' circus when Lord Burleigh makes a speech welcoming the lords, ladies, gentlemen, and children and Mr. Mills presents all the bareback riders, clowns, and trapeze artists with bunches of flowers after their acts. And you even see it in the political life of the country.

Although no nation is more experienced in political controversy than the British, public meetings usually have a cozy air of amateurishness. This is due to the fact that local parties are run by voluntary workers who have nothing to gain from victory except the excitement and the fun. The hall is usually cold, the

seats hard, and the table on the platform wobbly. Propaganda
leaflets are likely to arrive late and the microphone is likely to
break down. The man who stands at the door is usually on
familiar terms with most of the people who come in. The front
rows are always filled by the speaker's supporters and the seats
toward the back sprinkled with opponents who have come to
heckle; in the middle are those who are hoping for some fun.

But underneath the good-natured atmosphere opinions are
sharply divided and feelings run high. Today more people are
attending political meetings than ever before. Posters cry at
you all the way from city hoardings to village squares, and local
seats which before the war were unopposed are now hotly contested. The issues that grip the country are mainly domestic:
houses, prices, rationing, controls, and taxation.

Extreme statements such as the government claim that the
population is better fed than it was before the war and the Conservative claim that it is the worst-fed population in Europe
give plenty of scope within which to form one's own judgments.
And always present is the theme of freedom. Are the Socialists
curtailing it as the Conservatives claim, or extending it as the
government claims?

Many of the extravagant statements remind one of the fight
between New Dealers and conservatives when Roosevelt was
driving through his social legislation. Yet, although the changes
taking place in Britain are on a wider scale than in America the
bitterness is not so great. Political subjects are still argued on
their merits and personal attacks are always deplored. Some time
ago I attended a meeting held by the writer, Harold Nicholson,
who was fighting a by-election as a Socialist candidate. The
newspapers had made great play of the fact that his twenty-five-
year-old son, Nigel, had recently joined the Conservative party,
and at the end of Nicholson's speech a heckler rose and asked
him how he expected to convert outsiders when he had been
unable to convert his own son. Although the crowd was politically opposed to Nicholson, this was such an offense against
English good taste that cries of "Shame" and "Withdraw"
forced the interrupter to his seat.

The English scene is changing, but the English way of life remains; and what makes this way of life attractive is the character of the people.

CHAPTER 2

The English Character

You can beat your wife, you can go bankrupt,
you can run a bucket shop and the English will
still like you—But to bring the wrath of the pop-
ulace on your head—be impolite.

—HENRY JAMES

NO PEOPLE have more ardent admirers or more bitter detractors than the English. For centuries the complexities
of their character have been the subject of searching analysis.
Almost in the same breath they have been condemned for
coldness and lauded for restraint, criticized for their arrogance
and praised for their pride. They have been denounced as both
insular and interfering, and described as both ingenious and in-
genuous. As a people they are famous for minding their neighbors' affairs and as individuals for minding their own. No two
foreigners place the same emphasis on the same words, and a
Dutchman has cried out despairingly: "The English: Are they
human?"

What makes the English character appear so subtle and contradictory seems to arise from the curious line the Englishman
draws between the personal and the impersonal, the exact place
where conformity ends and individualism begins. In most countries so long as a man keeps within the law his principles are
the private concern of himself and his God, but in England they
are the concern of the nation as well.

Through the centuries England's survival has depended more
on the vigor of her people than on the superiority of her resources. She has needed to be served and served well. Public-
mindedness, therefore, has always been emphasized as a virtue.

But whereas other countries declare that virtue is its own reward the English have taken no chances. They have arranged a way of life in which virtue pays a higher return than in any other country in the world.

The subtlety of this arrangement has had a far-reaching effect on English values. Whereas in America money earns a man respect, in England it gives him the opportunity to earn respect; for the honors of the land are jealously reserved for those who directly serve it. This means that a naval officer has more prestige than a stockbroker, that a civil servant has more than a motorcar manufacturer, that a cabinet minister has more than a duke.

A successful career in the service of the state means a peerage or a knighthood but in the past it carried other benefits as well. For leading England's armies through Flanders John Churchill was created Duke of Marlborough and given a palace to live in; for defeating the French at Trafalgar Nelson's descendants were awarded a pension of £5,000 ($20,000)* a year, which is still being paid today.** After World War I Haig and Beatty were given gifts of £100,000 ($400,000). After World War II not only were all the prominent service chiefs raised to the peerage but cash awards were made to the three scientists who invented the device known as "the heart of radar" and to the inventors of the Bailey Bridge and the jet engine.

But honors are given not only for war service. Twice a year people from every walk of life and many professions including doctors, actors, scientists, and writers are singled out for awards. These awards are published in the newspapers and known as the New Year's Honors List and the King's Birthday List.

Almost all awards are made for public service, so much so that the famous Lord Melbourne many years ago loudly praised the Order of the Garter for having "no damn'd merit attached to it."

* Throughout the book, English currency has been converted at the rate of $4.00 to the pound, the approximate rate obtaining as this book goes to press.

** A bill recently passed in Parliament brings the pension to an end when the present recipient dies.

Because of the prestige that public service carries, there is a larger unpaid voluntary effort in Britain than in any other country in the world. In fact, the whole of local government runs on an amateur basis. British county councils, which correspond in activity and authority to the state governments of America, are composed of men and women who stand for election in the same way that American state senators do but who receive no salaries. This also applies to mayors and aldermen and all town and rural district councilors.

Today, besides local government representatives dozens of committees operate on a voluntary basis, many of which are so important that much of the legislation passed by the national government could not be carried out without their help. For example, during the war when food production was a vital necessity an act was passed declaring that any farmer who failed to produce a minimum amount of food owing to bad farming must be evicted from his land. Farmers were asked to serve on committees to see that this order was carried out. Today the law still stands, and farmers, landowners, and workers, who give their time on a voluntary basis, still enforce it.

In English public life character counts more than brains. It has always fascinated the French that England uses the word "clever" in a slightly derogatory sense. But this gives an impression which is only a half-truth, for many English politicians have taken first-class university honors, and the civil service boasts more names with academic distinctions than any other civil service in the world. What is true is that in the House of Commons brains alone will never take a man to the top, while character may. The "intellectual" who wishes to become a political leader must take care to establish his claim to other qualities as well, for the Englishman has an instinctive belief that brilliance and stability do not walk easily together, and stability is what he demands.

This is the reason facile lawyers often fail to make their mark in the House of Commons; the reason Sir Stafford Cripps, undoubtedly the intellectual superior of most of his colleagues, may never become Prime Minister; the reason Churchill has always been regarded with uneasiness in peacetime.

It is also the reason divorce remains a barrier to a public career. Politicians who have been named as guilty parties in divorce suits seldom receive high office; and with the rarest exception no divorced person may attend a function at Buckingham Palace or, for that matter, even have access to the Royal Enclosure at Ascot.

Stability, to the Englishman, implies restraint, and because of this, emotionalism is regarded as a weakness of character. Nothing embarrasses an Englishman more than an outpouring of the soul. Indeed, even when Edward VIII referred in his abdication speech to "the woman I love" a shudder went through the nation. This is why American plays and movies which stress the emotionalism of war are often unsuccessful in England; and why, inversely, the approach of a real-life crisis is usually greeted with such surprising calm. A year ago, when talk of a war with Russia was mounting, an American friend who was visiting London refused to believe that anyone was aware of the danger. "But the radio isn't making anything of it," she protested. "If this were America there would be 'flashes' every ten minutes." I assured my friend that she was mistaken and quoted the postmistress in a country village whose remark had summed up the English attitude: "There's nothing we can do about it, so what's the use of worrying?" I also tried to explain that to create agitation by radio bulletins would be regarded as a highly improper breach.

Boasting is not only frowned upon as a lack of restraint but considered an offense against good taste. The penalties it carries with it in the form of unpopularity are so severe that the Englishman has become famous as the master of understatement. War heroes seldom refer to their decorations, and boys who win distinctions at school sometimes do not even inform their parents. In political life, as well, modesty is thought so desirable that men like Attlee, who appear to have no personal ambition, are often the ones who climb to the top.

Public schools (the equivalent in America of private board-ing schools, such as Groton and St. Paul's) pay as much atten-tion to character as to scholarship. This is the reason such em-phasis is placed on games; the reason boys are expected to attend "early school" from 7:30 to 8:30 on empty stomachs; the reason the fagging system is still in operation. Under this system all smaller boys are assigned as "fags" to older boys. When a "fag" hears the cry "Boy" ringing through the corridor he must hurry to do his master's bidding, whether it's cooking his breakfast or lighting his fire or merely running errands. Every English public schoolboy thus learns what it is like to be servant as well as master.

Despite the stress laid on character, the English are remark-ably tolerant of failure. I remember once hearing an English-man rebuke his son for relating scornfully how he had found himself at the dinner table with a man who had recently come out of prison for forgery. "He has paid his debt to society hon-orably. How dare you adopt a patronizing attitude toward him!" thundered his father.

Tolerance is combined with a sense of humor which often expresses itself in surprising ways. Recently a tribunal was held to inquire into allegations of corruption in public life, and two members of the government were found guilty of having re-ceived gifts of whisky and clothes. In spite of the fact that no country demands a higher standard from its public servants, instead of being shocked the nation flung itself into the drama with astonishingly high spirits. Special writers were assigned to cover every aspect of the inquiry, newspaper circulations rose by the thousands, and from one end of the country to the other people competed with each other to invent new jokes. "This would never have happened if Attlee had been alive," cried some; others grinned happily: "We musn't grumble about the govern-ment. It's the best that money can buy."

Conformity ends and individuality begins in that curious sphere which the Englishman marks as personal. The very fact that the Englishman accepts the values laid down by the nation has given him a unique and striking independence which asserts itself in an insistence on privacy. It is here that to most foreigners the true complexities of the English character lie.

The English conception of privacy is subtle and delicate and its exact implications are as difficult for an outsider to understand as the Oriental conception of face. Respect for an individual's privacy forbids a man not only to intrude uninvited upon another's presence but to impose upon another's personality; it forbids him not only to pry into a man's personal affairs but to offend his sensibilities. To the Englishman privacy is the very essence of independence; it is the thread that binds his way of life together.

You see traces of it in the high wall he builds around his estate or the fence that separates his council house from his neighbor's; you see it in the strictness of his libel laws; his dislike of public restaurants, gossip, flats, and publicity; you see it in the faces buried behind newspapers in suburban trains, in the low voices in hotel lobbies, in the fact that advertising is banned from the radio. You see it in the politeness of the policemen, who call you "sir," and in the politeness of members of Parliament, who call each other "honourable gentleman"; and perhaps you see it even in the Englishman's love for animals. Writers have commented with awe that it is possible to live in an English village for years without knowing your neighbors, and during the war, when Duff Cooper, as Minister of Information, was audacious enough to send canvassers to take a questionnaire on problems affecting housewives, newspapers ran indignant headlines crying COOPER'S SNOOPERS.

Privacy to the Englishman does not mean solitude or unfriendliness. He enjoys crowds and social functions and his hospitality is not only noted for its lavishness but for its extensiveness. Yet he expects people to remain conscious of the barrier that protects him from intimacy. Americans often find this confusing, for to them the line between the personal and the impersonal is never clearly drawn.

During the war any visitor to an American front was shown all the snapshots of wives, children, and sweethearts that he had time to look at; and Red Cross hostesses were allowed to share a soldier's innermost thoughts in the letters they wrote home for him. But the only time I ever ventured to ask an English soldier so personal a question as whether he was homesick for his family he replied with an embarrassed smile: "Oh, they'll keep."

The conventions designed to protect an Englishman's privacy are therefore more misunderstood by Americans than by any other nationality. Americans are often chilled by English politeness and rebuffed by English reserve. To them politeness is a warm, friendly word that often embraces familiarity, but to the English it is usually mindful of respect. During the war I was at a headquarters in North Africa when an American lieutenant arrived to give the British colonel information on troop replacements. The American was gum-chewing and friendly. His voice had a cozy drawl and he stood talking to the colonel with his hand in his pocket. I saw the colonel's face redden and knew he thought the American was deliberately being rude. The colonel's voice took on a tone of icy politeness and a puzzled look came into the American's eyes. He knew something was wrong but could not understand what. Needless to say, after they parted each complained of the odious manners of the other.

The Englishman is often indifferent to whether he is liked so long as he is respected. Respect is as important to him as affection is to the American, a fact which is often misinterpreted as a sign of class-consciousness. Recently an American commission came to Britain to study and report on production. Several members were taken to the Midlands to visit a cotton factory. One of the group described to me the embarrassment he felt because the works manager led them through the factory elegantly attired in a black coat and pin-striped trousers, and was addressed by the workmen as "sir." "In America," my friend said, "a works manager would go through his factory in overalls and call his men by their first names."

I tried to explain that this attitude had nothing to do with servility; that British workmen had a very clear idea of their rights, as shown by the fact that they had built up the most powerful trade-union movement in the world. The British were by nature a polite people, and although they would think it disrespectful not to call the manager "sir," they would think it equally disrespectful for the manager not to call them "mister."

In England the advance from the surname to the given name is always slow and cautious, for this is the first step toward the Englishman's private world. But even when this world has been penetrated, reserve is seldom cast aside. In spite of a close relationship an Englishman would not criticize a friend's behavior unless the friend had invited him to do so. And I have often noted with amazement the restraint of English parents in inquiring into the affairs of their grown-up children.

Although English reserve often strikes the casual visitor as cold and unfriendly, once you live in England you find that it brings with it a curious freedom. Friendships are steadfast but unexacting, and remind you of Emerson's observation that a friend should be like a book—there to take down from the shelf when wanted.

Because people do not impose upon one another there is an easiness which encourages individualism and makes the eccentric an honored member of society. It frees people from the competitive urge to look, live, and behave exactly like their neighbors. New York salesmanship, which is usually concentrated in the phrase: "But madam, this is what everyone is wearing," would have to be revised in London, for the Ascot scene, with ladies in outfits ranging from tight black-lace frocks to flowing white organdies and picture hats, is proof enough of a rare independence of spirit.

The Englishman does not leave his Englishness at home even when he travels abroad. He sees nothing odd in putting on a dinner jacket in a remote village in China or wearing immaculate boots and breeches in a camp in the desert; and few circumstances are grave enough to prevent him from drinking his afternoon tea. During the war in North Africa I remember watching a British armored column moving up to the front. It was five o'clock on a cold winter evening. No lights were allowed

on the road but every time the column halted men jumped off
their trucks, attached little oil burners at the back of their vehicles, and began "brewing up" their tea.

The Englishman's insistence on preserving his own customs
usually sends him to countries where the British flag is flying
or where he can establish a little world of his own. Although
today several million British people are waiting to emigrate to
the Empire, during the last three years only 31,000 of them
have taken advantage of the American quota open to over six
times that number.

The English attitude toward foreigners has always been one
of superiority. The very fact that a man is not English is regarded as a handicap that immediately places him in a different
category. When France fell I returned to England on a ship
en route to Cornwall from the Cape, which had stopped at Bor-
deaux to take on extra passengers. There were nearly nine hundred of us aboard, a mixture of American journalists, English
businessmen, South African tourists, French holidaymakers. We
were attacked by German aircraft on the way, but arrived safely
to find the quay decorated with flags, and a host of kind ladies
dispensing tea and buns. One of these ladies gave me a form
to fill out, at the top of which was printed the word: "Refugee."
"I'm afraid there's a mistake," I said. "I'm an American journalist." The lady handed the form back to me. "Anyone who is
not English," she said firmly, " is a refugee."

Foreign names always arouse suspicion, for the English find
it hard to believe that anyone not brought up in England can
have the same standard of morality. Recently an English bicycle shop owner told me he had extended credit to a number of
Ukrainians who had just arrived in the country to work as agricultural laborers. "And they're paying their installments just
like English people," he added in an incredulous tone.

Today, although foreign labor is necessary to English recovery, lodginghouses often refuse to accept foreigners and in several industries trade unions have protested against their employment. Even when Princess Elizabeth was married you heard
the remark running through the general enthusiasm, "He looks

so nice. What a pity he isn't English." Americans escape some of this stigma because they speak the same language, but even more because their ancestors were English.

Needless to say, the Englishman's simple belief that what is English is right has always aroused antagonism. He has been accused of conceit and arrogance, and yet it is probably this faith which has saved him. Few observers who were in Britain when France fell will forget the astonishing reaction of the people. Instead of despondency, relief swept the country: "Now we're all together again. Now we're all right."

And today this same faith of one Englishman in another Englishman is playing a vital part in the battle for recovery. When I was in America a short while ago I was frequently asked how the British were adapting themselves to the position of a secondary power. The answer is that the British do not regard themselves as a secondary power. Although they are aware of their military weakness they believe this may be righted when their economic difficulties are overcome. And intellectually and morally they are determined to remain the leaders of the Western world. If character is what matters, they probably will.

No chapter on the English character would be complete without a reference to sport. Since the dawn of English history the people have had a passion for sport. English archers, besides discomfiting the French, were famous for the way they shot game and even birds in flight; in the Middle Ages, besides tilting with the chivalry of Europe, Englishmen of all classes indulged in bearbaiting, cockfighting, coursing, and wrestling; in spite of savage game laws poaching was a universal pastime. Later some of these sports were banned as cruel, but shooting and fox hunting took their place and flourished through social unrest and industrial revolution.

During the last two centuries, without losing their taste for blood sports, the English have also taken to games. Not only is there hardly a family in the land which has not an interest in some form of athletics, but the English have fired the rest of the world with their own enthusiasm. American football is a fine game, but it is only played on the American continent; "soccer" on the other hand, which is the name given to the more popular version of English football,* is played in every country from Japan to Brazil. Golf, lawn tennis, hockey, polo, table tennis, squash rackets, badminton were either invented in Britain or developed by the British; indeed, with the exception of pelota (*jai alai*), baseball, and bullfighting it is difficult to think of a sport or game anywhere in the world which does not also exist in England. Wild animals no longer live there, but the myriad and moth-eaten heads which adorn the walls of English clubs and country houses bear witness to the fact that no race travels farther or hunts more assiduously.

To foreigners this passion for sport has been a cause both of ridicule and of despair; the English have so often played while the world tottered that the French in particular have accused them of incorrigible irresponsibility. As late as 1938 I remember walking up Piccadilly with a distinguished French journalist and seeing a poster at an evening paper stall with the letters in large red type: ENGLAND IN DANGER. Munich was in the air, and the Frenchman, braving the traffic, rushed across the street to buy a paper. For several seconds he stood in the middle of the sidewalk scanning it. When I reached him he was muttering "Test Match, Test Match," and then in despair he turned to me and said: "Please, what is Test Match?" When I explained that it was a game of cricket between England and Australia, he threw the paper away in disgust, saying: "Really, these people are mad."

But the English do not think their interest in sport is mad. At school they are taught that Drake continued his game of bowls after the Armada had been sighted because he wanted time to think, and the tradition lingers. In between the wars, when crises occurred in London or at Geneva, the newspapers always seized upon the fact that Mr. Eden or Sir John Simon was playing golf, or Sir John Anderson or Sir Samuel Hoare was

---

* Rugby, the other version, was invented by William Webb Ellis who, in 1823, took the ball in his arms and ran with it with a fine disregard for the rules of football as played in his time.

skating, as a sign that all was reasonably well and the English at any rate had not lost their heads. Sir Austen Chamberlain's boat trips on Lake Locarno were taken in the same spirit. And as if to confirm how right they were, when faced with the task of designing a British pavilion for the Paris Exhibition in 1938, English architects chose to flank the entrance with a window of wax figures in hunting costume on the one hand and another window of more wax figures in shooting tweeds on the other; and to greet the visitor with a picture on the opposite wall of Mr. Neville Chamberlain, then Prime Minister, four times life-size, fishing. On this occasion even the French were amused.

The fact that this year two bills proposing to abolish blood sports were introduced by private Labor members of Parliament might seem to indicate a change. Up to a point this is true. There has always been a strong nonconformist objection to blood sports on the ground that it is unchristian to take pleasure by inflicting cruelty; and to nonconformism is added the voice of the small group of Marxist socialists to whom anything as unproductive as sport is anathema. Today there are strong objections. When food is scarce and the government is calling for the maximum production from everyone, the damage done by fox hunting and the expensive paraphernalia which used to be associated with it both seem out of place. But the charge goes no deeper. Otter hunting and coursing may go the way of bearbaiting and cockfighting, but the bill to abolish fox hunting had a bad reception even among Labor members of Parliament and many of those who represent urban constituencies learned for the first time how many men, even in towns, spend their Saturday afternoons in the country catching rabbits with a dog and ferret.

But for all the variety of sport which flourishes in England one game above all others reveals the English character, and that is cricket. Cricket is not the most popular game. A Test Match against the Australians, England's greatest rivals, will not draw more than 40,000 people, whereas a big game of football will draw 100,000. Nor is it the most lucrative game for players. Footballers are paid more per week than professional cricketers, and jockeys, golfers, and lawn-tennis players make far more money in a lifetime. Yet cricket is still the national game and famous cricketers are much more famous than players of other games. Only this year Don Bradman, the great Australian batsman, was knighted for his prowess.

The reasons for the pre-eminence of cricket are typically English. It is a game with a history, having been first played in the seventeenth century. It is an aristocratic game, for it has always been played by the gentry; yet it is also played in every village and in the back streets of every town. It is one of the few games in which players of the highest class can still be amateurs. Even more important, it is essentially the game of the English, as opposed to the Scots and the Welsh, and it is the game of the Commonwealth; for though other games are universal, cricket is only played where the inhabitants are mainly of English stock or where there has been British rule. Every year a touring team leaves England for one or other of the Dominions or the West Indian Colonies. At the same time Indians tour New Zealand or Australians the West Indies. Even the Egyptians, who had no love for British rule, love cricket.

It is not easy for an American to enjoy cricket. Occasionally, when a hard-hitting batsman is in and the ball is sent to all quarters of the field, the action is lively and the game full of incident. But for the most part it appears to follow a routine. The bowler bowls, and the batsman, armed with a flat-bladed club twice as broad as a baseball bat, strikes without apparent effort or difficulty so that the ball goes slowly or fast to one of the many fielders who has been placed to receive it. And so, hour after hour, in drizzle or sunshine, in wind or stifling heat (for cricket is played in the tropics), the game proceeds. In Australia, where Test Matches are played to a finish, one game lasted for nine days. In England big matches are usually limited to three days, but even the shortest game on the village green in the evening takes three hours.

To the English, cricket is an art. It is, they say, a game of infinite variety which depends partly on quickness of foot, hand, and eye but mainly on temperament and the weather. A match is not just a series of innings, each a hit-or-miss affair as in base-ball, but a campaign in which the successive duels between bats-men and bowlers are not individual fights but related phases of a battle. Skill is vital, but strategy, tactics, patience, and stamina, and above all the team spirit, are equally important. And the weather is the hidden reserve which wayward Providence may throw into the scales at a moment's notice and tip the balance against a seeming winner. For a shower of rain can so affect the bounce of the ball that bowlers who have been innocuous be-come deadly and batsmen who have been masters become as children.

Cricket is played from May till October. It is the only field game in which a man of sixty can be as useful as a boy of twenty and the only game in which all classes mix, for the squire and the parson are often regular members of the village side and peers have captained county teams in which all the other play-ers were professionals.

Its organization is as English as the rest of it. The Marylebone Cricket Club governs cricket, not according to any agreement or contract, but by custom. Its committee is elected by the members in London and its rulings are accepted without ques-tion in every country where cricket is played. "Lords" is the name of the headquarters ground, but it is called after the man who founded it and has no connection with the peerage. Yet any evening during the summer, on top of the pavilion, will be found men eminent in every walk of life from politics to the church, sitting in their shirt sleeves if it is hot and talking quietly and familiarly in the way that is peculiar to English clubs.

Cricket has become a ritual. Because it is long drawn out, because it needs mental as well as physical stamina, because luck plays a great part and the best player can fail utterly, because many decisions are in the hands of an umpire whose word must be accepted without question, because an individualist may ruin a side and a persistent man make one, most of the qualities which are called for in life are needed to play it. Cricket has therefore become part of the national vocabulary. "It isn't crick-et" or "playing with a straight bat" are phrases which to an Englishman convey at once something a little dishonorable or something good and thorough; parliamentary speeches are studded with cricket metaphors; and when in 1939 the correspondent of a daily newspaper wrote that if only Hitler had played cricket in his youth the war would never have happened, his readers laughed but were inclined to agree with him. It is vain for foreigners to hope to enjoy cricket themselves; but if they can come to an understanding of the enjoyment Englishmen derive from it they may come much nearer to an understanding of England.

PART II. GOVERNMENT

CHAPTER 3

The House of Commons

A very shrewd man of the world went so far as to
say that "the House of Commons has more sense
than anyone in it."
—BAGEHOT, *The English Constitution*

WHEN the results of the general election became known on
July 26, 1945, there was more visible consternation among
the English upper class than when bombs were falling on London. I went to a lunch party given by Lord Rothermere, whose
newspaper, the *Daily Mail*, had been one of the strongest supporters of the Conservative government. The luncheon was in
a private room at the Dorchester Hotel; a large blackboard stood
against the wall, on which the election results were chalked up
as they came over the tape. All the guests were Conservatives
and all of them had husbands, brothers, or close friends con-
testing seats.

As the first Labor gains began to trickle in the room was ap-
prehensive; then as news came of the defeat of the first Conservative cabinet minister, Mr. Harold Macmillan, followed
soon after by Mr. Brendan Bracken and Mr. Amery, then Liberal Sir William Beveridge, the apprehension turned to alarm.

27

Dismay was written on faces from one end of the room to the other; the only person still enjoying himself was the announcer, who, judging from the ringing voice with which he called out the results, was an ardent Socialist. One woman fought to keep the tears back, and another, cheeks pink with indignation, kept repeating: "How monstrous. How absolutely monstrous. And after all Winston has done for the country! The English people are the most ungrateful people in the world."

Others were too busy thinking about themselves to worry about Winston. One of them declared there would be no such thing as private property within two years, and another announced that he was going to leave the country for good as soon as he could pack his things. The gloom was now general, and people sat sipping their champagne and eating their lobster salad in a lifeless way. This state of affairs was relative, however, for suddenly Sir William Rootes, a motorcar manufacturer, arrived, and I heard him saying to his hostess: "What a relief to be in a cheerful atmosphere. I've just come from Lord Beaverbrook's lunch at Claridge's."

The Labor party had captured nearly 400 of the 640 parliamentary seats. For the first time it had full power. But even more significant, for the first time in the history of England members of the upper class no longer controlled the House of Commons. Such a radical departure from custom shocked many people far more than the thought of socialism. "If we must go left, let us at least go there led by gentlemen," one lady complained angrily. "This sort of thing is so un-English."

It was certainly untraditional; from the dawn of Parliament in the twelfth century onward, men of wealth or position had determined the political course of the nation. Even when the Labor party took office between the last two wars the upper class had managed to maintain a numerical superiority in the Commons. The fact that England was dominated by this powerful caste often puzzled outsiders, who found it difficult to understand not only how an oligarchy could flourish in a democracy but how a democracy had emerged from an oligarchy.

The answer was that English freedom was established as the result of a long bitter struggle between the upper class and the Crown. Unlike America, there was no great upsurge of popular feeling, no passionate cry for egalitarianism, no formal birth. First there was the rule of kings, which remained more or less absolute until 1641; then the rule of Parliament, in which the elected House of Commons was rivaled by the hereditary House of Lords; then, gradually, the usurpation of authority by the Commons, until in 1911, under the leadership of Asquith and Lloyd George, the Lords was finally stripped of major powers and turned into a revising chamber.

But democracy did not mean equality. While members of the oligarchy struggled among themselves to perfect democratic machinery and gave the lower classes the right to vote in the latter half of the nineteenth century, they also banded together to persuade the masses that the best way to exercise their newly acquired power was to allow their betters to govern them. "Sensible men of substantial means are what we wish to be ruled by . . . ," explained Walter Bagehot, the great constitutional writer.

The two great parties of the day continued to select their candidates from the upper classes; and since in England the sons of peers are "commoners" and eligible to stand for election, the Commons was nearly as wealthy and aristocratic as the Lords. The sentiment of the oligarchy was expressed in Bagehot's warning "that a political combination of the lower classes . . . is an evil of the first magnitude . . . ; that their supremacy in the state they now are, means the supremacy of ignorance over instruction and of numbers over knowledge. So long as they are not taught to act together, there is a chance of this being averted, and it can only be averted by the greater wisdom and foresight in the higher classes."

The oligarchy heeded Bagehot's words and ruled with such skill that seventy years later, in 1938, John Gunther was able to write: "Two percent of the property owners of England own sixty-four percent of the national wealth. These persons comprise a fluid and impregnable ruling class, or caste, which is one of the most remarkable phenomena in the world today."

It was remarkable for several reasons: first because it managed to hold tightly to the reins of government for over half a century after the franchise had become general, second because it believed passionately in its own virtue, and third because it was sensible enough to constantly refurbish itself with new blood. Although it was based largely on inherited wealth, aristocrats and gentlefolk automatically being members, it welcomed the newly rich and the newly powerful with outstretched arms. The self-made millionaire was the subject of merciless satire, but the public school was the accepted process of refinement guaranteed to make the sons of parvenus indistinguishable from the sons of bluebloods; and the public schools opened their doors to all who could pay the fees.

The House of Lords was also a way in. Every year peers were created on the recommendation of the government. Some were men who had distinguished themselves in medicine, science, at the bar, in the arts, or in various forms of government service, but many were merely the rich and ambitious—the coal merchants, the brewers, the shipping magnates who let it be known that they were ready to contribute generously to charity or party funds. It would have been considered foolish to leave them hanging in the air like ripe plums ready for the opposition to pluck.

The prerogative of the ruling classes was to rule, and opportunities lay before it like bonbons on a fancy dish. Politics offered the most glittering prizes, but diplomacy, the civil service, and the army and navy also carried considerable prestige. And if you liked pomp and ceremony there were governorships to be had from one end of the world to the other. As most of these careers were barred to outsiders, competition was not so severe that a man of reasonable intelligence could not hope to reach the top.

Great emphasis, however, was placed on character, and the standard of integrity was high and rigid. With understandable pride the rulers pointed to a system of justice that was the admiration of the world, and to a reputation for political incorruptibility enjoyed by no other great nation.

The fact that they persuaded the electorate to return them to power so consistently was tribute enough to their political skill; also to a tireless gift for propaganda. No group of people believed in the superiority of wealth and rank more fervently, and consequently no group of people extolled their own accomplishments more often or more convincingly. They referred to the system of oligarchic rule as "continuity" and "tradition" and even went so far as to accuse those who challenged it as being unpatriotic.

This was the great difference between American and British democracy; whereas America accepted egalitarianism as a fundamental precept, Englishmen made no such pretense. "The great advantage of being ruled by gentlemen," a politician's son explained to me, "is that most gentlemen are rich and it is more difficult to bribe a rich man than a poor man. Furthermore, a rich man will not cling to office the way a poor man will; he has many pleasures to fall back on, therefore he is more apt to obey the dictates of his conscience and act on principle than the professional politician."

Another concept, still widely held, was the belief that the English public school not only molded character but created it. A public-school boy was a definitely superior being. Only a few months ago an old gentleman indignantly told me at dinner that the Foreign Office examination board had turned down an Eton boy, the son of an old friend, in favor of a boy who had been to an ordinary high school. Someone suggested that perhaps the other boy had done better in his examinations. "Perhaps," he said, "but surely you don't want to send people abroad to represent England who drop their aitches." When someone else countered that most countries in Europe were no longer ruled by aristocrats and it was a good thing to get some new blood into the Foreign Office, the old man replied firmly that public-school boys had higher standards of behavior than other boys and it grieved him to think they were being cast aside.

This assumption of superiority was no mere conceit of the upper class. It was accepted by the great majority of the people and was the structure upon which the whole system was built. In 1938 when newspaper headlines announced one of the many international crises of the day, a woman who came in to look after my flat made a remark that could only have been made in England. "What do these dictators 'Itler and Mussolini think they're up to, causing decent people all this worry? The trouble is they're just common muck. Why, my old man says they're no better born than I am!"

This was the outlook that stemmed from the oligarchy and the outlook that kept it in power. Parliamentary seats continued to go to members of the upper class, and English love of continuity was noticeable in a number of constituencies which had been handed down from father to son for so many years that they were referred to as "family seats." In February, 1944, Lord Hartington, the Duke of Devonshire's eldest son, stood as a government candidate in the West Derbyshire by-election. In a letter supporting him Winston Churchill wrote:

My dear Hartington,
I see that they are attacking you because your family has been identified for about 300 years with the Parliamentary representation of West Derbyshire. It ought, on the contrary, to be a matter of pride to the constituency to have such a long tradition of such constancy and fidelity through so many changing scenes and circumstances. . . .

The rebelliousness which came to a head in the general election seventeen months later was already showing itself, for Lord Hartington was defeated by an Independent.

The M.P.'s who stood for re-election in 1945 had been in Parliament for ten years. Under ordinary circumstances a government must "go to the country" at least every five years; because of the war, however, the life of Parliament had been extended by special act.

The Conservatives held a large majority. They numbered 361

as compared with 166 Socialists and 87 in other parties. In those days the House of Commons was often referred to as "the most exclusive club in the world." In the summer, strawberries and cream were served on the wide terrace overlooking the Thames, and the scene often reminded one of a fashionable New York wedding reception with the female guests in flowered dresses and smart hats, and the M.P.'s wonderfully elegant in pin-striped trousers, with carnations in their buttonholes. It was a leisurely and agreeable place and in '37 and '38 you seldom went there without thinking how strangely removed it seemed from the trouble blowing up on the Continent only a few miles away.

To be a member of Parliament was a social distinction. Many worked hard but a good many more went into the House because it was the fashionable thing for a young man to do. They joined it as automatically as they joined clubs like White's or Boodles; it did not take up too much time, and it gave them the comfortable feeling of obeying the "tradition" of public service. However, seats were costly and a Conservative with a private income of less than £2,000 ($8,000) a year had little hope of attaining one. M.P.'s were paid only £600 ($2,400) a year, yet they were expected to finance their own election expenses and to contribute generously and regularly to party funds. In 1938 G. R. Hall Caine said in an interview to the *Sunday Chronicle*: "It is lamentable that Conservative seats should be put up for auction and sold to the richest candidate. Being a member for East Dorset has cost me £37,000 in the last seventeen years, and, deducting the amount received in salary, I have paid a net figure of £31,000. . . . . Many M.P.'s spend far more than I do in their constituencies." And in 1939 Mr. Duff Cooper stated in an article in the *Evening Standard*: "It is as difficult for a poor man, if he is a Conservative, to get into the House of Commons as it is for a camel to get through the eye of a needle."

From a social point of view the prewar House of Commons was a glittering assembly. Some idea of the wealth of the Conservative M.P.'s may be gleaned from the fact that, out of 43 Conservative members who died between the years 1931 and 1938, 33 members left a total aggregate of over £35,000,000 ($140,000,000). Of the 415 Conservative M.P.'s elected in 1935, 279 were educated at public schools (125 at Eton or Harrow), 181 held 775 company directorships, and 236 were knights, baronets, or relations by blood or marriage to the peerage. In 1938 the ministers who formed the government included a marquis, three earls, two viscounts, a baron, and a baronet.

If you enjoyed political talk there was no other capital in the world which provided it in so agreeable a setting as London. The House of Lords and the Conservative majority in the Commons were like a huge family with immense ramifications; everyone had been to school with everyone else, and everyone met everyone else at the same dinners, shoots, and week-end parties. All the great hostesses were politically minded and you rarely went to a social gathering without finding half a dozen ministers or would-be ministers present. Politics was the first sport of the land, and politics, conducted by gentlemen, meant good talk, good food, and good brandy.

Whatever the shortcomings of these luxury-loving men who decided the fate of the nation at such a momentous period in history, when war came they played their part; 146 Conservative M.P.'s joined the armed forces and ten of them were killed in action. That, too, was part of British tradition.

When Parliament began its opening session with the Labor party in full power for the first time, Winston Churchill, looking across at the government benches, is said to have murmured to a friend: "The wildest bunch of men who never cut a throat." Although the average American would find nothing unusual in the appearance of these M.P.'s, London hostesses protested sadly: "But my dear, you should see them."

Looking down from the visitors' gallery in the House of Commons on to the solid phalanx of Socialists you saw a cross section of ordinary men in ordinary business clothes very much like the sort of men you would find in Congress. But when you turned to the Conservative ranks you noticed the contrast. On those benches there was a hangover of elegance. There was self-made Sir William Darling in a black stock with a diamond pin and aristocratic Lord Hinchinbroke disdainfully immaculate in a collar stiffer and higher than any plebeian neck could carry. And around them were serried ranks of traditional striped trousers and black coats, of carefully brushed hair and polished shoes. When your eye wandered back to the Socialist benches you were suddenly aware of the unconventional note introduced by flannel trousers and tweed coats.

This informality seemed to pervade the whole building. In place of the elegance was a liveliness that reminded one of the bustle and turmoil of Congress. The great stone corridors resounded with the sharp click of hurrying feet; the entrance lobby was crowded with clerks, secretaries, and visitors. Sightseers who had come from the provinces to pay their first visit to Westminster stood gazing up at the ornate walls; ministers with dispatch cases hurried through on their way to the floor of the House. The general confusion was heightened by the fact that the several hundred new members were still losing their way in the labyrinth of corridors which all looked exactly alike. Attendants spent most of their time giving directions. One attendant who had been at the House for forty years and despite previous Labor governments clung to the belief that politics was exclusively a gentleman's profession, took pleasure in answering the queries of several M.P.'s by regarding them critically and saying in an over-polite voice: "Are you a member of Parliament, sir?"

The Labor members were a varied lot. Whereas in the last Parliament 50 percent of them were trade-union officials, this time the unions represented less than 25 percent of the total. The majority were drawn from the professional classes, 196 of them being listed as journalists, lawyers, doctors, technicians, teachers, and civil servants.

However, the class differences that divided the Labor and

Conservative benches were as sharp and clear-cut as ever. The results of a questionnaire* sent around soon after the election showed that 78 percent of the Conservative members, as compared with 17 percent of the Socialists, had attended public schools. This meant that nearly four-fifths of the Conservatives had the traditional background and environment of the "ruling class."

In striking contrast was the fact that 65 percent of the Labor M.P.'s were sons of manual laborers skilled and unskilled. Sixty-three percent of the Labor members went to work before the age of seventeen as compared with 10 percent of the Conservatives; and 43 percent of the Labor members attended no schools above the age of fourteen as compared with 1.3 percent of the Conservatives. Out of the Labor M.P.'s who received further schooling, half of them educated themselves by winning scholarships. In other words, most of the Conservatives had been born into their present state of life while most of the Labor M.P.'s had worked their way up from the ranks.

But the new House of Commons was not only a mixture of well-bred arrogance and gusty aggressiveness. It was also a mixture of rich and poor. Whereas most of the Conservatives were men of independent means and over a third of them held company directorships, most of the Socialists had no money except their salaries. As they received only $2,400 a year and had to pay their own postage and secretarial expenses it was not easy to make ends meet. One of the Socialists' first moves was to install bunks in the locker rooms where they could sleep when there were late sittings; then they abolished the tipping system in the restaurants, raised the salaries of the waiters, and instituted a lunch for 35 cents. The famous smoking room, where drinks were served, continued to be the chief gathering place for the Conservatives while the Labor members took over the tearoom, where less stimulating refreshments had the advantage of also being less costly. Soon after this they introduced a bill to raise

* The Present House of Commons: Its Educational and Social Background, by Nance E. Robertson and J. A. Waites.

their own salaries to $4,000 a year, a measure that was opposed by many Conservatives but passed by the large Labor majority. With the standard of living in the Palace of Westminster thus modified and the wages thus increased they settled down to the business of government.

A Frenchman once remarked that England was the only country in Europe capable of making a unique contribution to civilization, because it was the only country in Europe capable of going left and still retaining its traditions. This observation came to mind on the opening day of Parliament when the new Socialist members boisterously sang the "Red Flag," then sat down and elected a Conservative country gentleman as Speaker of the House. It was all in the best English manner. Let change take place, but let it take place within the existing framework.

However, even if members wished to substitute new and streamlined innovations for the age-old customs of Parliament (which they certainly do not), it is difficult to imagine how a new look could be introduced into a setting so gloriously old-fashioned. The Palace of Westminster, in which the Lords and Commons sit, is a huge, gloomy Gothic building that looks like a cathedral, with stone floors and stained-glass windows, gargoyles and huge forbidding murals. The keynote is discomfort. The committee rooms are badly lighted, with high ceilings and creaking wooden floors. No offices are provided for M.P.'s and there is not a comfortable chair in sight. You often see secretaries taking dictation on the narrow stone ledges that line the busy corridors, their papers strewn over the floor.

The chamber itself (borrowed from the Lords until the Commons chamber, destroyed by bombs, is rebuilt) is badly ventilated, and the heavily carved wood in which it is paneled is carefully designed to take away from the room the little light it might otherwise have. The Speaker, in black robes and white wig, is mounted on a throne at one end, and the government and opposition sit on red-leather benches on either side, facing each other across a narrow strip of carpet. On winter days when a pea-soup fog rolls in from the Thames members stare at each other through a thick yellow haze which dims the lights and gives the whole scene a weird, surrealist air.

And yet this strange, dark, ugly building has such a powerful personality that no member, however revolutionary, fails to be affected by it. The ghosts of seven centuries walk along the great echoing floor of Westminster Hall which leads into the passage that joins the Central Lobby. The link with the past, the feeling of continuity, is so impressive it seems natural that customs which mark significant stages in the Commons' long struggle for freedom should be jealously preserved.

For instance, on the opening day of Parliament when the King's messenger, "Black Rod," arrives with a message from his sovereign, the door of the Commons is always slammed in his face, and he must knock three times before he is admitted. Long ago Charles I with his spurs jingling strode into the chamber and demanded that five members who had spoken against the Crown be handed over to him. The members had been smuggled out by the river exit and the Speaker refused to divulge their whereabouts, making the famous reply: "I have neither ears to hear nor tongue to speak save as this House shall direct me." King Charles left, disconsolately muttering, "My birds have flown." And from that day to this the King has never been allowed to enter the Commons.

There are many of these customs. The House of Lords must always be referred to as "the other place," a rule which springs from the time when the Lords had the power to overrule the Commons, and the Commons defiantly refused to do more than barely acknowledge the existence of the Lords. It is also customary that in a debate no member shall designate another by name; he may only refer to him as "the honorable gentleman," a legacy from the time when if a member's name were known he might be sent to prison for criticizing the Crown.

The Speaker is the symbol of free speech and as such his office is treated with ceremony and deference. When he comes through the corridors on his way to the chamber in black knee breeches and fluttering robes, the police attendants cry in ringing tones:

"Make way for Mr. Speaker." As he passes everyone stands at attention and men take off their hats. More impressive still, particularly to American visitors, is the fact that even the police remove their helmets.

The feeling of continuity preserved by these ceremonies had its effect on the new members. Many of the Labor M.P.'s had come to Parliament with a gusty self-assurance, contemptuous of Conservatism in every sense of the word. But where the contempt sprang from ignorance the fascination of history soon exerted its spell. Before long you saw the most recalcitrant members leading groups of constituents through the corridors explaining points of interest with enthusiasm. And when a Socialist rose to speak in a debate, and in his ardor stepped forward onto the carpet that divides the two sides, there were immediate cries of "Order, order," from his own supporters; no member has been allowed to step on the center carpet since the days when debates grew so acrimonious that men were apt to draw their swords.

But it was not only history that made its impression on new members. The temper and atmosphere of the chamber itself was responsible for the greatest change. Outwardly you noticed that the rumpled shirts and unpressed suits usually worn by intellectuals as a proletarian gesture were giving way to clean collars and a general effort at tidiness. You also noticed that the dogmatic attitude of the most partisan members on both sides was gradually becoming tinged with politeness; and occasionally you even heard a reluctant word of praise for the opposition.

It has often been claimed that no political assembly in the world teaches a man to respect his opponent's point of view more quickly than the House of Commons. The reason for this is that the Commons, unlike Congress or the French Parliament, is first and foremost a debating chamber; debate requires the ability to listen and the ability to reason, and few politicians who are forced to open their minds on a subject become less tolerant as a result.

In the Commons a man's objective is not merely to make a speech but to make an impression. He must be able to reply to interruptions and yet not lose the thread of what he is saying;

a member who strays off the subject is called to order by the Speaker. If the arguments he uses are telling enough they will be answered by the minister who sums up the debate. If on the other hand he talks such trivialities or nonsense that he bores his audience he has the chagrin of seeing the chamber empty before him. Although the standard of wit and eloquence is high, sincerity and thoughtfulness will often carry a man much farther. The unforgivable sin is tub thumping; such tactics may have scored a great success in a member's constituency but if he uses them in the House he is apt to be howled down. One M.P. who began to shout at his audience was drowned out by cries of "Louder!"

The back-bencher who cannot express himself will have little chance of attaining office although there are a few exceptions in the case of outstanding administrators. The reason for this is that a British minister, unlike his American counterpart, is not an "outside appointment" but a member of the House. As such he must be able to withstand the cross fire of his opponents and defend the policy of his government on the floor of the House.

One of the most exacting features of a minister's life is "question time," which takes place every afternoon before the business of the day begins. During this hour ministers are subjected to a rigorous cross-examination. M.P.'s put down on the "order paper" whatever questions they wish to ask the various departments, and the minister concerned must be present to answer. But he must answer not merely the question which appears in writing, but any supplementary question the original questioner or another member may ask.

The result is often, in Mr. Churchill's words, "a debate in interrogatory form" and may last several minutes. And in such a debate a minister's wits are more roughly tested than at any other time, for his answers must be not merely accurate but quick and if possible witty. If he does not have his subject at his finger tips he is lost.

Many members of Parliament make question time their chief business, and groups of members sometimes lunch together to plan their campaign; a harmless-looking question asking for a set of figures or for information regarding some coming report may hide a sensation or even a scandal which will bring a minister down. More reputations have been lost at question time than in any other way.

Constitutionally "questions" are of great importance since they provide the principal means by which the ordinary citizen can check the bureaucracy. No question is too trivial for an M.P. to ask. Whether it is the failure of the War Department to provide private soldier Smith with a mosquito net in Singapore or a deduction of five shillings from Mrs. Jones's state pension because she took in a lodger, the civil service is on its mettle. "P.Q.'s," as they are labeled (parliamentary questions), are priority in every department, and in every case the circumstances are thoroughly investigated. For although the minister is responsible, it is a tradition that no department lets him down. He can lose his job whereas the civil servant who may have made the mistake is secure.

The greatest parliamentarian in the House today, and in fact one of the greatest England has ever known, is Winston Churchill. After the general election a number of friends tried to dissuade him from leading the opposition, arguing that it would be more dignified in view of his unique position if he retired from politics and concentrated on his writing. "Leave the House!" he exclaimed. "But I am a child of the House of Commons."

No one enjoys the cut and thrust of debate, the smoking-room gossip, the endless political shop more than Churchill. And no one prepares his speeches more carefully or treats the House with greater respect. When he comes into the chamber there is always a stir in the galleries and the whole atmosphere electrifies. He sits on the front opposition bench with his shoulders slightly hunched, his bulldog head thrust forward, and a hand cupping an ear that is getting a little deaf, straining to catch every word.

There is not a trick of the trade which he does not know. Quick to strike and quick to defend, few opponents score off him. Often, when he rises to speak, he begins in a deliberately low voice in order to command attention. Once there were cries from the Labor benches: "Speak up! Don't be afraid." He paused and surveyed them critically. The House grew still in anticipation. Then in a whisper, which could be heard from one end of the chamber to the other, he said: "I find I speak quite loud enough to silence any of you when I like."

Churchill's respect for parliamentary procedure does not prevent him from being provocative. He often whips the House into such an uproar that insults and abuse are hurled back and forth with the Speaker rising to maintain order. Following one of these hubbubs several letters appeared in the *Daily Telegraph* from readers deploring the fact that Churchill was not treated with greater deference. Little did they understand the man's temperament, for if the day ever comes when he fails to draw the fire of the other side he will consider his usefulness in Parliament at an end. In fact, his provocations are often such carefully planned traps that Labor M.P.'s are sometimes instructed by the "whips" not to interrupt him during a debate for he is certain to get the better of them. The same instructions have been given to Conservatives when Aneurin Bevan, the quick-witted, hotheaded Minister of Health, gets up to speak; next to Churchill he is the most eloquent speaker in the House.

No matter how much tempers fly in a debate no member is supposed to carry personal vendettas outside the chamber. This unwritten law may have developed as a result of Parliament's overcrowded rooms. It is awkward for a man to remain aloof when he is rubbing shoulders with an opponent in the library or forced to share a table with him in the restaurant. Whatever the reason, it is a curious fact that although in private life people may get so heated over an issue that they refuse to mix with those of opposite views, members of the House of Commons (with the possible exception of the Irish) always weather their differences with equanimity. When Churchill and Attlee are in the smoking room they often sit down at the same table and have a drink together.

Very few men ever tire of the House of Commons. Once a man has been an M.P. he will fight hard to hold his seat. Perhaps it is because England's constitution is unwritten so that there is always much to alter and always much to defend which in the end must suit all temperaments. Or perhaps it is because there is a fascination in the paradox of so many centuries of continuity and so many centuries of change. Kings have been dethroned, aristocrats shorn of their privileges, bankers and industrialists stripped of their power, and yet these things have been done peacefully, by and through Parliament which has been equal to them all.

For this reason even the most extreme radicals respect the great Chamber of the Commons and are content to frame their programs within its limits. As a Conservative remarked acidly: "If the Reds ever rule England they are certain to be known as 'His Majesty's Communist Government.' "

CHAPTER 4

His Majesty's Ministers

England is not to be saved by any single man.
—WILLIAM PITT

SHORTLY after the 1945 election a Conservative remarked mischievously: "Attlee is called the Prime Minister, Morrison thinks he is the Prime Minister, and Bevin is the Prime Minister." Since that time Sir Stafford Cripps has become a contender and Aneurin Bevan a runner-up.

These five men are the most powerful members of the government; they are almost equally well known throughout the country and almost equally experienced in assuming heavy responsibility. In the eyes of the public each has qualities which overshadow the others. Attlee is most respected for his character; Cripps for his brain; Morrison for his organizing ability; Bevin for his force; and Bevan for his oratorical brilliance. If you rolled all five into one you would have the statesman for whom the world has been searching for a long, long time.

Of them all Clement Attlee is the least dramatic. He is noted for two things: his integrity and his shyness. How did he become Prime Minister? It is seldom that the meek inherit the earth. Virtue is not a vote catcher and as a chief characteristic rarely takes a man to the highest office in the land. The designers of the American Constitution were so well aware of this that they made provision for the President of the United States to be chosen, not by direct popular vote, but by a group of eminent men elected for the purpose. They believed that these "electors" would be more inclined than the general public to make their selection on a basis of character rather than personality. But as everyone knows, the Founding Fathers' plan soon broke down. The electors became nothing more than puppets, which meant that the President was, in fact, chosen by the people. And popular appeal began to play a decisive part in a candidate's success.

In Britain the system is different. The public does not vote for a man but for a party. Issues are clear-cut and emphatic. The party that returns a majority of candidates to the House of Commons forms a government and the leader of that party, who is selected by his parliamentary colleagues, automatically becomes Prime Minister. But how did a man as retiring as Mr. Attlee become the leader?

Clement Attlee was born sixty-six years ago of well-to-do, middle-class parents who lived in the London suburb of Putney. He was one of seven children. His father, a solicitor, was a Gladstonian Liberal and his mother a Conservative. He was educated at Haileybury, a small public school, and at University College, Oxford. Politics did not concern him much; he accepted as a matter of course the atmosphere in which he lived.

I was a . . . Conservative [he wrote]. The Liberals of the type of Asquith, Runciman and McKenna were always distasteful to me. The violent nonconformist made no appeal. The "gentlemanly party" was to me far preferable. I was perhaps only half-consciously surcharged with class feeling. I thought then that quite definitely only gentlemen were fit to govern. I believed in the legend of the White man's burden and all the rest of the commonplaces of imperialist idealism. The well-to-do were, for the most part, what they were because of their virtue. . . .

A turning point came in his life when he was twenty-four years old. He made an excursion with his brother Tom to the East End of London to inspect Haileybury House, a boys' settlement run by his own school, "to see," as he put it, "how our money was being spent." It was a raw, foggy night and the mean streets of Limehouse looked even meaner in the dim, flickering lights. He had never seen a world of poverty before and was deeply impressed. Although he had begun a career at the bar he had not been particularly successful at attracting clients, and when the club manager asked him if he would give up some of his spare time to help with the boys he agreed to do so. Soon he was a frequent visitor and two years later when the manager retired stepped into his shoes. For the next fifteen years, except for the interlude of World War I which he began as a private and ended as a major, he lived in the East End. Attlee's settlement work led to socialism, his socialism to the street-corner soapbox, and the soapbox to Parliament. For twenty-nine years he has sat as the member for Limehouse.

Some claim that chance alone made him leader of his party; others that it was the natural reward of years of hard work in his constituency. This was what happened: In 1931 the Labor party suffered a severe defeat; only 51 Socialists and over 500 Conservatives were returned to Parliament. Almost all the prominent Labor leaders lost their seats, among them Morrison, Dalton, Greenwood, Alexander, and Clynes. The only three who survived were Lansbury, who became leader of the party, Attlee, and Stafford Cripps. As Cripps had only held legal office and was too aloof to be popular, Attlee was chosen deputy leader. In 1935 Lansbury resigned and recommended that Attlee take his place until after the general election which was due at the end of the year. "Clem is well able to handle anything that comes up," he insisted. Many newspapers, however, were caustic. The *Daily Mail* commented on the similarity of Attlee's head to that of Lenin and wrote patronizingly: "So the Leader of the Socialist Opposition is to be Major Attlee. I am afraid that he will not be so for long, but he deserves the success that is his momentarily."

The 1935 election brought 154 Socialists into the House. The party met to vote for a permanent leader. The names of Attlee, Morrison, and Greenwood were put forward. Attlee polled the highest, Morrison second, and Greenwood, supported largely by trade unionists, third. Greenwood dropped out and a second ballot was taken. Attlee's four years as deputy leader weighed in his favor. Greenwood's supporters went solidly over to him.

Certainly it would be difficult to imagine a greater contrast between two Prime Ministers than Churchill and Attlee.

Churchill reveled in his position; he loved power and recognition and squeezed every ounce of drama out of a dramatic five years. Attlee, on the other hand, gives one the impression of performing a duty; and in any given situation he may be relied upon to drain away whatever drama exists. When he served as deputy leader under Churchill during the war a cabinet colleague commented: "When Winston presides at cabinet we feel we are in the presence of history; the monologue goes on for hours and we come away as from a feast. When Attlee takes the chair it is a business meeting, and we get home for dinner."

It is an interesting fact that as children these two men had the same governess. A certain Miss Hutchinson left Lord Randolph Churchill's household to go to the Attlees. She has described Winston as "an extremely self-willed boy," but her opinion of Clement has never been recorded. According to Attlee himself, however, shyness was always a major characteristic. What is surprising is that nearly thirty years of public life have done little to minimize it. Even today when he meets a colleague in the smoking room of the House of Commons, or runs into one of his ministers in the passage, he is tongue-tied. His embarrassment is contagious and as a result many men who have great personal regard for him will go a long way to avoid him. Only when he is among a few people he knows well and with whom he can discuss cricket, army experiences, or the early days of the labor movement does he seem at ease. Then he has an inexhaustible supply of anecdotes and can be really witty.

Perhaps because he has suffered so much from shyness himself he is hypersensitive to the feelings of others. Once when he was giving a large dinner at 10 Downing Street, the seventeen-year-old schoolmate of one of his daughters was late in arriving. No one noticed her absence until the guests were seated and there was an empty chair. Mr. Attlee at once insisted that everyone fold his napkin, return to the drawing room, and take up his cocktail glass as though nothing had happened. The girl soon appeared and never knew what she had been spared.

Attlee as Prime Minister, however, is very different from the

Attlee one sees at social occasions. At cabinet meetings his meekness drops away and he becomes a martinet, rapping on the table and keeping order in a sharp, waspish way. And his sting can be dangerous for when he feels it necessary to dismiss a member of the government he does so ruthlessly. In England it has always been an unwritten law that you "kick a minister upstairs" by sending him to the Lords or perhaps deporting him to a colony as a governor. But Attlee has not bothered with this sort of appeasement; he has dropped both ministers and junior ministers alike and given them no alternative but a seat on the back benches.

Altogether, Attlee is far from a pedestrian character. When the century can be reviewed as a whole it may well prove that he has affected the history of the nation as decisively as Winston Churchill. With almost terrier-like insistence he has impressed his ideas of social democracy on a huge, unwieldy party that originally represented every shade of opinion. First and foremost he is a democrat. At all times he has refused to compromise with the extreme left. Lesser men might have hesitated in 1939 to take the drastic steps that Attlee did in supporting the expulsion of such eminent figures as Stafford Cripps and Aneurin Bevan from the Labor ranks for urging a Popular Front with parties which included the Communists. During his administration he has packed the junior offices of the government with moderates, for these are the men who will carry on the brand of socialism in which he believes. His speeches are thoughtful and reflect not only a creed but a philosophy. In January, 1948, he said:

Ours is a philosophy in its own right. Our task is to work out a system of a new and challenging kind which combines individual freedom with a planned economy; democracy with social justice. This task which faces not only ourselves but all the Western democracies requires a government inspired by a new conception of society with a dynamic policy in accord with the needs of a new situation. It could not be accomplished by any of the old parties, nor by a totalitarian party, whether Fascist or Communist. A Conservatism rooted in the past and looking backwards makes no appeal to the majority today. Even a reformed and liberalised Conservatism which nevertheless bases itself on class inequality, private ownership of the means of life, and the supremacy of the profit motive, makes no appeal to a generation that remembers the suffering of the interwar years and has seen what a nation can accomplish when everything was subordinated to the common good.

To Attlee freedom is both political and economic. He once summed it up saying: "I object to dictatorships whether in blue shirts, green shirts, red shirts or any other kind of shirt, but I object equally when they are in boiled shirts."

As everyone knows, Herbert Morrison and Ernest Bevin do not like each other. A feud has been smoldering between them for nearly twenty years which is supposed to have its roots in a clash of authority between Morrison, the Labor party organizer, and Bevin, the trade-union leader. Added to this, their personalities are naturally antagonistic, possibly because they have too much in common. Both are the sons of working-class men, both have struggled against poverty, both are on the right wing of the socialist movement, and both like power. Both are forceful, dictatorial, and supremely egotistical. However, a sign that the breach between them might be narrowing came in 1947 when Bevin went to America and a group of Labor back-benchers staged a "revolt" against his foreign policy. Herbert Morrison, as Leader of the House, squashed the insurrection quickly and decisively. When Ernest returned to London the first words of praise he had ever uttered for Morrison fell from his lips. " 'Erbert played the game," he said briefly.

Herbert Morrison is a short, square Cockney with one eye, a lock of hair that curls over his forehead, and a face full of pugnacious humor. He is fond of referring to his "Tory background," for his father, a policeman, was a die-hard Conservative. So much so that when Herbert began talking socialism at the age of fourteen and left-wing pamphlets started arriving in the mail for him, his father tore them up and Herbert left home. He had a series of jobs as a grocer's errand boy, a shop assistant, a window dresser, and a telephone operator. When he was twenty-seven years old he became the secretary of the Lon-

don Labor party at a salary of a pound a week. This was the
beginning of his political career. He organized the party with
such skill that it became the spearhead of the national movement; in 1934 it captured the London County Council (the
body that governs the metropolis of London) and has held it
ever since, although today the majority is only eleven.*

As Leader of the House of Commons, Morrison runs the
parliamentary Labor party. He decides what business will be
taken up, how much time will be given to debates, and what
tactics are to be adopted. He will direct the tactics of the next
general election. He believes that if Socialism is to survive it
must capture the support of the middle classes, and all his
speeches are carefully framed to this end. When someone like
Shinwell announces that he doesn't give a "tinker's cuss" for
anyone except the workers, or Aneurin Bevan declares that all
Tories are "lower than vermin," Morrison's anger reaches boiling
point.

His opponents speak of him contemptuously as a "Tammany
boss" and claim that intrigue and political maneuvers are the
only things that interest him. This is unfair for there is no firmer
democrat in the Labor ranks than Morrison. With Attlee, he
supported the expulsion of Cripps and Bevan from the party in
1939 for urging coalition with the Communists; and in 1943, in
spite of an uproar from many Socialists, he insisted on releasing
Fascist Sir Oswald Mosley from prison on grounds of ill health.
After the war, when there was pressure to prevent Mosley and
his followers from holding meetings, he supported his successor
at the Home Office in declaring that if Britain believed in freedom of speech she must uphold it.

Morrison's views on nationalization are regarded with im-
patience by many of his colleagues. He believes in "going slow."
He sees nationalization not as a means of breaking the power of
the capitalists, as some of his party do, but of increasing efficiency. "I don't want to socialize for the mere sake of socializing,"

* In the April, 1949, election, Conservatives and Socialists scored a dead heat,
each with sixty-four Councillors. But the majority of Aldermen, who only come up
for election every six years, are Socialists, thus giving Labor its majority.

he insists. "That wouldn't be sense. I want to socialize where
it is good public business to do so." His worship of efficiency
makes him one of the few Socialists who are not afraid to praise
the wartime Minister of Aircraft Production—that high priest
of Toryism, Lord Beaverbrook.

He also shows a magnanimity toward Churchill which the
latter finds hard to reciprocate. Every Thursday Winston, as
leader of the opposition, calls for a statement of the following
week's business, phrasing his words in a slightly different way
each time for the amusement of his colleagues. Herbert as
Leader of the House always replies to him, and then the fun
begins. As masters of sarcasm they are well matched. Insults
couched in stylish parliamentary language are hurled back and
forth, Churchill as savage as a bulldog and Morrison as agile as
a monkey.

During the war Churchill made full use of Morrison's ability,
inviting him to sit as a member of the war cabinet; and in 1943
he remarked: "We derive the greatest advantage from Mr. Morrison's counsels, and I hope we shall continue to do so for long."
However, when Morrison became instrumental in pressing for
a general election and breaking up Churchill's coalition, the
latter became as piqued as a small boy. He said that of all his
colleagues the one he was most glad to see the back of was
Morrison, and even went so far as to make a special appeal to
Morrison's constituents to "throw him out."

Some Socialist ministers were taken aback in 1945 by the
flood of new, independent, and unruly Labor M.P.'s who entered the House. But Herbert handled them with humor and
firmness. "Get this clear," he told the most obstreperous ones.
"You are not the government; no one is the government except
the government; and the government alone must govern."

Morrison is five years younger than Attlee but he has the
same birthday; perhaps astrologers can see something significant
in this.

Someone once remarked about Ernest Bevin: "He murders
the English language but mirrors the souls of millions of English

people." When this large, lumbering trade-union leader with a face as rugged as an Epstein sculpture was made Foreign Secretary in 1945 he went to Potsdam and inquired sharply of the civil servants present: "What is going to be done about S?" A note was circulated through the Foreign Office. "What about S?" "And who the hell is S?" expostulated an official in exasperation. The mystery was finally solved; Bevin was referring to Rudolph Hess.

The early life of Ernest Bevin might have been drawn from the pages of Charles Dickens. His father was a Somerset farm laborer who died before Ernest was born and his mother was a village midwife. At the age of six he was an orphan and at eleven was sent to work on a farm where he toiled from dawn to dusk for his keep and sixpence a week. Two years later he ran away with nothing more than the clothes on his back, to seek his fortune in the great port of Bristol. There were many men out of work in those days and the next few years were a hard, bitter struggle which contained an interlude to which Bevin has since referred as "the time when I found myself walking the streets unemployed and having to steal for my living." He got a job as dishwasher at a shilling a day, as a waiter, and later as the driver of a horse and van for a maker of mineral waters. For years he lived on fifteen shillings a week; he married on a pound a week and never earned over two pounds a week until he was twenty-nine.

His fabulous career as a trade-union leader began with his job as a van driver. His deliveries took him to the docks, where the unemployed lined up for work in the early morning light and often waited half the day before returning home empty-handed. He soon began addressing meetings and agitating on their behalf for "the right" to work. He joined the union as a member of the carmen's branch and before long became its chairman. In 1920 he won important wage concessions for the dockers in a public court of inquiry, earning himself the name of "the dockers' K.C." But his great work as a trade unionist was in amalgamating thirty-seven unions into one giant organization, the Transport and General Workers' Union, which today is the largest single union in the world, with a membership of over 1,600,000; and after that of becoming head of the mighty Trades Union Congress.

When Churchill became Prime Minister in 1940, Bevin was one of the first people for whom he sent. This was a dramatic move, for these two men were pitted against each other as bitter opponents when the latter was one of the leaders of the general strike in 1926. But Winston needed a man of unusual ability, and although Bevin was in his sixtieth year with no previous political experience, he persuaded him to enter Parliament and become his Minister of Labor.

Bevin's rise from obscurity and his powerful grip on three decades of history are due chiefly to an immense personality and an almost devastating conviction that he knows best. These two qualities stand out so clearly and sharply that one is apt to think of him as a man of simplicity, whereas in truth he is curiously complicated. With little education to draw from, his knowledge of human beings is derived entirely from direct observation. No man is a greater master of the art of bullying and bludgeoning, cajoling and persuading, in the use of first the velvet glove and then the mailed fist. His wiliness makes him a formidable opponent, and anyone who has seen him addressing a conference of many thousands of people cannot fail to be impressed by his technique; often long-winded and boringly repetitious in his opening, he never fails to introduce the sledge-hammer blows in the third act that generally succeed in pulverizing his enemies. In 1935, when the Labor party was in danger of a serious split due to the fact that its leader, George Lansbury, a saintly old man, was preaching pacifism in the face of the rising tide of fascism, it was left to Bevin to strip him of support. The conference hall was ringing with emotional cheers for the revered old man when Bevin rose and in a merciless speech snarled his disgust at him for taking his "conscience round from body to body asking to be told what to do with it." He swung the conference so completely that he broke Lansbury's leadership and in doing so saved the Labor party from ineffectualism and perhaps even disintegration.

As Foreign Secretary Bevin has commanded the support of all sections of the country, Conservative and Socialist alike, in much the same way Churchill commanded national support during the war. His chief critics have been on the extreme left of his own party, accusing him of playing into the hands of "capitalist America" and "fomenting war with Russia." Although Bevin has always been an enemy of communism he has tried repeatedly to reach agreement with the Soviet Union. Reluctantly he has abandoned this mirage and is now working for a united western Europe backed by the good will of the United States.

Many people criticize Bevin's caution and his tendency to blame others for his failures; they snicker at his egotism, his illiteracy, his indiscretions, and his gaffes. But most people like having him where he is. In these dangerous times there is something reassuring about this great bulky slow-moving man whose word is his bond and whose integrity is beyond dispute.

His vast experience of his fellow beings is worth the wisdom of many books, although Bevin himself often expresses regret at having been taken from the classroom at such an early age. Once, when he was expecting the Turkish ambassador a young man walked into his office. "What are you doing here?" asked Ernest. "I'm sorry, sir, but I've been sent to interpret. The Turkish ambassador doesn't speak English very well." "That's fair enough," sighed Bevin. "Neither do I."

Bevin's contribution to history already stands out clearly; he has taught the labor movement of the Western world that the great issue of the age is not socialism against capitalism but the survival of democracy. For that alone he will be remembered as a great Foreign Minister.

Sir Stafford Cripps is an international figure. As Chancellor of the Exchequer he not only directs how Marshall Aid money will be spent and carries the main responsibility for Britain's recovery but also has the task of co-ordinating the economy of western Europe.

He is the most brainy, the most eccentric, the least accessible, and the least sympathetic member of the cabinet. Winston Churchill once said of him: "There but for the Grace of God goes God." Because England is a country of superb contradictions it is not surprising to learn that this man, at one time on the extreme left of his party, is the son of a peer, spent his childhood in a forty-roomed house on a twelve-hundred-acre estate, and gave up a £30,000-a-year ($120,000) practice at the bar in 1939 to devote himself to the war effort.

Cripps is tall, thin, and forbidding, and looks every inch the part he plays as the apostle of austerity. He wears shoes without heels, believing that elevation is bad for his digestion; he is a vegetarian, he does not drink, he goes to bed every night at eleven and rises every morning at 4:30. He works sixteen hours a day. Attlee tells the story of a man who rang the doorbell of No. 11 Downing Street at 5:30 in the morning. A policeman came up to him and asked him what he was doing. "I have an appointment," replied the man. The policeman's eyes narrowed with suspicion. "Just move along," he ordered quietly. "But I have an appointment," the man insisted. "Now listen, I don't want to 'ave to take you to the station . . ." "If you don't believe me you can make inquiries yourself," the man cried angrily. "I have an appointment with Sir Stafford Cripps." "Oh 'im!" replied the officer. "Begging your pardon, sir. Go right up."

As a parliamentarian Cripps is both respected and feared. He does not suffer fools gladly and members of the opposition hesitate to risk his scathing retorts unless they are absolutely sure of their facts. His early unpopularity with his own party was due to an intellectual arrogance which he was unable to hide, but which now seems to be mellowing with political success. Even so, his conception of the give-and-take of conversation is usually for him to give and others to take.

The fact that he has never failed to supply an answer to any question is a trait which apparently advanced itself at an early age. When he was eight years old his brothers referred to him as "young Solomon" and nicknamed him "Dad." In those days Cripps's enterprise was on strictly private lines. His first business venture appears to have been when his parents had guests for the week end; he removed the cakes and buns from the drawing room, took them to the nursery, and put a sign on the door: "Tea: Sixpence." Although he may sound like an odious child it is perhaps worth recording that the only comprehensive articles about him in the London newspaper files are written by his two brothers, die-hard Tories; and both glow with praise.

Cripps was educated at Winchester and won a science scholarship for New College, Oxford. But his papers showed such unusual promise that he was persuaded, instead, to work in Sir William Ramsay's laboratory at London University. He did not pursue science long, however, and in 1913 became a barrister. During World War I he drove a Red Cross ambulance in France, later returning to England to work as a chemist in an explosives factory. In 1914 he joined the Labor party and became known in the Gloucestershire village where he lived with his wife and children as "the Red Squire of Filkins." He entered Parliament in 1931 and held the office of Solicitor General under Ramsay MacDonald.

Cripps was expelled by the Labor Executive from the party in 1939 for urging a Popular Front with all parties including the Communists. A Labor colleague, James Walker, M.P., commented caustically on the event:

> We must drop our Socialism
> To catch the Liberal votes
> And when we win our way to power
> We'll cut the Liberal throats.

However, the trade unions were firmly behind the Labor Executive in their decision. Ernest Bevin's Transport and General Workers' Union put out the following statement: "We are satisfied that the long and continuous efforts of Sir Stafford Cripps and his friends can only result, if successful, in undermining and destroying the Labor Party as built up after years of strenuous endeavour by the trade unions."

Although Churchill made use of Cripps during the war, sending him to Moscow as ambassador in 1940, and to India on a special mission in 1942, he was not an outstanding success. This may have been due to the fact that a sympathetic personality, the one quality which Cripps lacks, was an essential in these particular appointments. It is only since Cripps has been Chancellor of the Exchequer, a job to which he is eminently suited, that he has become a figure of international importance.

Those who work with him respect his intellect and his capacity for work but sometimes find his leadership somewhat exacting. He holds a meeting of his financial experts and under-secretaries every morning at nine o'clock which is referred to behind his back as "morning prayers"; and if anyone arrives even a minute or two late he has an unpleasant habit of nodding curtly and saying, "Good evening."

Cripps's lack of warmth may prevent him from becoming Prime Minister. That people seldom see themselves as others see them is illustrated by the fact that when a well-known American came to England recently someone asked Cripps what he thought of him. "A nice fellow," came the reply, "but he lacks the human touch."

Aneurin Bevan is the most controversial figure in the government. For years he has been something of a boy wonder. He went to work in the coal pits of South Wales at the age of thirteen, rose through the trade unions, and in 1929 came to Parliament as the member for Ebbw Vale. His soft Welsh voice, his immense laugh, his romantic appearance, and his fire and eloquence on the floor of the House immediately captured the imagination of political London. The press talked of him as a future Prime Minister while Conservatives, intrigued by this passionate, picturesque young man, at once bade him to their parties. He talked loudly of his burning hatred for the Tories but spent so many pleasant evenings drinking champagne at Lord Beaverbrook's house that Brendan Bracken described him as "Bollinger Bolshevik." But although "Nye" enjoyed the good things of life his political convictions remained steadfast. Once when he left Beaverbrook's house he remarked good-naturedly of his host: "You know, I'm afraid when we get to power we'll have to lock up that likable rascal Max!"

Representing as he does the left wing of the Labor party, many Conservatives believe that if Bevan became Prime Minister he really might begin locking people up. His violent abuse of the Tories, his boisterous spirits and scathing tongue have made him more hated by the opposition than any other figure on the Labor benches. Churchill referred to him during the war as "that merchant of rudeness," and when recently Bevan announced publicly that he considered the Tories "lower than vermin," Winston countered by saying that Bevan's title of Minister of Health should be changed to Minister of Disease and that he should submit himself as the first pathological case to be treated under the new medical scheme his department had introduced. "Nye and Winston are natural antagonists," commented an M.P., "because they're so much alike."

Churchill would be insulted at this comparison but so far as lack of stability is concerned it carries some truth. Both are brilliant, both are erratic, and both have personalities that arouse a mixture of admiration and hostility. One of Bevan's gestures which has done more to annoy the general public than almost any other is his insistence upon attending Embassy functions and parties at Buckingham Palace in a brown suit in order to show his contempt for convention.

Bevan's father was a miner and his four brothers and sisters, Blodwyn, Myfanwy, Arianwen, and Iorweth were also employed in the pits. When he was sixteen he memorized and recited long passages of Shakespeare in order to overcome a stutter which is occasionally still noticeable in his speech. Soon after he came to Parliament he married Jenny Lee, a pretty, vivacious Scottish M.P. who once remarked that politics was her career and marriage her hobby. At present she is a director of *Tribune*, the most forceful of the left-wing weekly magazines.

Although Churchill refused to give Bevan a job in his coalition government, as Minister of Health the latter has carried the immense burden of rehousing the nation, as well as inaugurating the first national health scheme the country has known. He has done both jobs with characteristic violence, arousing agitation and hostility, but Socialists insist that he has done them remarkably well.

Bevan is a member of the Labor party Executive and as a national figure has a large following, but his influence in the parliamentary Labor party is less marked. The extreme left intellectuals support him but the trade unionists and the moderates regard him with reserve. However, the fact that Bevan at fifty-two is a good ten years younger than other leading ministers causes members to prophesy that his turn to lead the country will come. "That is," they say, "if he grows up in time."

CHAPTER 5

Winston Churchill

I am a child of the House of Commons.
—WINSTON CHURCHILL

IF THE Conservatives win the next election, Winston Churchill, Leader of His Majesty's Opposition, will once again become Prime Minister of England. After the general election, when Tory fortunes were at their lowest ebb and the Socialists were proclaiming joyfully that Labor was "in" for twenty years, friends pressed Winston to relinquish his leadership of the party and to merely use the House as a platform for speeches on world affairs. "I don't see why I should give up my horse," he said stubbornly. "It may not be a very good horse, but at least it's better than being in the infantry."

Today no one is more pleased than Winston that he has clung to the saddle. After a year or two of quiet grazing his hired Tory beast showed signs of revival, and the master, always buoyant and imaginative, now visualizes a successful charge through the ranks of the government at the approaching election.

This does not mean that Winston is the darling of the Conservative party. Far from it. Many of his colleagues are alarmed by the use he is making of his charger. Sometimes their leader is galloping off to dictate a new chapter to his book; sometimes to direct activities on his three-hundred-acre farm in Kent; sometimes to hold a conference for the federation of Europe. They never know when he will come cantering into the House of Commons, and when he does, they never know what he will say. Although politics is still, as always, Churchill's major interest, he is not noted for his teamwork and his individuality is just as pronounced in opposition as in office. Just at the moment his party had issued a "charter" which declared that most of the existing controls must be retained as long as goods remain in short supply, Churchill cried out dramatically: "Set the people free," at once setting his own ranks in confusion.

Although as a young man Churchill deserted the Conservative party for the Liberals, flaunting his radicalism in the face of his former colleagues, long ago Sir Ian Hamilton, a close friend, said of him: "I have always felt that Winston's coat of many colors was originally dipped in a vat of blue; a good fast natural Tory background, none of your synthetic dyes."

This observation seems to have been astute, for today Winston represents the extreme right of the Tory party. His conservatism, which in former days would have been only too welcome, is at present proving an embarrassment to many of his supporters. They believe that the Conservative party has little chance of defeating Labor unless it can convince the electorate that it has abandoned its laissez-faire economy. The Conservatives, therefore, are divided into two groups: the progressives led by Eden and Rab Butler and the die-hards led by Churchill.

The fact that members of his party would like to see him relinquish his leadership to Anthony Eden has not escaped Winston's notice. He recently remarked to a friend: "When I want to tease Anthony I remind him that Gladstone formed his last administration at the age of eighty-four."

Whoever undertakes Churchill's biography will have to be a writer of unusual perception for there are few men in public life as incalculable and none as contradictory. Aristocrat, autocrat, and democrat, he is a blend of folly and wisdom, of sentiment and arrogance, of impulsiveness and detachment. Immensely human and yet entirely unconcerned with human beings except as they fit into a preconceived pattern of ideas, he is capable of playing the politician as well as the statesman and sometimes veers between these two roles with bewildering facility. The one constant note in his character is individuality. He specializes in drawing rabbits out of the hat and from his earliest days has defied the accepted maxims of behavior.

As a child he was regarded by his teachers not only as "the naughtiest small boy in the world" but as a dunce as well. He entered Harrow at the bottom of his class and left, six years later, still in the Lower School. The only flair he showed was for journalism, but as his contributions to the school paper consisted mainly of attacks on the masters, they were not greatly appreciated. Although lampoons were innocently signed "Junius Junior" he was called up before the headmaster, J. E. C. Welldon, and asked for an explanation. "But they're anonymous, sir," he replied. "Anonymous or not," snapped Welldon, "if any more appear I'm going to beat you."

Winston's apparent stupidity was accompanied by a lack of contrition that his teachers found unforgivable, and a bumptiousness that his schoolmates found intolerable. In order to protect himself when he walked down the street it is claimed that he sometimes found it convenient to keep his back toward the wall. Although such treatment did not lessen his self-confidence he describes his school days as "the only barren and unhappy period" of his life.

Winston was born in the heyday of Victorian privilege when wealth or rank were necessary credentials for the world of politics. As the grandson of the Duke of Marlborough and the son of Lord Randolph Churchill, the famous leader of "Tory Democracy," the silver spoon in his mouth had "the House of Commons" plainly written on it. His father was so disgusted with his scholastic record, however, that he declared he would not waste another penny on his education and instead of sending him to a university entered him for Sandhurst. Even though Winston was thrilled at the prospect of a military career he started off in a disappointing fashion. He passed his examination with so low a mark that the only place open to him was in the cavalry, which was limited to men of independent means and therefore always had a number of vacancies.

Soon Second Lieutenant Churchill of the 4th Hussars was

sent to India with his regiment; and soon his irrepressible aggressiveness had made him as unpopular with his fellow officers as with his schoolmates. A field marshal, who was a captain at the time, recalls an occasion when Churchill and several of his colleagues were invited to dinner at the Viceroy's Palace. Pomp and ceremony blazed at such functions, and rules of procedure were observed with meticulous care. The young army officers were kept at one end of the huge reception room while the great ones of India, the governors and princes, or "heaven-borns" as they were called, talked politics at the other end. Winston listened impatiently to the banal conversation of his contemporaries, then strode down the length of the room, pushed his way into the circle, and began to give them advice on how to run the country. "That sort of thing," the field marshal explained, "did not contribute to his popularity."

Winston remained in the army only four years, but short-lived as his service was it was packed with change and adventure. Soldiering at that time was obviously far removed from the grim business it has become in this century. In those days cavalry officers got nearly six months leave a year; it was permissible for an officer to write articles for the press and still retain his commission, and possible for a young man of Winston's connections to vary monotony by switching at fancy from one regiment to another. Thus you see Lieutenant Churchill moving from the 4th Hussars to the 31st Punjab Infantry; from there to the 36th Dogras and then to the 21st Lancers, usually in the capacity of an "officer correspondent." You see him dashing off to Cuba during his leave to cover the rebellion for the *Daily Graphic*; dashing off to a Pathan revolt in the Himalayas during another leave for the *Daily Telegraph*; and during a third leave to Kitchener's army in the Sudan for the *Morning Post*.

The spate of articles and books he wrote on his adventures, climaxed by his capture and escape from the Boers after he had resigned from the army, aroused mixed storms of praise and abuse. Many deplored what they termed his "passion for the limelight" and attacked his insolence in criticizing his superior officers rather than sticking to his regimental duties.

However, Winston remained impervious. He was now a well-known figure with several thousand pounds of earnings in the bank and a world market for his writing. But journalism was no longer enough. His interest in politics had been aroused and the House of Commons was his objective. He wrote: "It is better to be making the news than taking it; to be an actor rather than a critic."

During the past few years he had made a concentrated effort to gain a knowledge of history, philosophy, and literature. He read greedily, expressing regret for the years he had wasted at school. Even though he succeeded in educating himself more thoroughly than most university students he complains even today that his education is like a Swiss cheese, "smooth on the surface but with too many holes in it."

In 1900, at the age of twenty-six, he was elected Conservative member of Parliament for Oldham. Thus he had at last embarked on the career that his father, who had died some years before, had hoped for him as a child.

I first met Winston Churchill in 1938, six months before the Munich agreement. He was not a member of the government, but even outside it he was still the most colorful and controversial figure in English political life. I had sat in the gallery of the House of Commons and watched the chamber crowd to hear him speak. In the distance he looked extraordinarily old-fashioned in his black coat, his winged collar and bow tie, and even his rolling prose suggested a more leisurely and cultivated century. But what he had to say was not of the past; when he leaned forward to warn his colleagues of the dangers of Nazi Germany he became the incarnation of a pugnacious and perennial John Bull. You felt the imagination of the House stir with the brilliance of his words, but unfortunately the magic ended with his eloquence. When you went into the tearoom half an hour later you heard people chattering about what he had said with an alarming lightheartedness.

Churchill spent most of his time at his country house Chartwell, in Kent, and one Sunday his son took me there for lunch.

I remember being surprised by his round pink face. I had not expected such a formidable man to have such a cherubic appearance. Later I heard that a woman had once told him that her baby looked like him, to which he replied firmly: "All babies look like me." I was also surprised by the fact that even in private conversation his phrases were as rounded and polished as when he was speaking in the House. He delighted in the use of such Victorian expressions as "I rejoice," "I am greatly distressed," and "I venture to say," which were emphasized by the impediment in his speech that prevented him from pronouncing distinctly the letter s.

During lunch the conversation centered on world affairs, and he expressed his fear that England would refuse to show her hand until it was not only too late to avoid war but too late to win a war. He talked with the brilliance I had expected but I later learned that I was lucky, for when he is preoccupied or moody he makes no attempt at conversation. Small talk does not interest him and he is incapable of repartee; it is a question of either silence or a monologue, and nothing in between.

After lunch I was taken upstairs to see his large, high-ceilinged, oak-beamed study. He showed me several stacks of manuscript of the history of the English-speaking people which he was then writing. "I doubt if I finish it before the war comes," he said morosely, "and if I do, the part the English-speaking people will play will be so decisive I will have to add several new volumes." He paused. "And if it is not decisive no more histories will be written for many years."

As Churchill talked one could not help being struck by the restless energy and frustration of the man. In spite of his writing, his weekly contributions to the press, his long and masterly speeches in the Commons, one was aware that only a quarter of his resources was being used, and one felt that he was like a mighty torrent trying to burst his dams. At that time he had been out of office for nine years. "A genius without judgment" was the phrase heard most often in connection with him. "The trouble with Winston," people said, "is that you never know what he will do next."

Although today it is commonly believed that his exile was due to his anti-Nazism this was not altogether true. He was excluded from Ramsay MacDonald's national government in 1931, two years before Hitler came to power. And in 1935, when there was talk of his joining Baldwin's Conservative government, he suddenly backed the cause of Edward VIII and Mrs. Simpson, arousing such a storm of disapproval that his chances of restoring himself to favor were again eclipsed.

The truth of the matter was that Churchill was not a popular figure. His arrogance and aggressiveness still provoked the same hostility that had followed him from his earliest days. He wounded sensibilities without even knowing he had done so, for ideas, not people, were the only thing that interested him. Tactless and impetuous, he had not learned the virtue of at least giving the appearance of co-operation and as a result he was branded as "a troublemaker." When Bonar Law became Prime Minister in 1922 he said: "I consider Churchill a formidable antagonist. Nevertheless, I would rather have him in opposition than on my side."

Much of this prejudice was based on Churchill's past. His political career had been anything but orthodox. After having sat as a Conservative M.P. for four years he crossed the floor of the House in 1904 and joined the Liberals, an act which caused as much of a sensation then as if a Conservative should join the Socialists today.

Under various Liberal coalition administrations he held the ministerial posts of President of the Board of Trade, Home Secretary, First Lord of the Admiralty, Chancellor of the Duchy of Lancaster, Minister of Munitions, Secretary of State for War and Air, and Secretary of State for the Colonies. Then in 1922 he crossed the floor of the House again and returned to the Conservatives. It is a tribute to his talents that he was rewarded in 1924 with the position of Chancellor of the Exchequer, for party loyalty is taken very seriously in England and rebels are not often forgiven. Once when Churchill was referring to his past he said with a twinkle in his eye: "Anyone can rat, but it takes a certain amount of ingenuity to re-rat."

However, although his ability had been used he was distrusted by many people and frequently referred to as "an opportunist." Added to this, the working classes had not forgotten that when he was Home Secretary he had called out troops to break industrial strikes; they also blamed much of the unemployment of the same period on the fact that as Chancellor of the Exchequer he had been responsible for England's return to the gold standard.

Thus, in the decade preceding World War II Churchill found himself with bitter opponents among Conservative, Liberal, and Labor leaders alike. What was so disarming about him was the fact that he never got used to unpopularity; it always surprised him. Once he wrote mournfully: "I have never joined an intrigue. Everything I have got I have fought for. And yet I have been more hated than anybody!"

During this unhappy period in Churchill's life his chief solace lay in writing. He has always enjoyed hard work and is capable of turning out an immense amount of material in an astonishingly short time. But his literary achievements, distinguished as they were, always seemed to him secondary to political success. World affairs was the only topic of conversation that never bored him, and during those days of exile a flow of statesmen, journalists, and foreign emissaries were invited to Chartwell to give him firsthand information on the latest happenings.

Churchill's reputation for luxury always seemed to me greatly exaggerated. Comfort was essential to him but he cared nothing for society. He insisted on a good bed, good food, good wine and brandy, and good cigars. Occasionally he dined out but he seldom spent a week end away from his own house where things were ordered to his taste.

Any deviation from comfort, arranged in the name of pleasure, filled him with gloom. For example, Megan Lloyd George tells the story of a time many years ago when her father and Winston went on a trip to North Africa. A prominent prince of the desert gave a large dinner in their honor. The feast was served in the open and the guests sat in a circle on the ground around a huge caldron of steaming food. There were no forks and knives and everyone was expected to help himself from the common bowl. Lloyd George enjoyed anything out of the ordinary and at once flung himself into the spirit of the occasion. But Winston sat silent and glowering, refusing to make a move of any kind. Some of the guests eyed him nervously for fear their host would take offense at his sullen mood. Suddenly he rolled up his sleeves and with a fierce defiance plunged his arm into the bowl growling: "Come on, Megan, to hell with civilization!"

Winston was every inch a Prime Minister. Occasionally I had the honor of being invited to 10 Downing Street for lunch. A low-ceilinged room below the ground floor which, I believe, was once the servants' hall had been turned into the dining room, and there were seldom more than seven or eight guests. Winston usually came into the room in a blue siren suit looking remarkably like a Teddy bear with an air as autocratic as a monarch. I used to watch the guests struggling between surprise at his comic appearance and awe at his dignity. The success of the lunch depended entirely on what sort of mood he was in; sometimes he ate in such sullen silence your heart sank as you imagined that the war had taken some grave turn for the worse; other times he was buoyantly talkative and held the table with a brilliant monologue.

Winston had at last found his destiny. The world looked to him for a lead, and all the pent-up energy of the immense machine that throbbed in his heart and mind was being brought into play. He no longer knew the frustration of ideas that could not be brought alive, vitality that could not be spent, ingenuity that could not be called into play. The tremendous task that had fallen to him equaled his stature as a man.

The whole of 10 Downing Street throbbed with a restless energy it had never known before and probably hoped never to know again. The routine of government was turned topsy-turvy. Churchill stayed in bed half the morning dictating and stayed up half the night talking. Every afternoon, after lunch, he had a nap. Chiefs of staff, civil servants, ministers had to adapt themselves to this routine as best they could. Most of them had to be at work at nine or ten in the morning; even so, woe betide them if they were not men enough to come when he sent for them after dinner to stay up until the early hours of the morning. The only man who persistently stuck to his guns and always bade Churchill good night at 11:00 P.M. was Field Marshal Alexander.

Week ends, too, became a novelty. During the blitz Chequers, the Prime Minister's official country residence, was regarded as too obvious a target for the German bombers to be safe and Churchill was persuaded to abandon it. He accepted the offer of Ronald Tree to spend his week ends at Dytchley, one of the most beautiful houses in England. Every Friday Churchill and an entourage of ten or twenty guests, secretaries, civil servants, generals, ministers, and distinguished foreign emissaries moved to Oxfordshire. The Trees kept only a few rooms for themselves and turned the rest of the house over to the Prime Minister. In these luxurious surroundings, with the best cook in the land and drink flowing freely, many plans for the war were laid.

The main relaxation of the week end was the showing of a film every Sunday after dinner. Churchill watches a film with schoolboy enthusiasm; he enjoyed *Lady Hamilton* so much he insisted on seeing it eight times, and a few months later its producer, Alexander Korda, received a knighthood. Churchill, however, was not always left in peace to see his films. Frequently he was interrupted by urgent messages. The news that Hess had landed in England is said to have arrived during a Mickey Mouse.

Only a few miles from Dytchley stands Blenheim Palace, the family seat of the Marlboroughs and the house in which Churchill was born. Occasionally he took distinguished Americans to see it. One wonders what they thought of this immense palace built by Queen Anne as a gift from the nation to that famous soldier, the first Duke of Marlborough. Although during the war Blenheim was occupied by Military Intelligence the present Duke retained one wing of the house. There is a story, probably apocryphal, that when Churchill was eager to show a group of Americans the room in which he was born he led them down a long corridor and opened the door. "This is it," he said. He was at once greeted by cries of female protest for the room had been turned into the Ladies' Room.

No one denies that Churchill was a great war leader, but the charge most often leveled against him is that he *enjoyed* the war. I do not see how anyone can pretend otherwise. From youth his imagination had been stirred by the great battles that had decided the history of Europe, by the relentless struggle for power between men of different nations and different creeds. Churchill was a fighter and the stakes were high; for the first time in his life he had the opportunity to employ all his genius and energy in a cause in which he passionately believed.

But anyone who imagines that he carried the burden lightly is mistaken; there were times when the weight was almost crushing. In the autumn of 1940 I motored to Chequers one day for lunch. Mrs. Churchill was away and only his daughter Mary and daughter-in-law Pamela were there. Just before lunch was announced one of Churchill's private secretaries came into the room and handed him a message from the Foreign Office. He read it standing before the chimney piece in the drawing room. Then, unexpectedly, he handed it to me. The message was a report from Berlin stating that Pétain had agreed to turn over to the Germans the use of all airdromes and ports in unoccupied France.

Churchill was plunged into a state of gloom. He came into the dining room but ate very little and sat halfway through the meal, with his elbows on the table, holding his head in his hands. The secretary who had brought the news reminded him that it was only a report from Berlin and likely to be untrue, but the old man would not be consoled. "If it is true, it's a bitter blow," he said.

At last lunch mercifully ended and Churchill went out for a walk. I left at about four o'clock and before I went he came back in the drawing room as vigorous and lionhearted as ever. He had received a message that the report was false.

A few months later I went again to Chequers, this time to be the godmother of Randolph Churchill's son, Winston Jr. The christening took place in a small chapel about a mile from the house. Owing to a breakdown of my car I did not arrive until the ceremony had begun, and found a place reserved for me between Mr. Churchill and his son. I had always heard that the Prime Minister's emotions were easily stirred and at times he could be as sentimental as a woman, and on this occasion I had proof of it, for he sat throughout the ceremony with tears streaming down his cheeks. "Poor infant," he murmured, "to be born into such a world as this."

After the christening we returned to Chequers for lunch. Only the family, Lord Rothermere, and the two godfathers Lord Beaverbrook and Brendan Bracken were present. Beaverbrook rose and proposed a toast to the baby, then turned to Churchill, whose birthday had taken place the day before, and proposed a toast to him. Beaverbrook was eloquent and reminded us that we had the honor to be in the presence of a man who would be remembered as long as the civilized world existed. Once again I looked up to see Churchill weeping. When he was called on to reply he rose and, in a voice unsteady with emotion, said: "In these days I often think of Our Lord." Then he sat down.

I have never forgotten those simple words, and if he enjoyed waging the war let it always be remembered that he understood the anguish of it as well.

Churchill's overwhelming defeat at the general election of 1945 was ironical not only because he was at the summit of his power and fame but because no statesman dramatized the superior qualities of the British people more romantically than he. During the war, when someone congratulated him on a broadcast, saying: "You are giving the people the courage they need," he replied quickly: "You are mistaken. They already have the courage. I only focus it." To have been rejected by a people toward whom he felt such pride and possessiveness was a bitter blow.

During the first years of his premiership Churchill declared privately that he would never commit the mistake Lloyd George had made in seeking to retain power once the war was over. But those close to him were skeptical when he took over the leadership of the Conservative party in 1942. Many criticized his action, declaring that since he had assailed the Tories so bitterly in the prewar years it was undignified to grasp the reins at the first opportunity; others insisted that as the head of a great coalition government he should remain above party politics.

It would have taken a man of far greater detachment than Winston to have refused to offer himself to the electorate when all the world was acclaiming him. Although leading Conservatives were uncomfortably aware that a new wind was blowing through England, they believed that Churchill's fame could keep them in power. Churchill believed this too. Like most great men he lived in an atmosphere of adulation and flattery and had little contact with the rank and file of the population. He was supremely self-confident. Although from time to time he was pressed to make some positive statement on domestic policy, he was not interested in internal affairs; a conservative "five-year plan" was put forward under the guidance of Lord Woolton but it contained few constructive proposals. It was perhaps typical of the arrogance which had led Churchill to political disaster so often before that he should think he could win an election on personality alone. "His tragedy," an opponent remarked, "is that although the public will sometimes follow his ideas, they will never follow *him*." While the Socialists went into action with a carefully planned program, Conservatives fought the battle equipped with little more than Churchill's photograph.

The election was a boisterous and exciting affair. The weather was fine, the war with Germany was over, and the people were in a happy frame of mind. Soon drab, austerity-minded Britain was plastered with election posters and the quiet countryside was resounding to the noise of loud-speaker vans. In public halls, pubs, and village squares enthusiastic candidates expounded their faiths. In London the unofficial Conservative "nerve center" was Lord Beaverbrook's flat on Park Lane. "The Beaver" was Churchill's closest friend and chief adviser. One night I visited him after dinner, and during the course of the evening three Conservative ministers dropped in to solicit Beaverbrook's support in securing them appointments when the new government was formed. Beaverbrook enjoyed his importance and probably exaggerated the influence he exerted.

The campaign was memorable for the fact that it was an astonishing revelation of Churchill's dual character. Overnight the statesman vanished and in his place appeared an excited and irresponsible politician hurling invective and abuse at his opponents and offering nothing constructive of his own. Churchill sounded the first gun in a radio broadcast telling the country that socialism would mean a "Nazi state" and "a Gestapo." I heard this broadcast at Lord Rothermere's house and remember the silence when he had finished. "If he continues like that," said Lord Rothermere, "the election is as good as lost."

People were shocked, because Churchill had paid many tributes to Attlee, Morrison, Bevin, and other Socialist leaders when they were serving in his coalition government; to turn on them so wildly in order to cadge votes was considered "un-English." Some people attributed his tactics to Lord Beaverbrook's influence, and others to his own notoriously bad judgment. I could not help recalling the lines H. G. Wells once wrote: "There are times when the evil spirit comes upon him and when I think of him as a very intractable, a very mischievous, dangerous little boy, a knee-worthy little boy. Only by thinking of him in that way can I go on liking him."

The public was inclined to regard his abuse as a political stunt and the working class remained skeptical of his interest in domestic affairs. They remembered the high prices and the unemployment that followed the first war and listened for reassurances which were not forthcoming. In one speech Churchill referred to milk for babies. The comments of the people in a village in which I was staying were: "What's 'e know or care about babies' milk?" one woman said. "Guns is 'is specialty and any time there's a war we're glad to let 'im run it but when 'e talks about babies' milk we know someone's told 'im what to say and it's not 'im speaking at all."

Although it was obvious that opinion was hardening against him, even the pessimists believed he would win a majority of fifty seats. The results of the Gallup poll published in the *News Chronicle* showed a Labor landslide which proved to be accurate within 1 percent, but Britain was not "poll-conscious" and few people paid any attention to the figures. Two days before polling day I heard Churchill address an enormous gathering at the Walthamstow Stadium on the outskirts of London and was amazed at the amount of opposition and heckling he received. He was interrupted so often he could scarcely get through his speech. When he had finished, his daughter Sarah invited me to a private room to have beer and sandwiches with them before he went on to his next engagement. As a war correspondent for the past eight years I had seen a number of countries invaded and overrun by the enemy and when Churchill saw me he exclaimed: "What a bad omen! For the first time I have my doubts about this election. You only appear when the established regime is crashing to the ground!"

Neither he nor I had any idea how prophetic his words were to prove. He arranged a small dinner party in advance to celebrate his victory on the day the results were made known. One of the guests told me afterwards she had never sat through a more depressing meal. Churchill's daughters were in tears and the old man himself sat immobile as though too stunned to speak.

Defeat burned deep into Churchill's soul. He felt that he had been badly used by an ungrateful population, but he concealed his bitterness and took care not to allow vindictiveness to creep into his speeches. And he still retained his sense of humor. When a friend suggested that he should make a tour of England so that the thousands of his own countrymen who had never seen him could have a chance to honor him he growled: "I refuse to be exhibited like a prize bull whose chief attraction is its past prowess."

He faced the new House of Commons with the pride and courage for which he is famous, and on the opening day of Parliament hundreds of members cheered him singing: "For he's a jolly good fellow." He was extremely courteous to the new Prime Minister but every now and then he could not resist a private joke. When, after the election, Attlee went to Washington and in his absence there were altercations between his ministers, Winston is said to have remarked: "When the mouse is away, the cats will play."

In spite of the insults Churchill hurled at his opponents during the campaign, once the fight was over he was ready to resume friendly relations with them. He expects others to regard a political battle as he does: as a good healthy English game after which everyone shakes hands in the accepted sporting fashion. His peculiarly disarming quality of forgive and forget was expressed when he had bronze plaques made, adorned with the oak and the acorn, which he sent to all those who had served in his wartime government. Socialists whom he had branded as future Gestapo leaders were surprised to receive these souvenirs with their names inscribed and bearing the words: "*Salute the greatest of all Coalitions. 1940–45.*"

Today Winston is buoyed by the hope of returning to No. 10 Downing Street at the next election. In spite of his activities as leader of the opposition, historian, painter, farmer, and crusader for European federation, he still burns with restless energy, hankering after the great political prize that slipped from his grasp in 1945.

When he comes into the House there is a ripple of excitement in the gallery and you feel the pulse of the chamber quicken. As belligerent and impulsive as ever, his deliberately scathing remarks still succeed in provoking his opponents to angry rejoinders; at the same time, ever since his defeat there has been a curious gentleness toward him. He is too partisan to play the role of elder statesman, but his fellow members recognize him not only as a great man but as a great character without whom the House of Commons will never have the same flavor again.

Although Britain is passing through the greatest domestic crisis she has ever faced, Winston exerts little influence on internal affairs. Although in his early days as a Liberal he helped to launch the social services, today he gives the impression of regarding them, and labor relations as well, as preoccupations for far more detailed and pedestrian minds. His imagination soars only at world affairs, conflicts between whole nations, not groups of men—the continuous struggle for power on which the whole of civilization depends.

The one consistent thread that runs through Churchill's life is his approach to foreign affairs. In spite of impulsive and contradictory views on other subjects he has never departed from his conception of what Britain's foreign policy must be, and in this matter he has been the purest of traditionalists. In 1907, Sir Eyre Crowe, a member of the Foreign Office, wrote:

> The only check on the use of political predominance has always consisted in the opposition of an equally formidable rival or a combination of several countries forming a league of defence. The equilibrium established by such a group of forces is technically known as the Balance of Power, and it has been an historical truism to identify England's secular policy with the maintenance of this balance by throwing her weight now on this scale, now on that, but ever on the side opposed to political dictatorship of the strongest single state or group of states at a given time.
>
> If this view of British policy is correct, the opposition to which England must inevitably be driven by any country aspiring to such a dictatorship assumes almost the form of a law of Nature. . . .

Study British history and you will see that this simple formula has been followed at each great crisis in the life of the nation. Five times Britain has been seriously threatened and five times Britain has fought in partnership with a coalition of nations; first against Philip II of Spain, second against Louis XIV of France, third against Napoleon, fourth against the Kaiser, and fifth against Hitler.

Before the last war was over Churchill was already preoccupied with Britain's position in a Europe dominated by Russia. I went to lunch at 10 Downing Street in 1944, the day after D-Day. The papers were full of the great landing and most people could talk of little else. Churchill came into the room dressed as usual in his blue siren suit, and the guests expected him to comment on the invasion, but he scarcely referred to it; he was worried and moody. Suddenly in the middle of lunch he launched out on an angry discourse on foreign affairs. He was annoyed by left-wing attacks on a speech he had made which had been interpreted as conciliatory to General Franco and by criticism of his attitude toward the Italian monarchy. "When this war is over," he growled, "England will need every ally she can get to protect herself against Russia. I'm sick of these parlor pinks, always criticizing the internal regimes of countries. I don't care a whit what people do inside their own countries as long as they don't try to export their ideas, and as long as their relations with Britain are friendly. Spain is ready to make her peace with Britain and I am ready to accept it; the Italian monarchy is friendly to Britain and I would like to see it preserved. The idea of running foreign affairs on personal prejudices is criminal folly."

Churchill's passionate concern with ideas rather than men has probably been, at one and the same time, his greatest strength and his greatest weakness. His present efforts to federate Europe are an extension of the classical policy he has pursued so faithfully. Historically his conception must be correct, but in building up his concert of nations will he ignore the human struggle within those nations, and in so doing set up a pack of cards? And will he succeed in his concert of nations?

One cannot give the answer. One only knows that as long as he lives his influence on world affairs will be splendid, bold, and in the interest of freedom-loving men.

CHAPTER 6

The House of Lords

In fact, we may say that they (the House of
Commons) are a growing plant and we (the
House of Lords) are cut flowers.
—LORD STANSGATE, *Hansard*, JUNE 9, 1948

IN FRONT of one of the entrances into the Palace of Westminster stands a doorman dressed in a scarlet coat and a
black top hat. This gentleman guards the portals that lead into
the House of Lords. When you step inside, the quiet almost
reminds you of a cathedral. A sharp contrast to the crowded
lobby and the proletarian noise and confusion of the Commons.
Instead of being asked your business by a suspicious six-foot
policeman, an attendant in black knee breeches with a huge
gold chain across his coat bearing the royal arms inquires if he
can be of assistance; when you say you have a ticket for the
visitors' gallery he leads you across a marble floor, past rows and
rows of coat pegs each proudly bearing the name of a peer, up
a flight of stairs, across a huge banqueting hall where parliamentary receptions are occasionally held, and finally he turns
you over to another gentleman with a gold chain who checks
your name and calls for an attendant to show you to your seat.

From the gallery you look down on a small oblong room with
a throne at one end flanked on either side by benches covered
with dark red cloth. Although the chamber is not large the
benches are seldom more than half full; the presence of forty
or fifty members is considered a good attendance. What strikes
you most is the fact that it is an old man's chamber. Almost all
the heads are bald, white, or graying; there is a generous sprin-

kling of earphones and canes, and it is not unusual for two or three of their lordships to be fast asleep in their seats.

The atmosphere of leisure and affluence suggests the palmy days of less than half a century ago when the Lords wielded great power and England was ruled by one class alone. But any suggestion that the assembly belongs to a past era is hotly resented. When, during a recent debate on the Parliament Act, a Labor peer asserted that members of the Commons were in closer contact with the rank and file of the population than members of the Lords, an imperious old gentleman retorted sharply: "Nonsense! We live among them!" And one at once had visions of the imposing country house with the tenants' cottages grouped together within the large walled-in estate.

Although there are 844 peers in the United Kingdom, at the present time only 619 of them are entitled to sit in the House of Lords. They include all the peers of England who are over twenty-one, who have proved their titles, who have taken the oath, and who are clear of the bankruptcy courts; sixteen Scottish and eight Irish peers who are elected by the general body of Scottish and Irish peers; the Archbishops of Canterbury and York and twenty-four bishops known as "the lords spiritual"; and nine Lords of Appeal who are appointed for life and who act as Supreme Court judges.

Although 75 percent of the members of the Lords are men who have inherited their titles, and the majority of these are landowners, it would be wrong to give the impression that the House is an entirely feudal institution. Over 160 members are "lords of the first creation" or, in other words, commoners who have been raised to the peerage. These men give the House its tang, for in character and ability it would be difficult to find a more mixed lot; they range from the self-seeking to the self-sacrificing, from the inept and foolish to the clever and wise.

This is due no doubt to the fact that the paths leading to the Lords are strangely varied. First, you can become a peer by outstanding services to the state: to wit, the great soldiers, sailors, and airmen of the last war such as Air Marshal Lord Portal,

Admiral Lord Cunningham, Field Marshals Lord Alexander and Montgomery; or you can become a peer by distinguishing yourself in some such field as medicine, literature, or science, or by accumulating a fortune as a brewer, an industrialist, or a press proprietor and contributing to the funds of the party in power. Lastly, you can become a peer by rising from the lower house. But your service in the Commons must be one of two things: either long and faithful or short and disastrous. If you do badly as a minister your Leader will undoubtedly relieve you of your duties, much to your colleagues' relief, and gently kick you upstairs.

In spite of this infusion of new blood into the Lords, the upper chamber remains overwhelmingly conservative. There are only seventy-one declared Liberals and only forty-three Socialists. This is not surprising in view of the predominance of landowners and the fact that even a majority of the "lords of the first creation" have a public-school background. Furthermore, nearly half the peers in the United Kingdom are over sixty years of age, which does not encourage them to develop radical tendencies.

The House of Lords is the highest court in the land and theoretically all its members are entitled to sit as judges. In practice, the actual work is done by the Lords of Appeal who are appointed exclusively for the purpose. The function of their lordships, therefore, is solely to amend and revise legislation (with the exception of money bills) passed by the Commons; and they have the power to delay legislation for two years.

Needless to say, the upper house with its immensely conservative background is eulogized by the upper classes. It may strike Americans as a curious anomaly in a democracy that men who represent no constituencies and 75 percent of whom owe their positions to inheritance can block legislation presented by elected representatives of the people. But many English people, particularly those of the upper classes, have an outlook toward privilege different from that of Americans. For centuries privilege has been an integral part of the British system, and there is still a lingering, deep-rooted belief that men of birth, breeding, and financial means are more reliable and objective than those who are familiar with adversity. Indeed, when I interviewed a prominent civil servant at the House of Lords who kindly consented to give me information, he was curious to know why I wished to make a distinction between peers whose titles had come from their fathers and those whose titles had been awarded for merit. "What you Americans never seem to understand," he said, "is that in England political ability is often inherited."

Notwithstanding this, few Conservative politicians would care to get up on a public platform and argue the merits of inheritance. They picture the Lords in quite a different light. The reason the upper house functions so well, they claim, is because the great bulk of peers, commonly referred to as the "backwoodsmen," never appear. The average attendance is only seventy or eighty members and even less than that on dull days; but these few are the pick of the lot. They are the most distinguished and the most public-spirited; they give the House its reputation for being a body of experts. The fact that they receive no salaries and represent no constituencies frees them from any outside pressure, and as a result (contend the Conservatives) debates in the Lords are on a higher level than in the Commons.

It is perfectly true that the upper house contains many famous men who represent a wide range of expert opinion. To name only a few, there are Lord Halifax and Lord Simon, ex-Foreign Secretaries; Lord Catto, chairman of the Bank of England; Lord Beveridge, author of the famous social insurance report; Lord (Bertrand) Russell, philosopher; Lord Beaverbrook, press proprietor; Lord Lindsay, Master of Balliol College, Oxford; Lord Vansittart, ex-permanent head of the Foreign Office; Lord Linlithgow, ex-Viceroy of India; Lord Nuffield, industrialist; Lord Citrine, ex-trade-union chief; Lord Swinton, Lord Rosebery, Lord Margesson, Lord Winster, and many other ex-ministers of the Crown.

From this galaxy one might expect the debates in the Lords to be sparkling and trenchant, and indeed on great occasions there are sometimes great debates. But to the casual visitor the House has a curious lifelessness, perhaps because most peerages come to men when they have completed their life's work and all passion has long ago been spent. This does not mean that the upper house has little to contribute. Debates in the Lords are valuable for their analytical qualities in much the same way that an expert lawyer's advice is valuable. In revising and amending legislation the Lords have made many contributions. But if one is searching for statesmanship in the broad sense of the word one begins to wonder if detachment is a virtue in politics after all. When one examines the long record of the Lords and finds how many of the great progressive measures of the past have been opposed, one cannot help but question their persistent claim to wisdom.

There have been many clashes between the Lords and Commons, and for over a century now, whenever an issue has arisen, the question has been asked: "Should the Lords be reformed, and if so, how?" Needless to say, the curious composition and powers of the Lords were never contrived; like most things English they emerged slowly from the mists of time.

Originally the Lords acted as an advisory body to the Crown. In the Middle Ages the King called the feudal lords of the land together to seek advice and to help him raise money for his wars. He also called the knights and burgesses who were directly responsible for collecting the taxes, but the latter soon found it convenient to meet separately to discuss what should be said to the King and to elect a Speaker to say it. Thus began the Lords and Commons.

Gradually the functions of the two Houses became defined. As time went on, the burden of raising funds became exclusively the business of the commoners, whereas the lords not only gave the King advice but attempted to guide his actions. While the Lords struggled with the Crown for supremacy, the Commons struggled with the Lords for authority.

However, it was not until 1689 when the battle against the Crown was won and Parliament stood supreme that the rivalry between Lords and Commons began to develop in a serious way. Although the Commons passed a resolution declaring that money matters had always been their particular concern and that the upper house must vote yes or no on financial bills and not attempt to amend them, the Lords had great power. The very fact that they could throw out a budget meant they could bring the Commons to a standstill and curtail any measures of which they did not approve. But even more important was the fact that so many of them owned land which carried with it the right to nominate members in the Commons. Some of the constituencies were nothing but fields with only a few inhabitants, yet landlords solemnly chose candidates to represent them. These seats were known as "rotten boroughs" and one of them, Old Sarum, was held by William Pitt.

It was not until 1832 that Britain took its first step toward modern democracy. The Commons insisted on the abolition of the rotten boroughs, a redistribution of parliamentary seats, and an extension of the franchise to a limited number of householders. The Lords opposed the bill vehemently, and the only way the Commons could make it law was to prevail upon the King to use a royal prerogative to create enough new peers to outvote the recalcitrant ones. The threat was sufficient to make the Lords give way, and the Duke of Wellington redefined the powers of the upper house as a "revising and suspending" chamber, warning them that they must not interfere with the will of the people.

However, the Reform Bill by no means ended the great influence of the upper house. Although the most flagrant examples of corruption were done away with, such as the rotten boroughs, the Lords still managed to exert pressure to see that their kinsmen were elected to the Commons. In other words the ruling class ruled and among them this amazingly compact little group controlled both Houses. For instance, the Duke of Bedford sat in the Lords and his brother, Lord John Russell, the Prime Minister, sat in the Commons. In *The Transition from Aristocracy* Christie writes: "When Lord John Russell formed the Administration of 1846 his opponents alleged that it was

mainly composed of his cousins. Certainly his relatives had their
share of spoils of office; the Home Secretary and War Secretary
were his cousins; the Colonial Secretary and the Chancellor of
the Exchequer were his sons-in-law, and his father-in-law was
the Lord Privy Seal."

Although a certain amount of interfamily antagonism continued between the two Houses throughout the nineteenth century, it was not until a Liberal government was voted into power
by an electoral landslide in 1906 that a climax was reached. The
Lords were aghast that such a radical government had grasped
the reins of office, and their fears increased when they saw the
program of reform the new cabinet intended to put into effect.
When Mr. Lloyd George presented his budget to them they
ignored the century-old warning of the Duke of Wellington not
to thwart the will of the people and threw it out lock, stock,
and barrel.

This time the Commons decided that the power of the upper
house must be drastically and permanently cut. They introduced
a Parliament Act depriving the Lords of all rights as far as financial matters were concerned; they also declared that although
the peers could veto bills introduced by the Commons, after two
years had elapsed and three readings had taken place, the bills
would become law with or without their consent. They forced
the Lords to sign their own sentence by prevailing once again
on the King to threaten them with enough new peers to outvote them.

Today, once again, there is an issue of Commons versus
Lords. And like most of the issues of the past this one is political rather than constitutional. Although it is worth noting
that the Lords have never once opposed a conservative House
of Commons and have become refractory and obstinate only
when liberals have been in power, no one could accuse them
of trying to thwart the "will of the people" during this Parliament.

They have been a model of behavior, dutifully passing Socialist legislation that was anathema to them. But the very fact
that it was anathema aroused Socialist alarm. In the spring of

1948 when the government was approaching the last twenty-four months of its term in office, the Socialists began to fear that their lordships might exercise their right to delay legislation for two years. This would bring the government to a standstill (and halt the nationalization of steel) or force it to seek immediate re-election against its will. In order to forestall any such eventuality the Commons promptly introduced a retrospective bill cutting the Lords' delaying powers from two years to nine months.

This preventive war aroused a storm of anger among Conservatives. One lady, indignant that anyone should tamper with such a sacred institution as the Lords, said to a Labor M.P. in my hearing: "I think it's so ungrateful of you. After all, the Lords have been most awfully good to this House of Commons!" The Conservative Central Office issued a booklet on the subject, declaring in effect that an attack on the upper house was an attack on "democracy." It pointed out that half a dozen Socialist M.P.'s had even gone so far as "to regret that the government did not intend to abolish the House of Lords on the grounds of it being a 'feudal anachronism.' " This incident was described as "betraying a degenerate attitude of mind unhappily common on the nether fringe of the Socialist movement."

Tory politicians adopted a less hysterical attitude. They argued, and with reason, that the government had no right to reduce the powers of the Lords without once again examining the question as a whole. They suggested that a committee should be set up consisting of government and opposition leaders in both Houses. This was agreed to.

The question of reform brought a spate of letters to the newspapers. Ardent advocates were the eighteen peeresses-in-their-own-right who had never been allowed to sit in the House of Lords merely because they were women. As one peer put it: "Think what a frightful bore it would be. Why, we would even have to build a ladies' cloakroom!" Other reform advocates were the small group of Conservative M.P.'s who are heirs to titles and therefore will be forced to move to the upper house one day. This, to a clever young politician, is nothing less than ca-

tastrophe, for the highest offices such as the Premiership, the
Treasury, the Home Office, and usually the Foreign Secretaryship are barred to peers on the grounds that ministers of such
important departments must be able to answer questions on
the floor of the Commons. Quintin Hogg, M.P., son of Lord
Hailsham, wrote the following letter to the *Times*:

Sir:

For twenty years I have been wondering how I might avoid sitting in the
House of Lords as an hereditary peer. There is no means of achieving this,
since, unfortunately, besides being the heir to an hereditary title, I am a
man. Legislation is now proposed to subject women to the same disability
whereby they will be debarred from standing for or sitting in the House of
Commons. Have the influential body of men and women who signed the
letter in your columns today consulted the ladies concerned? Or has the
plot to relegate them to the political ghetto so far reserved for the eldest
sons of peers emanated solely from the passion of the moment for equality
of sacrifice?

The committee of all-party leaders sat for some months and
their proposals for reforming the House of Lords were as follows:

1. The Second Chamber should be complementary to and not a rival to
the Lower House, and, with this end in view, the reform of the House of
Lords should be based on a modification of its existing constitution as opposed to the establishment of a Second Chamber of a completely new type
based on some system of election.

2. The revised constitution of the House of Lords should be such as to
secure as far as practicable that a permanent majority is not assured for any
political Party.

3. The present right to attend and vote based solely on heredity should
not by itself constitute a qualification for admission to a reformed Second
Chamber.

4. Members of the Second Chamber should be styled "Lords of Parliament" and would be appointed on grounds of distinction or public service.
They might be drawn either from Hereditary Peers, or from commoners
who would be created Life Peers.

5. Women should be capable of being appointed Lords of Parliament in
like manner as men.

6. Provision should be made for the inclusion in the Second Chamber of

certain descendants of the Sovereign, certain Lords Spiritual and the Law Lords.

7. In order that persons without private means should not be excluded, some remuneration would be payable to members of the Second Chamber.

8. Peers who were not Lords of Parliament should be entitled to stand for election to the House of Commons, and also to vote at elections in the same manner as other citizens.

9. Some provision should be made for the disqualification of a member of the Second Chamber who neglects, or becomes no longer able or fitted, to perform his duties as such.

The above proposals were acceptable to the parties as a basis of discussion as far as the composition of the House was concerned, but they could not agree on what the powers of the Lords should be. Conservative leaders were willing to see their right whittled down to a year's delay but would not go farther than that; the government argued that a veto of even one year could render the fourth year of the Commons ineffective and insisted on nine months as the maximum period. On this the talks broke down. Perhaps discussions will be resumed at the third reading of the bill. If not, Bagehot's prophecy made nearly eighty years ago may prove correct. "The danger of the House of Lords certainly is, that it may never be reformed," he wrote. "Its danger is not in assassination but in atrophy; not abolition but decline."

The majority of their lordships rarely attend debates unless the subject happens to be one which particularly interests them. A debate on the press will draw the press Lords; a debate on criminal justice, the lawyers and judges; a debate on agriculture, the landowners. Only a handful of peers hold office or aspire to hold office and can therefore be described as "serious politicians." And this group, like the House as a whole, reflects the fact that youth is sadly in a minority.

The three most important peers on the Labor benches are Lord Addison, Leader of the House of Lords, who is nearly eighty; Lord Jowitt, the Lord Chancellor, who is sixty-four; and Lord Hall, First Lord of the Admiralty, who is sixty-eight. All three of these men began their political careers in the House of Commons and all three have at least one quality in common: great personal charm.

Christopher Addison is the son of a Yorkshire farmer and William Jowitt of a London solicitor. Both began their political career as Liberal M.P.'s and both joined the Labor party between the two wars. Addison is amazing for his age; a short man with a shock of white hair and lively brown eyes, he neither looks nor acts over sixty. Astuteness combined with the great gift of amiability has made him popular on all sides of the House, which is no small achievement considering that he must constantly face a hostile majority.

Jowitt, on the other hand, is regarded by the opposition with a certain amount of suspicion. After a long and successful practice at the bar, a period as Attorney General under the second Labor government, he has reached the pinnacle of his career, the distinguished office of Lord Chancellor. To see him on the woolsack is alone worth a trip to the House of Lords, for he fits the part well enough to suit the most exacting casting director in Hollywood. Dressed in his black robes, with a white wig framing his gaunt, handsome, aristocratic face, he has just the right air of weariness about him as he sits lackadaisically in his chair, a hand dropping languidly over the side. He has a quick, versatile mind, a remarkable memory, and is fond of relating anecdotes of past experiences at the bar. The criticism usually leveled at him is that he views politics less from principle than a lawyer's brief. His wife, who was originally a Conservative, has followed him loyally through Liberalism to Socialism. I once heard this attractive and vivacious lady remark gaily to a luncheon partner: "If you want to know anything about party politics, ask me. I've been a member of every one of them."

Lord Hall began life in a very different way. He went into the coal mines of his native Wales at the age of twelve and worked for seven shillings and sixpence ($1.75) a week. A miner for nearly thirty years, he vividly recalls the cruel slash in wages which led to the famous coal strike of 1920. He and his comrades tramped the streets in search of work and bitterly swore that no son of theirs would ever go into the pits. "Aye," he says, "and what's more we kept our word."

But the hardships of his early days have left no trace of bitterness, and as a result he is one of the most beloved figures in political life. "George Hall is a saint," an M.P. once remarked. "Do you know if he has performed any miracles?" "Yes," replied another. "He has persuaded the Admiralty to allow working-class boys to compete in the Dartmouth entrance examinations."

But Lord Addison and Lord Hall will probably retire from politics after the next election; and perhaps even Lord Jowitt. What then of the younger men? The Socialists have a star in the solid shape of Lord Pakenham, forty-two-year-old Minister of Civil Aviation. During the past four years Pakenham has moved from being an unpaid assistant to Arthur Greenwood, to lord in waiting to the King, to Undersecretary for War, to Chancellor of the Duchy of Lancaster, to his present ministerial post. And when Lord Addison retires he will undoubtedly take over the leadership of the Lords and step into the cabinet.

Most English people love an eccentric aristocrat, and when the latter is also a clever raconteur with an irrepressible sense of humor he becomes something of a fable. Such is Lord Pakenham. Born of an English mother and an Irish father, his early life followed the usual upper-class pattern of Eton and New College, Oxford, where he took first-class honors. He made his political debut at the Conservative Central Office, and his Tory friends are fond of claiming that he still might be "one of them" if it were not for the accident of fate which led him to a Fascist meeting in the early thirties where he found himself involved in a brawl and was hit over the head with an iron chair. After regaining consciousness, they say, he was a confirmed Socialist.

For nearly ten years Pakenham taught government at Oxford and in 1945 he contested the Oxford City constituency held by Quintin Hogg, an old Etonian schoolmate. He was defeated by Hogg and when, a few months later, the Prime Minister offered him a peerage he accepted it, partly because he is the heir to an earldom and one day will be forced to go to the upper house in any case.

If the test of a true intellectual is a wonderfully untidy appearance Lord Pakenham passes with distinction. Although he is a man of considerable wealth there are few people who care less for comfort. When he was working for Greenwood he often found it convenient to sleep on the floor of his Whitehall office, and at eight o'clock in the morning he would stroll across the park to the Athenaeum Club for a shave, clad only in pajamas and overcoat, oblivious to the stare of passers-by.

Pakenham's independence of mind is not only reflected in his political life and his personal eccentricities. In 1940 he became a Catholic, which seemed as strange to his left-wing colleagues as Socialism had to his Tory friends. Astuteness mixed with vagueness, worldliness with idealism, cynicism with religious fervor are all facets of his character.

His rapid rise in the House of Lords is due to a brilliantly quick intellect which enables him to master the details of complicated legislation with unusual facility. It is also due to his tact, and his unashamed use of flattery, by which he has captured the approval of many of his opponents. If the upper house is ever reformed and Lord Pakenham has the opportunity to enter the Commons, the highest offices may not be beyond his reach; that is, so long as the left wing of the Labor party does not gain control.

The handful of Socialists in the Lords are square pegs in round holes. They sit in seats surrounded by the rear guard of the privilege they are trying to destroy, stubbornly claiming that so long as the House exists Labor must be represented. To the bulk of their lordships they are curious anomalies. The man who reflects the true spirit of the upper house, and reflects it to his finger tips, is the leader of the conservative opposition, the Marquis of Salisbury.

Salisbury is a member of England's most famous political family, the Cecils. His ancestor William Cecil, later Lord Burghley, was Chief Minister under the great Queen Elizabeth; and Burghley's son Robert, the first Lord Salisbury, was for many years her faithful adviser. According to Lytton Strachey, when the Queen was dying she rose from the chair where she had lain for several days, struggled to her feet, and remained standing for fifteen hours to ward off the terrible moment of finality. Even when she succumbed to the cushions which had been spread out to receive her she refused to be moved into her own room. Cecil hovered about anxiously. Finally he said boldly: "Your Majesty, to content the people, you must go to bed." "Little man, little man," replied the Queen, " 'must' is a word that is not used to princes."

The Cecils have maintained their tradition of public service. The present Salisbury's grandfather, the third Marquis, was three times Prime Minister of England. He was deeply Conservative. Referring to his party's views on constitutional reform he said: "We have no program because we are very skeptical of the benefits of raising such political questions at all. As a party we do not advocate organic change. Admitting that organic change is sometimes inevitable, we regard it as an evil, and we do not desire to give it any assistance we can avoid."

This old gentleman would certainly regard the present Salisbury as a dangerous radical for "Bobbety," as he is known to his friends, has gone so far as to admit in a recent radio broadcast that laissez-faire capitalism is finished and some sort of planning is here to stay. However, his followers do not take these utterances seriously; in the House of Lords he not only continues to satisfy them that he is as sound a Conservative as Cecils have always been, but mesmerizes them into leaving most decisions of policy in his hands.

To foreigners Salisbury is something of a puzzle. If you met him at dinner you would find yourself talking to a thin, dark man unprepossessing except for a charming smile. He would not strike you as particularly witty, particularly clever, or particularly dynamic. Yet most Conservatives sing his praises with an enthusiasm that is rare in England and talk of him as "a great man." His record is good but not unusually distinguished.

Before the war he served as Undersecretary of Foreign Affairs and resigned with Anthony Eden as a protest against "appeasement." During the war he served as Dominions Minister and might have gone to India as Viceroy but for the ill health from which he has always suffered.

What then is Salisbury's fascination for the English? The answer, I believe, is that he justifies to most members of the upper class the British hereditary sytem. He is public spirited; he is a man of honor and integrity; he proves the virtue of the aristocracy. The fact that he is a Cecil, of course, helps. As one Conservative lady, a peeress of some intellectual distinction, remarked to me: "Wouldn't it be wonderful to be a Cecil and know that everything you did was right!"

CHAPTER 7

The Civil Service

The creation of this service was the one great
political invention in 19th century England.
—GRAHAM WALLAS

IT is sometimes said that it is the civil servants and not the
politicians who run Britain. For although the civil servants
might be able to get along without the politicians, the politicians
could not get along without the civil servants for even a day.
A nineteenth-century Chancellor of the Exchequer once remarked ironically that the politician was elected to tell the civil
servant what the country would not stand.

No description of Parliament would be complete without a
description of the civil service for it is the hidden girder on
which the government rests. It operates behind the scenes in a
shadowy world of anonymity. Even the most informed section
of the British public would not be able to name more than one
or two of its chief officials; and yet these men carry almost as
much responsibility as American cabinet ministers.

The explanation is not difficult to find. In all democratic
countries the civil servant's job is to administer the laws laid
down by the elected representatives of the people. But whereas
in other countries these tasks are often assigned to men who are
appointed by politicians, in Britain they are kept tightly in the
hands of professionals. As a result the British civil service enjoys
great prestige and has the pick of the ablest brains in the country; it is undoubtedly the most highly skilled, highly experienced,
and highly disciplined organization of its kind in the world.

It operates as a law unto itself. Its positions are open on a strictly competitive basis and offer permanent security to those who hold them. The young man who enters the service in his twenties remains in it until he retires at sixty. Promotion, however, is not automatic, but is awarded on a basis of merit. He will only reach the top posts if he distinguishes himself; then he receives a knighthood and a salary of £4,500 ($18,000) a year.*

Even the original entry into the civil service is difficult, for the administrative branch is easily the most exclusive intellectual club in the country. The written examinations are so exacting that only men who have won the highest university honors can hope to pass them. Besides this, great emphasis is laid on character. A candidate must submit at least four, and sometimes more, recommendations written by schoolmasters and people in positions of authority, who have known him through various stages of his life. The rigorous code of ethics under which the service operates was hinted at in a report issued in 1928: "A civil servant is not to subordinate his duty to his private interests: but neither is he to put himself in a position where his duty and his interests conflict. He is not to make use of his official position to further those interests: but neither is he so to order his private affairs as to allow the suspicion to arise that a trust has been abused or a confidence betrayed . . . the public expects a standard of integrity in conduct not only inflexible but fastidious. . . ."

Although today the civil service is one of Britain's most dignified institutions, its respectability is only eighty years old. Until the middle of the last century it not only was run by political patronage but was corrupt and inefficient as well. Cabinet ministers assigned the most important positions to friends or impecunious relatives or men whose political support they wished to enlist. As Britain began to expand into an industrial power the faulty machine creaked and groaned so dangerously under the increasing burden of government that civil service

* This is part of the new salary scale which comes into operation in November, 1949.

reform became one of the great controversies of the age. Educationalists and intellectuals played a leading part, and Gladstone, the great Liberal statesman, who was then Chancellor of the Exchequer, appointed two eminent men, Sir Charles Trevelyan, the grandfather of the present historian, and Sir Stafford Northcote, to investigate the matter.

Their report "On the Organisation of the Permanent Civil Service" was published in 1853. They did not mince their words. They claimed that because the top posts were filled from above the service only attracted "those whom indolence of temperament or physical infirmities unfit for active positions. Civil servants," the report went on, "were habitually superceded because they were incompetent and incompetent because they were superceded."

The idea of abolishing patronage raised such a storm that it nearly swept Trevelyan out of his club. "I went to Brooks," wrote his brother-in-law, the famous Lord Macaulay, on March 4, 1854, "and found everybody open-mouthed, I am sorry to say, against Trevelyan's plans about the Civil Service." And a few days later: "The news is worse about Trevelyan. There is a set made at him by men who will not scruple to do their utmost." People cried out that low people "without the breeding or feelings of gentlemen would demoralize the public service," and that a democratic civil service and an aristocratic legislature would result in calamity. This was countered by Sir James Graham, First Lord of the Admiralty, who insisted that it would be the "greatest boon to the nation since bread was freed from taxation," and John Stuart Mill, who declared that it was "one of the greatest improvements ever put forward by a Government." However, the civil servants who enjoyed their high offices and the politicians who had appointed them fought it tooth and nail and succeeded in gaining widespread public support. "The pear is not yet ripe," wrote Macaulay sadly. "I always thought so. The time will come but it is not yet come."

However, it came sooner than Macaulay supposed for the Crimean War broke out and W. H. Russell's dispatches to the

Times soon contained alarming descriptions of the mismanagement and confusion of the War Department. Clothing, medicine, bandages, and even kitchen equipment had failed to arrive. Florence Nightingale worked feverishly to obtain supplies through private channels and overnight became a national heroine. Her condemnations of officialdom succeeded in at last galvanizing public opinion, and in 1855, by an Order in Council under Lord Palmerston's government, a Civil Service Commission was finally established.

This, however, was only a beginning for Gladstone was no longer Chancellor, and the new ministry did not share his enthusiasm for reform. Although candidates were to be subjected to examination, their nomination still remained in the hands of politicians. The battle, therefore, continued, and less than two months after the Commission had been set up a motion was moved in Parliament: "That this House views with deep and increasing concern the state of the nation, and is of the opinion that the manner in which merit and efficiency have been sacrificed, in public appointment, to party and family influences, and to a blind adherence to routine, has given rise to great misfortune, and threatens to bring discredit upon the national character, and to invoke the country in great disasters." Gladstone, who had written to a friend in the previous year that "the reorganisation of the Civil Service is my contribution to the picnic of Parliamentary reform," argued that any remedy which did not include open competition would be futile, while Disraeli, although he supported a professional service, opposed him. It was not until 1870 that Gladstone finally triumphed and the service was placed on the competitive basis on which it now rests.

Today entrance to the civil service is determined by the Civil Service Commission, composed of five commissioners who are appointed by His Majesty's Government. Although the Commission is under the control of the Treasury in matters of policy, it is completely independent in carrying out its duties and always begins its reports: "May it please Your Majesty. . . ." Its work consists of making the rules of entry, drawing up the examination papers, and selecting the candidates. Sir Stanley Leathes, a former First Commissioner, wrote: "There is a measure of luck, there is a margin of error, but subject to these and the limitations of personal capacity and opportunity, the fate of the candidate is at his own disposition to make or to mar."

The service is divided into three main branches, clerical, executive, and administrative, each of which requires a different educational standard. The administrative class is the most important and is what people usually have in mind when they talk of the civil service as a "career." The majority of candidates enter this class by open competitive examination between the ages of 21½ and 24. However, it is also possible for men to work their way up from other branches; every year nearly 20 percent of the places in the administrative class are filled by the executive class, and 40 percent of the places in the executive class are filled by the clerical class.

The candidates who enter the administrative class by the direct route have their choice of two methods of selection.* Method I was in operation before the war, and consists of a very stiff written examination and an interview. Method II was originally devised for men whose studies were interrupted by military service and is known to the public as "the country-house week end." About twenty candidates spend two days together at a house in Surrey but not, as the commissioners stress indignantly, during the week end, where they are tested in groups of seven or eight. They are given intelligence tests, projection tests, general knowledge papers, written examinations, and exercises which they are asked to work out in committee. One of the most famous of these is known as "the island story." They are told that an island has just been discovered in a certain part of the world and asked to work out plans for populating it, governing and administering it. During the week end every candidate is interviewed separately by the three judges, who

* Women are eligible for the civil service on the same terms as men.

each send a report to the commissioners. The boy then appears for a final interview in London at which his fate is decided.

Method II was inspired by the tests employed by the army during the war for selecting candidates for commissions. Although it is still regarded as an experiment to be tried out for ten years from 1948 onward, Ernest Bevin was so pleased with the results during the reconstruction period that he asked the Commission to use this method only in selecting recruits for the Foreign Service. This does not mean a lowering of the intellectual standards, for no candidate is allowed to enter by Method II unless he has taken a university degree with high honors.

The British watch their civil service with a vigilant eye; no matter how perfect it becomes as an instrument it will always be a target for criticism. Today the charge most often leveled against it is that the majority of its recruits are from well-to-do families. There are about four thousand men in the administrative class today. Nearly 60 percent have been to public schools and nearly 80 percent to Oxford and Cambridge, which is the same, proportionately, as it was before the war. The answer is that these schools and universities still provide the best education that England can offer, and until the general level is raised throughout the country they are likely to continue to take first place.

The second charge, which has largely died down since the "week end" examinations were initiated, is that too much emphasis is placed on brains and not enough on personality. This at once raises an argument as to the exact way in which the line should be drawn, for few people would like to see the academic requirements seriously altered. When the civil service examinations were first introduced Lord Macaulay wrote: "Early superiority in literature and science generally suggests the existence of some qualities which are securities against vice—industry, self-denial, a taste for pleasures not sensual, a laudable desire for honourable distinction, a still more laudable desire to obtain the approbation of friends and relations: we, therefore, think that the intellectual tests about to be established will be found in practice to be also the best moral test that can be devised." Most British people still agree with this contention.

A young man entering the administrative branch of the civil service begins as an assistant principal with a salary of £400 ($1,600) a year. He is not permanently confined to any one department. He may be moved from the Home Office to the Ministry of Labor, and from the Ministry of Labor to the Commonwealth Relations Office. Although during the early stages of his career promotion is mainly worked out by seniority, once he has become an assistant secretary he has the chance to rise rapidly if he can prove his worth. If he is sufficiently outstanding he may become the head of a department by the time he is forty.

Because the Treasury controls the purse strings of all departments it long ago constituted itself as a sort of paterfamilias, with powers of guidance and co-ordination in matters of personnel as well as finance. The head of the Treasury is the head of the civil service. Although promotions are the responsibility of the minister in charge of a department, acting on the advice of his chief civil servant, appointments to the top positions are usually made after consultation with senior officials at the Treasury; and for certain appointments the approval of the Prime Minister himself is required.

Once a civil servant has become the head of a department with the rank of permanent secretary, he is in a position to exert great influence. For his job is not only to carry out the policy of his minister but to supply his minister with the expert knowledge and advice on which to form a policy.

In Britain, unlike America, it is the constitutional duty of a minister to introduce legislation. And because a minister "makes" policy he must spend many hours in the House of Commons explaining and defending it. Since he cannot possibly have the same detailed information as the professional, it is essential for him to work in the closest touch with his officials.

In every debate in the House of Commons a small stall behind the Speaker's chair is always filled with civil servants. Often a cabinet minister whispers to his parliamentary private secretary, who is always a back-bench M.P., and then you see the latter get up and stroll over to the civil servant to verify facts or telephone the department for information.

The civil servant's approach must always be strictly practical. He must never express a political bias or for that matter even think in political terms. He is expected to serve any minister of any political party with unswerving and absolute loyalty. This does not mean, however, that he must agree with his chief. Far from it. The good civil servant states frankly and forcibly any objections he may feel, and does his best to dissuade his minister from taking what he believes to be the wrong course. The late Sir Austen Chamberlain, a former Foreign Minister, once described in *Public Administration* how he took a course of action of which his permanent secretary disapproved. "And then," wrote Chamberlain, "my eminent friend discharged the second valuable function of the civil servant. 'Well,' he said, 'if you will do a silly thing, of course you must, but is it essential for you to do it in that silly way?' And having done his utmost to dissuade me from doing it, he then showed me how to do it with the least friction and the smallest disadvantage."

Thus the civil servant must have almost superhuman qualities. He must be tactful yet persistent, energetic yet patient, imaginative yet obedient. He must always remain in a subordinate position to his political chief, but to make up for this he has the advantage of exercising influence over a long period of time. Whereas the politician may lose his job at any moment, the civil servant cannot be removed except for serious moral misbehavior. The politician takes the credit, but the politician also takes the blame.

The fact that, in Britain, civil service memoranda are always tied up in red tape gave birth to an expression which the English-speaking world would find it hard to do without. The British like to grumble about their civil service, and yet if they were challenged by foreigners they would defend it vigorously for they know that its virtues constitute the backbone of their political stability. As Napoleon once remarked: "No one has any interest in overturning a government in which all who have any merit are in their right places."

CHAPTER 8

The Crown

> There can be no doubt that the English Monarchy has a power of expressing and representing national emotion that may be above rational explanation.
>
> —D. W. BROGAN

BRITISH political life is wrapped up in the glamorous, make-believe authority of the Crown. His Majesty's government rules the kingdom and His Majesty's forces defend it; His Majesty's ships sail the seas and His Majesty's mint turns out the coins of the realm; His Majesty's postal officials collect the mail and His Majesty's ministers dispatch their business in envelopes marked: "On His Majesty's Service." Every session of Parliament opens with the King's Speech; diplomatic correspondence is carried to foreign capitals by the King's Messenger; and even roads are known as the King's Highway. At public dinners a toast is drunk to the King's health and at public gatherings ranging from theaters and night clubs to balls and political rallies the program closes with the strains of "God Save the King."

Yet everybody knows that the King's political power is polite fiction; that he reigns but he does not rule. He neither selects his ministers nor tells them what to do, and nobody attaches either blame or credit to him for the way the nation's affairs are conducted. Nevertheless, the very fact that democracy and monarchy move so easily in double harness is a distinguished example of the British genius for marrying new ideas to old institutions; but the secret of this genius cannot be put down to the invention of a novel system. The constitutional monarchy does not work by rhyme or reason or, for that matter, by any logical process whatsoever. It works only because everybody bends over backward to make it work.

By the strict letter of the law the King has dozens of prerogatives which he could exercise if he wished. He could make every man and woman in the kingdom a peer; he could dissolve Parliament; he could pardon all prisoners and make all aliens British subjects; he could recall all ambassadors and refuse to commission any officers for the armed forces, and make peace with a foreign power by ceding one of the colonies. But even more important, he could prevent a bill from becoming law by refusing to sign it; Edward VIII's Abdication Act was legal only when he himself put his name to it. Of course if the King exercised any of his prerogatives against the advice of his ministers, no matter how "legal" they are held to be, the government would at once declare a general election and the issue of monarchy versus democracy would be fought, which would undoubtedly spell the doom of the Crown. And for this reason the King carefully remains within the undefined but well-understood boundaries that limit a constitutional sovereignty.

But the fact that the King has no political power does not mean that he has no political influence. According to Bagehot the King has three rights: the right to be consulted, the right to encourage, and the right to warn. He receives regular visits from his cabinet ministers and is informed of all matters under discussion. Throughout a long reign he survives many politicians and many administrations, and the very permanency of his position often gives him a wisdom and detachment which can carry great weight. Whereas a politician's firsthand knowledge is limited by his term of office, the King draws from the experience of a lifetime.

Because of the many people the King is supposed to receive and the large number of engagements he is expected to fulfill the task of also keeping himself well informed requires a vigorous schedule. His days begin with an 8:30 breakfast during which he reads the newspapers and examines his mail. At 9:45 he sends for his private secretary and deals with state papers. An hour later he sends for a second secretary and deals with invitations, requests, and inquiries and from 11:30 to lunchtime has audiences with ministers, foreign ambassadors, and public servants. There are often official guests for lunch, and in the afternoon he probably has an outside engagement. If not, business is done with the royal household, and after tea he reads Foreign Office telegrams and periodic reports from governors general and handles matters concerning his estates and private correspondence. The half hour from 5:30 to 6 is usually reserved for the visits of cabinet ministers, and in the evening there is often another outside engagement. But although the King is expected to digest all current legislation his direct concern with political matters is the least important of his duties.

The Crown fulfills a triple function. First and foremost the King is indispensable as the symbolic head of the state, for without him the whole complicated pattern of British constitutional procedure would fall to pieces. He is important, second, as the head of society, and third, as the embodiment of virtue. The insistence on virtue as a royal characteristic is a comparatively recent development which has arisen during the last 100 years as the King's power has waned and obviously springs from an insistence that if the King cannot serve the nation by his authority he must serve it by his example. And with the exception of Edward VII's eight-year reign and Edward VIII's one-year reign the monarchy has dutifully conformed to the prescribed pattern ever since Victoria was crowned in 1837. This was the reason, of course, why no political party raised a finger to keep the Duke of Windsor on the throne and why the present King is so popular. George VI performs his public duties conscientiously, and his family life is a model of propriety. His daughters are not only pretty but as well behaved as a monarch could wish. They attend church on Sundays, they do not smoke, they see the right people, say the right things, and remain always mindful of their position as royalty. It could not be otherwise. Just how exacting the public is in its demands was recently revealed by the cries of protest from Puritan Scotland when Princess Elizabeth attended the races in Paris on a Sunday.

But virtue by itself is not enough. The British public want to enjoy their monarchy as well as respect it. They like the golden coaches and the scarlet uniforms, the swords and coronets, the ermine-trimmed robes and red carpets, the pomp and ceremony, glitter and paraphernalia that go with the Crown. And this is where the King fulfills his function as the head of society. The more often he appears the more popular he becomes, for his presence turns any occasion into a gala event.

The public expects the King to race his horses in the Derby and to take part in the regatta at Cowes; to attend the theater and the opera; to present a silver cup to the victorious football team at Wembley; to drive into the Royal Enclosure at Ascot in an open landau. Crowds line the streets when he proceeds in state to open Parliament, or attends divine service at St. Paul's; and a jubilee or a royal wedding, a silver anniversary or a coronation is a great day in the life of the nation.

The King entertains at state dinners and holds a number of receptions and garden parties at Buckingham Palace each year. But these functions are not limited to fashionable and exclusive society. Although many peers and peeresses are present, cabinet ministers, M.P.'s, local officials, eminent doctors, actors, and writers are also invited. The Lord Chamberlain, master of the invitations list, never loses sight of the strict national code which declares that the best British society is composed of those who serve Britain.

The British people pay generously for the glamour with which monarchy supplies them. The King has three "official" residences: Buckingham Palace, Windsor Castle, and Holyrood House in Edinburgh. Besides this he maintains three private houses on his own: Royal Lodge at Windsor, where he spends his week ends, Sandringham in Norfolk, where he goes to shoot in the winter, and Balmoral in Scotland, which he visits in the summer. Princess Elizabeth lives in Clarence House and Queen Mary in Marlborough House, ex-ducal mansion in the heart of London.

The royal bill comes to approximately $2,244,000 a year. Originally the King received his annual revenue from Crown lands but George III complained that they did not bring him enough money and agreed to yield them to the state in return for a yearly sum from Parliament.* This sum is known as the "civil list." It is fixed at the beginning of each King's reign and remains unalterable. However, whenever a royal event takes place, such as Princess Elizabeth's marriage, an application is made to Parliament for an annuity to meet increased expenses. But the expenditures are never itemized or "debated" on the floor of the House. A "select committee" consisting of twenty-three M.P.'s is appointed by the Prime Minister to inquire into the royal finances and agree upon a sum; this committee does not reveal any of the evidence submitted to it in regard to the expenditure but merely asks Parliament for its approval, submitting as a guide the main headings under which the money was spent in the previous reign.

In the days of Queen Victoria radical Sir Charles Dilke declared that the civil list was excessive and asked that it be looked into, but he was defeated by 276 votes to 2; and when ten years later he voted against an annuity to Prince Leopold, the Queen was so angry she used her influence to prevent him from being appointed to any cabinet post except the one connected with the Local Government Board, where she was unlikely to come into contact with him.

When Princess Elizabeth's annuity was before Parliament in January, 1948, criticism again rose but the King's reaction is unlikely to have been as violent as his great-grandmother's. The select committee asked Parliament to provide the Princess with a sum of £50,000 ($200,000) a year, whereupon a number of Socialists put down an amendment to have the amount reduced by £5,000. This was done as a protest against the fact that the Princess was planning two large houses, one in London and one in the country, at a time when the nation was desperately short of building materials and labor. However, in view of the fact that the King had already announced that he had saved £100,-000 from the civil list because of the wartime curtailment of

---

* Today the Crown lands have appreciated so enormously in value that their revenue to the Treasury is nearly four times the total amount of the civil list.

entertaining, and that he was returning this sum to the Treasury
so that the taxpayers' burden would not be increased, the protest
was branded by many as "a shabby gesture" and received little
sympathy in the country. The amendment was defeated by a
vote of 291-165.

These are the amounts that are now paid:

I. His Majesty's Privy Purse	£110,000	($ 440,000)
II. Salaries of His Majesty's Household and Retired Allowances	£134,000	($ 536,000)
III. Expenses of His Majesty's Household	£152,800	($ 611,200)
IV. Royal bounty, alms, and special services	£ 13,200	($ 52,800)
Total	£410,000	($1,640,000)
Parliamentary Annuities		
Queen Mary	£ 70,000	($ 280,000)
Princess Elizabeth and the Duke of Edinburgh	£ 50,000	($ 200,000)
Trustees of the children of His Late Majesty King George V	£ 31,000	($ 124,000)
Total	£151,000	($ 604,000)

Although the monarchy relinquished Crown property a century ago there are still a number of things on the statute books
which the Crown can claim. The Crown owns any land which
is left bare by the slipping away of the sea, and any island which
suddenly springs up in territorial waters; it owns the foreshore—
the land between high and low watermark—subject to the right
of the public to use it for navigation or fishing. Wreck in its
various forms belongs to the Crown; also the property of any
person who dies without leaving kin; also treasure trove, which
is carefully defined as gold or silver coin, plate, or bullion which
has been hidden in the earth or in a secret receptacle with the
intention of being recovered later; if the property has merely
been abandoned it can be claimed by the finder. The Crown*

* Although originally these possessions belonged to the King personally, by custom they have become the property of the state even though the word "Crown" is
still used. Swans and sturgeon can still be claimed by the King, perhaps because they
are of little use to the Treasury.

also owns white swans swimming in open or common rivers, provided they are wild and unmarked; and it owns sturgeon and whales captured in territorial waters as opposed to the open sea, with a special proviso that the whalebone goes to the Queen for her stays. At the beginning of George V's reign a sturgeon was caught in Cardigan Bay and at once offered to the King by the enthusiastic villagers. But although His Majesty thanked them profusely the creature never saw its sovereign and is reported to have finished its earthly existence unmourned and unsung on a laboratory dissecting table.

The King of England not only lives more regally than any other King in the Western world but sits on the most famous throne. *Burke's Peerage* traces his ancestry back to Egbert, King of Wessex in 825. A thousand years of history is a long stretch to contemplate but when it is reduced to the simple terms of kingship and you suddenly realize that the present monarch is only the nineteenth sovereign since Henry VIII, only the thirty-third from Richard the Lion-Hearted, and thirty-eighth from William the Conqueror crowned in 1066, instead of complaining how little the human race advances you marvel that it can have accomplished so much in the lifetime of only three dozen men. These links with antiquity produce awe and even reverence, for they place the members of the royal family in a category by themselves.

This is important, for the fascination of royalty lies not only in the glamour of their paraphernalia but in the fact that they are different. The public does not wish to picture royalty like themselves but themselves like royalty. Thus in performing their duty English royalty take care to preserve the aura that sets them apart. Although their public life is immensely public their private life is secluded. They do not mix in smart London society and their circle of friends is severely restricted. The Queen and the Princesses even take care to look different. They rarely wear such ordinary colors as brown, dark blue, or black. Regardless of rain, sleet, or wind, they appear in pale pinks or pale blues, in lavender grays or yellows, topped by elaborate, feathery, unreal hats.

The British people follow their lives with interest and excitement. They have few serious rivals for whereas athletes and actresses and statesmen fade from the public scene when they pass their prime, the monarchy is as perpetual as the statues in the park. At the wedding of Princess Elizabeth an American reporter asked an English girl why she would wait in line twenty-four hours for a Princess and not for a Prime Minister. "Prime Ministers come and go," she retorted, "but the Princess and I will be here for a long, long time."

Just as wine increases its bouquet with age, the royal family increases its popularity as each reign advances. When I settled down to live in London at the end of the war I was astonished to find that the press printed pictures of the King, Queen, or Princesses nearly every day. In the beginning this seemed monotonous and even irritating, but I discovered that it catches hold of you like a drug; you do not realize you are becoming enmeshed in the royal lives until you suddenly find that the fact that Princess Margaret has acquired a new beau or Princess Elizabeth has let down her skirt to achieve the New Look is a matter of absorbing interest. Now I am looking forward to the time when Prince Charles cuts his first tooth and I dare say by the time he goes into the navy I shall regard him as my own son. And I am only a beginner. People born and bred in Britain not only are launching into a new era with the Princesses but have grown up with the King, and their fathers grew up with the King's father and their grandfathers with Victoria. The love of royal family life is in their blood. A good many people do not confine themselves merely to reading about them but go so far as to keep scrapbooks of their doings. This startling fact was recently revealed when the Labor party ran a picture of a baby entitled: "Healthy Babies of 1949." The pamphlet had not been issued more than a few hours before an indignant woman rang the *Daily Express* and declared that she had thought she recognized the baby and when she "looked it up" in her royal album she discovered it was none other than a picture of the Duchess of Kent's son photographed some twelve years before. The Labor party apologized profusely and explained that the photographer had sent the wrong picture.

There is no republican movement inside Britain for the simple reason that the monarchy is too useful. Although a few Socialists claim to favor a republic "in theory," none of them advocate it as a policy. Glamour that serves a utilitarian purpose is much too strong a card to toss away. Whenever the British wish to display their solidarity with a foreign power they have only to send the royal family on a tour or a state visit to excite the popular imagination in a way that no politician or ambassador could do. Long ago Bagehot wrote: "Royalty is a government in which the attention of the nation is concentrated on one person doing interesting actions. A Republic is a government in which their attention is divided between many who are all doing uninteresting actions. Accordingly so long as the human heart is strong and the human reason weak Royalty will be strong because it appeals to diffused feelings and Republics weak because they appeal to understanding." That there is some truth in this no one would deny for who would dare to pit the popular appeal of Mr. Attlee, President Truman, or M. Schuman against that of Princess Elizabeth?

But the King is not King of England alone. He is also King of Canada, Australia, New Zealand, South Africa, Pakistan, and Ceylon. Although these countries are fully independent, each accepts a Governor General who deputizes for the King; the latter signs their laws, formally appoints their ministers, and opens Parliament, and in every way deputizes for the King. When the King visits any of his Dominions the Governor General recedes into the background and the King himself reigns. The Dominion ministers are *his* ministers and when he is in the Dominions he acts according to their advice—and never without it—just as in England he acts on the advice of the British government. The present King has already made extended tours of Canada and South Africa and if it had not been for illness would have spent several months in Australia in 1949. As these visits are expected to become more frequent in the future, his kingship in the Commonwealth, far from being a fiction, is becoming increasingly real.

Although the oath to the King is mainly sentimental,* many people argue that the attachment is so strong that it is the King in fact who holds the Commonwealth together. But not everybody accepts this view. Others claim that the true source of Commonwealth allegiance lies rooted in a common democratic political heritage, and point out that although the Republic of India was not willing to take an oath to the King, she wished to retain her tie with Britain; and now that a formula has been found, the Republic of Ireland may also formally announce her adherence to the Commonwealth.

Despite these problems there is no doubt that in parts of Canada, Australia, and New Zealand and among people of British stock in South Africa loyalty to the King has a fervor stronger even than the fervor in Britain. And this is often shared by people in the colonies. Recently when the fiery Jamaican leader Bustamente came to England he had an interview with the King which he described as the highlight of his life. When he returned home and was asked what the King had said to him, he placed his hand over his heart dramatically and said: "What passed between my Sovereign and me is sacred."

But the monarchy is not only useful in serving British interests abroad: by transcending political differences it binds its own people together and plays a large part in creating the stability for which they are famous. Many years ago Sir Stafford Cripps cried out excitedly that when the Socialists came to power they would "probably have to overcome resistance from Buckingham Palace."

On the contrary, Buckingham Palace has undoubtedly proved an asset to the Socialists. The fact that the King is on his throne and the members of the Labor Government are His Majesty's ministers has had a curiously soothing effect on the most con-

---

* In May, 1949, when Governor Dewey visited England he shocked members of Parliament by referring to Canada, Australia and New Zealand as "colonies"; like many Americans he was unaware of the fact that the Dominions are entirely independent nations, even as far as declaring war is concerned.

servative elements of the public and served to diminish rather than emphasize the many changes taking place.

Although the people know that the politicians rule them, their instinctive loyalties lead them to the throne. This was demonstrated on the day the European war ended. Thousands went to 10 Downing Street to cheer the great architect of victory, Mr. Churchill; but thousands more went to Buckingham Palace to cheer the King and Queen. The Crown has no rivals. It is the symbol of the nation.

PART III: THE PARTY SYSTEM

CHAPTER 9

The Labor Party

All history is that of man's rebellion against his
original state.

—BERTRAND DE JOUVENEL

LIKE America, and unlike France, British politics have always
operated on a "two-party system." Although there is nothing to prevent anyone from forming a new party the British
people have never been one for splitting hairs; generally speaking they are for or against an issue, and generally speaking their
sentiments have found expression in the party in power or the
party in opposition. For two hundred years Whigs and Tories,
or Liberals and Conservatives ruled Britain. The rise of the
Labor party in the last fifty years has resulted not in the rise
of a third party but, almost like a law of Nature, in the eclipse
of the Liberal party. Today the Liberals can claim only thirteen
members of Parliament out of a total of 640; the Labor party
rules Britain and the Conservative party forms the opposition.

The political faith of the Labor party is socialism, but the particular brand of this socialism often puzzles foreigners. A few
months after the general election of 1945 a French political
writer came to England to study the program of the new gov-

ernment. When he advanced his ideas on socialism to a group
of Labor M.P.'s he was told somewhat airily: "But that's continental socialism, not *British* socialism."

British Socialists are apt to regard Karl Marx with the same
superior air that Americans whose ancestors came over on the
Mayflower regard those who followed at a later date. They remind you that the seeds of the British labor movement, which
led to socialism, had been planted before Marx was born, and
that although the latter spent many years in London collecting
data for his major work *Das Kapital*, he has had surprisingly
little influence on British thought.

In other words, British socialism is not Marxist. Indeed, now-
adays many Socialists shudder at the very mention of the name,
for whereas Marx advocated violence in changing the existing
order the majority of English radicals believe stoutly in constitutional means, regarding social progress as an evolutionary
and not a revolutionary process.

It is perhaps typical of Britain that the working class is as
mindful and proud of its own traditions as is the aristocracy of
its traditions. Conservatives depict the greatness of eighteenth-
and nineteenth-century England in terms of Wellington, Peel,
Rhodes, Disraeli, and Chamberlain, while Socialists counter
with the names of Robert Owen, Robert Blatchford, William
Morris, Keir Hardie, and the intellectuals who comprised the
Fabian group. Which men will be considered to have made the
greatest contribution in five hundred years' time depends on
the course of civilization. But whatever the verdict, the story
of the British labor movement will remain a fascinating saga.
It is remarkable because it was consistent and dogged; because
it did not resort to violence; and because it has emerged today
as the strongest and most stable working-class organization in
the world.

The labor movement began as the struggle of the working
classes to establish their rights and advance their interests in a
country which had been ruled by a powerful oligarchy for nearly
eight centuries. The first vision of democracy was inspired by

that rebellious Englishman Tom Paine, who became a friend of Washington and Jefferson and whose remarkable pamphlet *Common Sense* fanned the flames of the American Revolution. The French Revolution with its cry of "Liberty, Equality, Fraternity" also made a profound impression on English radicals. But these were only the intellectual stirrings; the real force of the movement sprang from the desperate conditions in which the working-class population found themselves at the beginning of the nineteenth century when Britain started to evolve from an agricultural country into the greatest industrial power the world had known.

The industrial revolution began with the invention of the steam engine, the power loom, and the spinning jenny; during the same period the "Enclosure Acts" wiped out thousands of small holdings and placed over five million acres of common grazing land, where cottagers kept their geese and cows, in the hands of private owners. Suddenly deprived of their livelihood, peasants were forced to seek work in the factories that were springing up in Lancashire, Yorkshire, the Midlands, South Wales, and parts of Scotland. The new towns were ugly, unsanitary, and black with smoke. Because of the cutthroat competition among manufacturers for foreign markets wages were driven as low as possible. The average working day was fourteen hours, not including mealtime. Children of three and four were employed in the cotton mills, and it was a common practice to employ boys of six in the coal mines because they could crawl through shafts too narrow for grown men.

The misery and poverty of this era have been handed down to posterity in the novels of Charles Dickens and Charles Kingsley. But one of the most striking firsthand accounts was written by Robert Dale Owen, son of the great reformer, who was taken by his father in 1815 on a tour of the industrial areas:

As a preliminary measure, we visited all the chief factories in Great Britain. The facts we collected seemed to me terrible almost beyond belief. Not in exceptional cases, but as a rule, we found children of ten years old worked regularly fourteen hours a day, with but half an hour's interval for the midday meal, which was eaten in the factory. In the fine yarn cotton mills they were subjected to this labour in a temperature usually exceeding seventy-five degrees; and in all the cotton factories they breathed atmosphere more or less injurious to the lungs because of the dust and minute cotton fibres that pervaded it. In some cases we found that greed of gain had impelled the mill-owners to still greater extremes of inhumanity, utterly disgraceful, indeed, to a civilized nation. Their mills were run fifteen and, in exceptional cases, sixteen hours a day, with a single set of hands; and they did not scruple to employ children of both sexes from the age of eight. We actually found a considerable number under that age. It need not be said that such a system could not be maintained without corporal punishment. Most of the overseers openly carried stout leather thongs, and we frequently saw even the youngest children severely beaten. We sought out the surgeons who were in the habit of attending these children, noting their names and the facts to which they testified. Their stories haunted my dreams. In some large factories from one-fourth to one-fifth of the children were either cripples or otherwise deformed or permanently injured by excessive toil, sometimes by brutal abuse. The younger children seldom held out more than three or four years without serious illness, often ending in death. When we expressed surprise that parents should voluntarily condemn their sons and daughters to slavery so intolerable, the explanation seemed to be that many of the fathers were out of work themselves and so were, in a measure, driven to the sacrifice for lack of bread; while others, imbruted by intemperance, saw with indifference an abuse of the infant faculties compared to which the infanticide of China may almost be termed humane.

This was the background against which Britain's working-class movement began, a background unknown to nineteenth-century Americans with the untapped resources of a vast continent before them. Although there were repeated attempts by British workers to force employers to grant better working conditions, the government was frightened that the revolutionary ardor of France and America might prove contagious and in 1790 and 1800 declared all trade unions illegal. Not only were jail sentences imposed but defendants were forced to bear evidence against each other; by use of the common law against conspiracy these penalties were increased to sentences of years and even public whippings. As the working classes did not have the right to vote there was no hope of political redress.

Such severe repression lasted little more than a generation; in 1824 trade unions were legalized; and from 1833 to 1850 a group of factory laws was passed regulating the hours of work of women and young people and prohibiting the labor of children under nine. Gradually foreign competition relaxed, wages increased. Most of these reforms, however, were too gradual to eradicate the bitter memories of the past; the workingman's crusade had begun and it continued to develop throughout the century. Many personalities left their stamp upon this movement, but those who actually shaped it were three fascinating and diverse characters: Robert Owen, capitalist; Keir Hardie, coal miner; and Sidney Webb, intellectual.

It is a curious paradox that the "father of British socialism" should have been a rich businessman. Robert Owen's rise in the world was romantic and meteoric. Born in 1771, the son of a village ironmonger, he went to work at the age of ten as a draper's apprentice and twenty years later became manager and part owner of the largest cotton mill in Britain. But here his life deviated from the normal pattern of English capitalist. Instead of founding a family dynasty he became a reformer.

He turned his mills at New Lanark, Scotland, into model concerns which soon aroused so much interest that people came from all over the world to examine them. Not only did he rebuild many of his workers' houses, open schools for their children, establish shops where food was sold at cost prices, but he redesigned his workrooms, shortened the hours of labor, abolished the current system of fines and punishments, and refused to take any profits from the industry other than 5 percent on the money invested.

Although a friend once remarked to Owen, "Thou needest to be very right for thou art very positive," Owen had none of the superficial qualities usually associated with reformers; he was neither impetuous, nor angry, nor unhappy, but an affable, good-natured man who made friends easily, and numbered among them such eminent personages as Lord Palmerston, the future Prime

Minister; Queen Victoria's father, the Duke of Kent; and the
Archbishop of Canterbury—all of whom alluded to him pleas-
antly as "Mr. Owen the philanthropist."

But Owen was not content to be merely a man of good deeds.
His intellectual processes went deeper than that. In 1812 he
published a book entitled *A New View of Society* which caused
a sensation both in England and on the Continent, and was
reputed even to have been studied by Napoleon at Elba. In this
book Owen revealed the philosophy that inspired his actions.
"Man's character," he claimed, "is formed *for* and not *by* him."
It was the duty of the state, therefore, to educate each one of
its citizens; to maintain full employment in times of depression
by providing useful work such as road building and repairs on
public property; to encourage a system of old-age pensions; to
remove children from evil home environments and provide
schools and playing fields for them.

These suggestions fell on astonished ears for in those days the
poor were regarded not as deserving unfortunates but as a
scourge against which the well-to-do were obliged to protect
themselves. The theory advanced by the economist, Malthus,
that the population would always outstrip the means of subsistence was the accepted doctrine of the day; and because
of this the whole emphasis of society was concentrated on lowering rather than raising the amenities of the poor as the only
method of discouraging their breeding; hence the severity of
the poor laws and the degrading squalor of the workhouse.

Owen struck at the Malthusian theory boldly, declaring: "The
fear of any evil to arise from an excess of population, until such
time as the whole earth shall become a highly cultivated garden
will, on due and accurate investigation, prove a mere phantom
of the imagination, calculated solely to keep the worker in un-
necessary ignorance, vice and crime. . . . It is the artificial law
of supply and demand, arising from the principle of individual
gain in opposition to the wellbeing of society, which has hith-
erto compelled population to press on subsistence."

This was the beginning of Owen's socialism. At first he hoped by example and teaching to persuade other capitalists to adopt his views. At his own expense he printed and distributed innumerable propaganda pamphlets; on one occasion he sent out so much literature that all the London mail coaches were twenty minutes late in starting. However, he soon discovered that although people discussed his ideas few were ready to carry them out. He complained bitterly that even his own cotton mill partners refused to co-operate with him. "They objected to the building of schools," he wrote, "and said they were cotton spinners and commercial men carrying on business for profit, and had nothing to do with educating children; nobody did it in manufactories; and they set their faces against it, and against all my measures for improving the conditions of the work people. They objected to all improvements I had in progress for the increased comforts of the villagers, to my scale of wages for the people, and of salaries to the clerks and superintendents."

In 1817 Owen came reluctantly to the conclusion that his reforms would not be brought about by preaching to the rich, but that a radical change in the system was needed whereby "competition should give way to co-operation," and that this could only be made effective by a popular movement. He therefore expounded his conception of "co-operation" from one end of England to the other. He advocated the setting up of co-operative villages, where the poor could form themselves into independent communities, farm the land jointly, and sell and buy their produce in shops owned by themselves. Everywhere he preached the idea of joint ownership for the benefit of the whole, a world in which the capitalist would have little place.

His followers were known as "Owenites" and soon co-operative societies began to spring up all over England. In 1824 he went to America and founded a co-operative village in Indiana, which he christened "New Harmony," but which did not survive long in a country where there was still room for every man to make his own fortune. Although he was treated with great respect in America and entertained by the President and the Secretary of State, he returned to England to find himself no longer regarded as a distinguished man but as a lunatic. His influential friends dropped him and the next few years of his life were bound up exclusively with the working classes.

His attention turned to the trade-union movement which had been developing rapidly since the repeal of the Combination Acts. In 1833 he urged that one "Grand National Consolidated Trade Union" should be formed embracing all existing unions. By controlling strikes and promoting the co-operative movement this master union would forward the "interests of the industrious and productive classes." The union was duly set up and met with a great initial success; at the beginning of 1834 it was estimated that there were at least a million trade unionists in Britain, a larger membership than at any time until the close of the century.

This was the climax of Owen's career, for a depression soon gripped Britain and the "great consolidated union" fell to pieces under the new wave of poverty and misery that prompted men to accept work under any conditions rather than support their leaders. Owen died at the age of eighty-seven, believing in spiritualism and tipping tables in dark rooms. But the influence of his early life laid the foundation for the three great forces that provide the lifeblood of the Labor party of today: the trade-union movement, the co-operative movement, and the intellectual conception of socialism based on educational reform and high wages.

If Robert Owen was the prophet of the Labor movement, Keir Hardie was the architect. Although Hardie was born two years before Owen died, the climax of Owen's work was reached in the 1830's and Hardie's achievements did not begin until the 1880's.

The fifty-year interim was an era of riches, respectability, and great statesmen; of poverty, strife, and unrest. It was the England of Queen Victoria, and the England of Charles Dickens. Although working-class agitation was un-co-ordinated and often ineffective it was unflagging and persistent. The Chartist movement which demanded the reform of Parliament and an extension of the franchise flared up and died; the first co-operative stores, jointly owned and run on a non-profit-making basis, were established; trade unionism rose from the low ebb it had reached in the thirties to become in the eighties an organization which once again could boast over a million members. During this period socialism as a philosophy played little part. Although Karl Marx published his manifesto in 1848 and Henry Hyndman, an old Etonian (who Bernard Shaw claimed must have been "born with his top hat on"), formed the Social Democratic Federation based on Marx's teachings, few English people were attracted by a program of revolution and violence.

Keir Hardie's contribution lay in crystallizing the labor movement into one main force; he spent the greater part of his life persuading his fellow trade unionists not to rely on Liberals or Conservatives for the reforms they desired, but to organize a political party of their own. In 1893 he formed the Independent Labor party, forerunner of the Labor party of today.

Unlike the kindly Robert Owen to whom worldly success came so easily, Hardie's early life was a desperate fight against poverty, and the bitter memories he carried all his life made him a vehement apostle of the "class" struggle. Born the son of a Glasgow ship's carpenter, he went to work at the age of seven as a baker's message boy for four and sixpence a week. Twice he was late to work, the second time after sitting up all night with a sick brother. When he reached the bakery he was fired and docked a week's wages. His vivid description of his feelings some fifty years later showed how deep a mark the incident had left:

I had reached the age at which I understood the tragedy of poverty, and had a sense of responsibility for those at home far beyond my years. I knew that, despite the brave way in which my mother was facing the situation, she was feeling the burden almost too great for her to bear, and on more than one occasion I had found her crying by herself. . . . The news stupefied me, and finally I burst out crying and begged the shopwoman to intercede with the master for me. The morning was wet and I had been drenched in getting to the shop and must have presented a pitiable sight as I stood at the counter in my wet patched clothes. She spoke with the master through a speaking tube, presumably to the breakfast room I remembered so well, but he was obdurate, and finally she, out of the goodness of her heart, gave me a piece of bread and advised me to look for another place. For a time I wandered about the streets in the rain, ashamed to go home where there was neither food nor fire, and actually considering whether the best thing was not to go and throw myself in the Clyde and be done with a life that had so little attraction. In the end I went to the shop and saw the master and explained why I had been late. But it was all in vain. The wages were never paid. But the master continued to be a pillar of the Church and a leading light in the religious life of the city!*

At the age of ten Hardie went into the coal mines near Glasgow as a trapper, and for the next twenty-five years worked as a miner and a miners' leader. As a young man Hardie was a Liberal and his aims were summed up by a simple declaration: "I am anxious and determined," he said, "that the wants and wishes of the working classes shall be attended to in Parliament." Historians searching for the reasons that led to the eclipse of the Liberal party need go back no farther than this; if the Liberals had had the wisdom to adopt working-class men as parliamentary candidates it is doubtful if the Labor party would have ever come into existence. But in those days M.P.'s were paid no salaries; only men of wealth and, preferably, men of public-school education were acceptable. When Hardie realized that the Liberals, in spite of their talk, had little intention of extending political opportunity to men like himself, he began to agitate among the trade unions to form a party of their own.

In 1887 he stood as "miners' candidate" for North Ayrshire, and although he was defeated his speeches made a deep impression.

The Liberals and Conservatives have, through their organizations, selected candidates [he said]. They are both, as far as I know, good men. The point which I wish to emphasize, however, is this; that these men have been selected without the mass of the people being consulted. Your betters have chosen the men, and they now send them down to you to have them returned. What would you think if the Miners' Executive Council were to meet in Kilmarnock and appoint a secretary to the miners of Ayrshire in that way? Your candidate ought to be selected by the voice and vote of the mass of the people. We are told that Sir William Wedderburn is a

* *J. Keir Hardie,* by William Stewart.

good Radical and that he is sound on the Liberal programme. It may be all true, but you do not know whether it is or not. Will he, for example, support an Eight Hour Bill? Nobody has asked him, and nobody cares except ourselves. Will he support the abolition of private property in royalties? Well, he is a landlord and not likely to be too extreme in that respect. Is he prepared to establish a wage court that would secure to the workman a just reward for his labour? Nobody knows. . . .

Hardie continued to fight elections as an "Independent Labor" candidate, and the Liberals, realizing their mistake, finally offered to back him financially if he would stand as one of them. But by this time it was too late; the division had taken place in Hardie's mind, and in 1892, when he was thirty-five years old, he was elected to Parliament as Independent Labor. His mining colleagues raised the money to maintain him and escorted him triumphantly to the House of Commons in a charabanc with a brass band. Dressed in brown trousers, a purple muffler, and a deerstalker's cap he must have presented an extraordinary sight. The press made pitiless fun of him and overnight he became a national character. But his sincerity and dignity soon made an impression on his fellow M.P.'s; Bernard Shaw described him enthusiastically as "the damndest natural aristocrat in the House of Commons."

Two years later Hardie formed the Independent Labor party. Although his party had the sympathy of the trade unions, most of them still supported the Liberals, and were not willing to give it full backing. Hardie worked unceasingly to convert them and at the turn of the century the Trades Union Congress at last passed a resolution in favor of calling a conference of "co-operative trades union, and other working class organizations in order to consider ways and means of returning more Labor members to Parliament."

At the conference a Labor Representation Committee was set up which, six years later, became the Labor party of today.

Sidney Webb has often been described as the "man who captured the soul" of the Labor party. The Labor party did not embrace socialism until eighteen years after it was founded; and when it did, its socialism was the socialism of the Fabians, that remarkable late-Victorian, left-wing society of intellectuals dominated by Sidney and his wife Beatrice, by George Bernard Shaw, Graham Wallas, Annie Besant, and, for five or six turbulent years, H. G. Wells.

If Sidney Webb was not the most brilliant of the group, he was intellectually the most thorough and politically the most effective. In appearance he was curiously ugly, with a huge head, bulging eyes, a Lenin-like beard, and a small tapering body; his wife once described him as "the delight of caricaturists" but Shaw insisted that his profile was an "improvement on Napoleon III."

Sidney was already well known as a socialist when he married Beatrice Potter, a tall, striking girl, daughter of wealthy upper-middle-class parents and, incidentally, a sister of Lady Parmour, mother of Sir Stafford Cripps. For some time Beatrice' name had been associated with that of Joseph Chamberlain and historians may well speculate as to the course history might have taken if such a dominating character as Beatrice had become the stepmother of Joseph's son, the future Prime Minister, Neville.

Beatrice turned her back on London society when she was twenty-five and began collecting material for a book on the co-operative movement. This led to her meeting with Sidney. The letters written during their courtship are famous for their lack of romance, consisting mainly of a solemn exchange of ideas on social investigation; and these were followed fittingly by a honeymoon spent in Glasgow looking up trade-union records.

Although many people described the Webb alliance as a "union of two machines," and the fruits of this alliance were such somber children as the standard works on trade unionism, industrial democracy, and the co-operative movement, as well as the founding of the London School of Economics, the marriage was long and happy. The Webb household at 41 Grosvenor Road, London (later bitingly lampooned by H. G. Wells in *The New Machiavelli*), became the center of the liberal and radical intellectual life of the day. Beatrice carefully recorded in her diary her impressions of all the cabinet ministers, writers, and M.P.'s who moved in and out of her circle. Lloyd George and young Winston Churchill were occasional guests and of the latter she wrote: ". . . restless—almost intolerably so, without capacity for sustained and unexciting labour—egotistical, bumptious, shallow-minded and reactionary, but with a certain personal magnetism, great pluck and some originality—not of intellect but of character. More of the American speculator than the English aristocrat. Talked exclusively about himself and his electioneering plans—Wanted me to tell him of someone who would get up statistics for him. 'I never do any brainwork that anyone else can do for me'—an axiom which shows organizing but not thinking capacity." However, later her opinion of Winston changed for she wrote: "He is brilliantly able—not a phrasemonger, I think. . . ."

Although Beatrice was capable of great powers of analysis, she was interested in people as well as ideas, whereas Sidney was a man of pure reason. Oliver Stanley once described him as "a man with blue books in his veins." Little else appealed to him aside from his work. Writing of him recently Kingsley Martin said: "His mind was stored with accurate and valuable information, neatly arranged and strung together on a single strong thread." He read and digested books at a superhuman rate; it was said he could read and remember two hundred pages an hour, and a story was told of his reading the whole of *Chambers's Cyclopaedia of English Literature* in the train between London and Edinburgh. He seemed to remember everything that was useful to his purpose and to know nothing that was not.

After his death a correspondent described a walk with Sidney Webb in the garden at Passfield Corner. Webb halted at the end of a row of fine sweet peas, and said: "Those are very pretty; I don't know whether they are the sort we eat, do you?" His notions of literature and art were also rudimentary. When, after his death, tributes were paid to him in the House of Lords, one speaker recalled the sole occasion on which it was known that the Webbs went to hear a Wagner opera. Webb was asked if he had enjoyed it. "Oh yes," he said, "we had a most enjoyable evening. We happened to be sitting just behind Herbert Samuel. I was able to have a most useful conversation with him in the interval on the incidence of sickness in pregnancy."

It is difficult to imagine two men more opposite in character than the serious, humorless Sidney Webb and the provocative, mischievous Bernard Shaw, yet as well as being great friends they worked together as the driving force of the Fabian Society. The mission of the Fabian Society was to propagate ideas. The trade unions boasted few intellectuals and were concerned mainly in gaining practical, everyday concessions, whereas the Fabians were interested in proposing ways and means by which the system itself could be reformed, and fighting for the precepts which lay behind the immediate agitation of the day.

The Fabians strongly repudiated the continental conception of socialism, which was based on revolutionary methods. They declared that socialism was first and foremost an extension of democracy and must only be brought about by slow and constitutional means. In 1889 they reprinted the lectures of their leading members in a book entitled *Fabian Essays* which today is in its sixteenth edition. An excerpt from Sidney Webb reads as follows:

Advocates of social reconstruction have learnt the lessons of Democracy, and know that it is through the slow and gradual turning of the popular mind to new principles that social recognition bit by bit comes. All students of society who are abreast of their times, Socialists as well as Individualists, realize that important organic changes can only be (1) democratic, and thus acceptable to a majority of the people, and prepared for in the minds of all; (2) gradual, and thus causing no dislocation, however rapid might be the rate of progress; (3) not regarded as immoral by the mass of the people, and thus not subjectively demoralizing to them; and (4) in this country at any rate, constitutional and peaceful.

In another essay Shaw put the same point of view in a more lively way:

The young Socialist is apt to be catastrophic in his views to plan the revolutionary programme as an affair of twenty-four lively hours, with Individualism in full swing on Monday morning, a tidal wave of the insurgent proletariat on Monday afternoon, and socialism in complete working order on Tuesday. . . . You cannot convince any man that it is impossible to tear down a government in a day; but everybody is convinced already that you cannot convert first and third class carriages into second class; rookeries and palaces into comfortable dwellings; and jewellers and dressmakers into bakers and builders, by merely singing the "Marseillaise." . . . The necessity for cautious and gradual change must be obvious to everyone here, and could be made obvious to everyone elsewhere if only the catastrophists were courageously and sensibly dealt with in discussion.

Even though the Fabian Society was never large in numbers it poured forth an astonishing amount of propaganda as part of its "policy of permeation." For some years the Fabians paid small attention to the Labor party, hoping to convert the Liberals to their program; but although they had a good deal of influence on Liberal legislation, "permeation" met with more success among the trade unionists. In 1918, with the war drawing to a close and a general election once again in sight, Arthur Henderson, the leader of the Labor party, asked Sidney Webb to draft a program. The program was entitled "Labor and the New Social Order"; and from that day forth the labor movement was committed to socialism.

Sidney Webb served under two Labor governments as a cabinet minister. When, in 1929, he moved from the Commons to the upper house his wife described him as "that fantastic personage Lord Passfield" and announced firmly that she would still be known as Mrs. Webb.

Beatrice Webb died in 1943 and Lord Passfield four years later. Before he died, however, he was awarded one of the highest decorations in the land, the Order of Merit. The fact that Socialist Sidney Webb received this distinction at the recommendation of Conservative Winston Churchill, then Prime Minister, was a monument in itself to Sidney's belief in "the inevitability of gradualness." He was buried in Westminster Abbey.

Today the Labor party is an immense, complicated, puzzling, and contradictory organization, thoroughly British in the sense that on paper it should not work at all, and yet surprisingly enough it does. It has a membership of roughly five million people, which is nearly a sixth of the voting strength of the nation. About four and a quarter million of these are working-class men and women who support the party through their trade unions; a hundred thousand are members of co-operative societies affiliated to the Labor party; and six hundred thousand are independent party members.

The charges periodically hurled against the government are (a) that the Labor party dictates policy to members of Parliament and (b) that the Labor party is dominated by the trade unions and therefore the trade unions dictate policy to members of the government. On the face of it this ought to be the case but in practice it is not.

The Labor party is governed by a National Executive Committee which is composed of twenty-seven members elected annually at the party conference. Eleven seats are allotted to trade unionists, one to a co-operative society, one to a leader of the parliamentary Labor party; the rest go to constituency parties and women members with a place left open for the treasurer. If the trade unionists came to the conference as a solid trade-union "bloc" with an exclusive ax to grind they could easily win a majority, but they come as separate unions with independent and conflicting views; and they come not to boost trade-union interests but to play their part in the Labor party. Out of the twenty-seven members elected to the National Executive at the last conference sixteen were members of Parliament. Far from the party controlling the politicians, the reverse is true; while the conference delegates let off steam by passing resolutions, cabinet ministers and M.P.'s decide the policy.

The national party has an income from membership fees and trade-union subscriptions of about £300,000 ($1,200,000) a year, most of which is spent on organizers' salaries, office rents, and propaganda; the rest goes to a general election fighting fund. The task of raising any extra sums for the general election, as well as keeping the various elements within the party in harmony, lies with Morgan Phillips, the party secretary. A small man with a quiet voice, Phillips started life as a coal miner. For many years he worked as a party agent and just before the war was appointed to his present job. Hard-working, shrewd, and sensitive to the wishes of his leaders, he is given a free hand in running the national machine. As a bitter foe of communism he played an important part in persuading his chiefs to deal firmly with the dozen fellow travelers in the Labor party who sent a telegram of encouragement to the Italian party leader Nenni. This resulted in the expulsion of John Platts-Mills and inspired the *Daily Express* to indulge in the paradox of running an article likening Phillips to Joe Stalin.

The divisional Labor parties have a great deal of independence in their relationship to the national party. As they are responsible for financing their candidates at the general election, they have a free hand in selecting whom they want, but the candidates they nominate must be endorsed by the National Executive; conversely, national headquarters can make recommendations but the local parties are under no obligation to accept them. The usual method of choosing a candidate is to invite three or four applicants to appear before the local executive committee. Each is asked to make a twenty-minute speech and answer questions from the floor; after all have been heard a vote is taken.

Once a candidate has become a member of Parliament, so long as he supports the underlying principles of the Labor party he is largely free to act according to his conscience. If he consistently opposes certain planks in the program which he has originally accepted he may be asked to explain his views to the local executive committee, but it is very rarely that a local party will withdraw its support from a member of Parliament.

In the case of serious breaches the Executive Committee of the national party acts. During the last ten years this committee has expelled six M.P.'s from the Labor party. Five of the six were ousted for advocating closer co-operation with other parties including the Communists. They were Sir Stafford Cripps, Aneurin Bevan, and George Strauss, who were voted out in 1939 and reinstated shortly after; Pritt, who was expelled in 1941, and Platts-Mills, in 1948. The sixth, Alfred Edwards, was dropped for campaigning against the nationalization of steel. Although an M.P. who is expelled from the party no longer has the right to sit on the Labor benches, he of course remains a member of Parliament, and there is nothing to prevent him from standing at the next election as an Independent. However, it is an interesting fact that in recent years only one Labor M.P. succeeded in winning an election without the backing of the national party, and that was Pritt in 1945.

The parliamentary Labor party operates as a unit on its own, distinct from the Labor party. It is composed entirely of members of Parliament and has its own chairman and party secretary. It holds meetings every fortnight, which are attended by both lords and commoners, and where government policy is discussed. The Prime Minister and a number of cabinet ministers are usually present and in this way keep in close touch with the opinions of back-benchers.

Party discipline is maintained by the "whips." Although most of them hold office as "Commissioners of the Treasury" their duties are to see that government business gets through the House. They keep ministers informed of trends of opinion within the party and do their best to dissuade members from voting against the government when they disagree on points of principle. In such cases members are asked to abstain.

Every week M.P.'s receive a printed paper stating the week's business. The various bills to be voted on are underlined; two black lines means that M.P.'s should be present and three black lines that no excuse short of illness will be acceptable. The latter is always alluded to as "a three-line whip."

When the whip is only one or two lines M.P.'s of opposite parties who do not wish to stay at the House sometimes arrange to "pair." They inform their whip's office and their votes are canceled against each other. This custom innocently serves as a barometer of the political temperature; when issues are heated acquaintanceships are acknowledged by curt nods and "pairing" becomes almost nil.

Labor back-benches are not always easy for the whips to "keep in order" for among the stolid trade unionists sparkle a number of intellectuals who liven the House with a mixture of brilliance, impulsiveness, eccentricity, unreliability, and restlessness. Perhaps the most well known is Richard Crossman, assistant editor of the *New Statesman,* who organized a revolt against Bevin's foreign policy in 1947 which cost him his chance of acquiring office; then there is Michael Foot, a contributor to the *Daily Herald* and assistant editor of *Tribune,* whose political articles are famous for their passion, eloquence, and polish; Richard Stokes, a Catholic industrialist who champions lost causes; R. G. W. Mackay, the fervent advocate of a Federated Europe; Ian Mikardo, a fluent and forceful speaker with an expert knowledge of industry. The extreme left is led by fellow traveler Konni Zilliacus, a plump innocent-looking little man, half Finn and half American, who advocates British friendship with Russia on strictly Russian terms. The Labor party has refused to endorse Zilliacus as a candidate for the coming election, which makes it improbable that he will reappear in the next Parliament.

With the possible exception of "Kim" Mackay it is unlikely that any of these men will be given jobs under the Attlee regime; but if "Nye" Bevan ever reaches 10 Downing Street their chance may come.

No chapter on the Labor party would be complete without mentioning that fabulous concern, the Co-operative Society. This movement is based on a political philosophy; at the same time it has built up, on a nonprofit basis, one of the most amazingly successful commercial enterprises of the century; it works closely with the Labor party; at the same time, in the usual complicated English fashion, it is independent of it.

The co-operative movement has the largest single chain of grocery and provision shops in the world. It began just over a hundred years ago from the inspiration of Robert Owen, who preached that workingmen would only succeed in freeing themselves from poverty and want by co-operative effort. His ideas were improved upon and put into practice in 1844 by a group of Rochdale weavers who raised £28 to start a grocery shop on the principle that the customers would run it and share the profits.

Today the co-operative movement is composed of 10,000,000 members who probably represent two out of every three families in the United Kingdom. There are over 1,100 societies and 25,000 retail stores, which employ a quarter of a million people. During the war these societies distributed 32 percent of the nation's dairy products; 15 to 20 percent of its coal; 16 percent of its groceries, bread, and confectioneries; 12 percent of its meat; and 10 percent of its footwear. In 1947 it did over £400,-000,000 ($1,600,000,000) worth of business, about 6 percent of the *total personal expenditure of the United Kingdom* for the same year.

The success of the Co-operative Society contradicts the teachings of almost all businessmen. Each individual society, which controls anywhere from 1 to 494 retail shops, is run by the members of that society, and anyone who buys a £1 ($4.00) share automatically becomes a member. Although customers are allowed to hold up to £200 ($800) worth of shares no customer may have more than one vote, and the shares do not entitle a customer to extra profits but are merely a form of investment.

The members vote every eighteen months, and in some cases every three years, and elect a committee from among themselves which is responsible for the policy of the shop and the appointment of the general manager; the committee members receive no payment for their services but operate on a purely voluntary basis and general managers receive salaries which range from £1,000 to £2,000 ($4,000 to $8,000) a year.

At regular intervals all profits, apart from money set aside for reserves, are returned to the customers in the form of dividends worked out on a percentage basis according to how much they have spent.

Most American businessmen would deny that any committee could run a successful commercial venture, much less a committee of unpaid workers with no single person in a more authoritative position than another. And yet the enterprise of the Co-operative Society did not halt with the retail trade. At the end of the last century it decided to enter the wholesale business and during the last fifty years has penetrated every field from agriculture to manufacturing, from banking to transport. In the words of Sidney Webb:

They have their own arable, pasture and fruit farms, and their own creameries, butter and bacon and biscuit works, cocoa and jam and sauce and pickle factories, their own flour mills and bakeries; their own dress-making and shirt-making and tailoring workshops, and even a corset factory; their own cotton mills and clothing factories; their own hide and skin and boot and shoe and brush and mat and soap and lard and candle and furniture works; their own tin plate works and metal ware and crockery factories; their own printing establishments and their own newspapers; their own tea estates in Ceylon, their own buyers in foreign countries and their own ships on the sea; their own thousands of distributive stores, their own arrangements for insurance, their own banks and even their own common libraries.

Today the Co-operative Wholesale Societies have a loan and share capital of nearly £200,000,000 ($800,000,000) and do an annual business of over £270,000,000 ($1,080,000,000) a year. They employ sixty thousand people and their business is controlled by twenty-eight directors who are elected annually by ballot of the committees that run the retail stores. Sometimes they are men who have served as general managers, sometimes committee members, sometimes employees of the wholesale societies. They are paid a salary of about £1,400 ($5,600) a year.

The basis of the co-operative movement is social and economic, but it also runs one political party; and here is where the confusion sets in. In a certain number of localities the co-ops have local party organizations which are separate from the management committees that run the shops. Many of these groups are affiliated to the local labor parties, yet on the national level the Co-operative party retains a hair-splitting independence. It is not "affiliated" with the Labor party, but since its political aims and ideas are so much the same it has a "gentleman's agreement" not to oppose Labor candidates at election time, in return for which a small number of Co-op candidates receive Labor backing.

At the present time there are twenty-two Co-operative M.P.'s in Parliament. They sit on the Labor benches, vote as Labor M.P.'s, and even become Labor ministers: to wit, A. V. Alexander, the Minister of Defense.

But if the Co-operatives are so completely in accord with Labor policy why do they continue to function as a separate party? That is the sort of question only an American would ask. "Because," comes the answer, "we like to preserve our identity." And that is the sort of answer only an Englishman would give.

The co-operative movement proves two astonishing facts: first, that enterprise does not always require the stimulus of the profit motive; and second, that it is possible to build up and run a fabulous commercial concern by committee work rather than individual authority. Throughout the organization power is so widely diffused that no single person or even group of persons can be said to control or dominate it.

It offers the Socialists their most striking argument that nationalization is workable.

CHAPTER 10

How Socialist Are the Socialists?

We will never sacrifice the liberties won by our
forefathers to narrow dogma.

—C. R. ATTLEE

B RITISH SOCIALISTS support the monarchy; they do not
object to titles; they are not opposed to the individual ownership of property. They believe in a large measure of private
enterprise and in the incentive of more money for more work.
They also believe in government control of the basic industries
and in a society where opportunity is equal. Foreigners whose
knowledge of socialism is based on the Marxian conception
often find these facts surprising and even contradictory. After
being in London a month an American journalist who had
come to England to investigate the "social revolution" asked
plaintively: "But what is socialism anyway?"

First of all, British Socialism is as British as kippers or treacle
tart. Like Conservatism it has been fashioned from the experience of Britain's long transition from a feudal to a modern
state, and like Conservatism it is peculiar to Britain and Britain
alone. For this reason Americans, who approach British politics
from a purely American point of view in which free enterprise
and equality of opportunity are linked automatically and almost
inevitably together, find the choice that confronts them in the
two British parties baffling. Although the Conservatives believe
in free enterprise they also support a social system based on
privilege; and although the Socialists believe in equality of
opportunity they also support a planned economy. Neither of

135

these philosophies fully satisfies the American conception of democracy.

The difference in outlook between the two nations stems from the difference between British and American capitalism. And to understand the aims of Socialism it is important to make that distinction clear at the start. Whereas the history of the United States began with a Declaration of Independence which asserted that all men were equal, and the way of life emerged hand in hand with the capitalist development of the country, British capitalism was imposed on a long-established pattern of society.

The great landowners and wealthy squires who succeeded the barons and knights of feudal days regarded themselves as the natural rulers of the country. As the nation evolved from agriculture, trading, and banking to an industrial state, these men were clever enough to absorb the newly rich manufacturers, by which means they strengthened and perpetuated themselves as a ruling class. While the workingman had virtually no political representation, the new capitalists, combined with the old landed gentry, supplied the nation with its civil service and members of Parliament. And unlike America, political power became concentrated in the same hands that ruled the business world.

Had the redistribution of wealth been as consistent as it is in America this class monopoly might have been disintegrated. But once the first great boom of the nineteenth century was over, the propertied interests solidified into what was almost a caste system. Whereas in America fortunes were usually broken up by being divided among all the members of a family, in England the law of primogeniture kept large fortunes intact.

Primogeniture enabled a father to leave all his property, as well as his title, to his eldest son. This practice, which is still observed today, dates back to feudal times when titles and estates carried with them obligations which could not be fulfilled without large possessions. Even though the landlords who succeeded the feudal barons no longer incurred the obligations, they retained the custom of primogeniture in order to preserve their estates; and the industrialists, flattered at being accepted into aristocratic circles, faithfully followed the pattern. They built vast country houses and often left their money in unbreakable trusts to be handed down generation after generation. Death duties were introduced over fifty years ago in an effort to split up these big estates, and Sir William Harcourt, Liberal Chancellor of the Exchequer, proclaimed: "We are all Socialists now"; but in 1938 it was estimated that 2 percent of the population still owned 64 percent of the national wealth.

The well-entrenched society into which the manufacturing class was admitted regarded business as a distasteful occupation. The bulk of the ruling class lived on inherited wealth and therefore was able to pursue the more agreeable and unpaid pastimes of politics, sport, or letters. Unearned incomes were a badge of respectability and even the term "gentleman" was defined in the Oxford dictionary as "a man of wealth and leisure." In a book entitled *The Case for Conservatism* Quintin Hogg, regarded as one of the most progressive Conservative M.P.'s writes: "Nor have the Conservatives the smallest objection to the existence of a leisured class which uses its leisure well. On the contrary, however short the working hours of life become, Conservatives believe that a leisured class has much to bring to society—both in culture and wisdom."

This outlook greatly influenced the sons of the newly rich industrialists. First and foremost they wished to be gentlemen. Even though the control of the nation's vested interests passed into their hands, many of them accepted money as a basis of security, pleasure, and public service rather than as a means of promoting new business ventures. This attitude, often extolled as an English virtue, meant that in many instances industry suffered. The British coal mines are a classic example. The coal owners numbered among them some of the richest men in England, and yet when Lewis Douglas, the American ambassador, explained to the United States Senate the reasons that had led to the nationalization of the mines he emphasized that, while between the two wars American coal owners had put back an average of 75 percent of their profits for re-equipment, in England an average of only 25 percent had been returned.

The example of many British capitalists' turning their attention away from business and yet continuing to live on income drawn from it caused much discontent. This was further aggravated by so many businesses being closed concerns. Outsiders with ability could rise to managerial positions but the directorships and control usually passed to family connections or family friends.

Competition was also limited by lack of education. The men who ruled England sent their sons to the famous and expensive public schools where they received an education second to none; as a result little attention was paid to bettering the state system. The schools were badly equipped and the teachers poorly paid; until 1918 the school-leaving age for the vast majority of children was twelve, and until 1946, fourteen. Only children clever enough to win scholarships received a further education.

In spite of these handicaps many men rose to positions of eminence by their own outstanding qualities; many more, however, felt their abilities wasted by the scales being weighed too heavily against them. If the capitalist class had been as flexible as it is in America, if there had been the same redistribution of wealth and the same opportunity for ability regardless of family connections, and above all, if economic power had not been linked so closely with political power, it is doubtful if the Labor party would have come into being. At the end of the last century most trade unions were staunchly Liberal; although the Liberals introduced much social reform their refusal to accept workingmen as candidates led directly to the formation of the Labor party.

The concentrated effort of the war against Hitler emphasized the interdependence of all classes; it finally crystallized the growing feeling among the working people that they were entitled to a large share in the nation's councils and a larger share of the nation's wealth. At last the Socialists were able to convince the population that only by breaking the grip of the ruling class would their aims be achieved. Socialism, as an extension of democracy, became the creed of the day.

Someone once described politics as "the art of what is possible." Because British Socialism is based firmly on a belief in the parliamentary system of government it is not a rigid set of principles but a compromise between the theoretical and the practical; and its ideas are subject to constant revision and modification by public opinion.

There is probably no elected assembly in the world more sensitive to political criticism than the House of Commons. When the American Constitution was framed it was decided that the three branches of government, the executive, legislative, and judicial, should each have the power to check and balance the others. In Britain the House of Commons is absolute. If it wished, it could abolish the House of Lords; and if the King were ever unwise enough to withhold his signature from a bill, which has not happened since the days of Queen Anne, the result would probably be the end of the monarchy.

The very fact that the House of Commons is absolute and there is not even a written constitution as a final appeal has had the effect, curiously enough, of serving as a brake. Governments are always conscious of the fact that they are not merely instruments of party but are legislating for the country as a whole. They know that if they use their powers unwisely and fail to govern by persuasion and compromise their only alternative is force; and this would mean the whole breakdown of the democratic system, as almost happened with the general strike in 1926.

The government, therefore, pays the opposition leader a handsome salary to oppose and closely heeds the arguments of minorities. A measure that would provoke active resistance from any considerable section of the people would never be introduced even though nothing would be easier than for a government with a large majority to make it law. For example, although Socialists believe theoreticaly in the nationalization of the land they recognize that it will not come about until a large majority of farmers are willing to work it, which places the prospect in the far future.

This outlook marks the difference between British Socialism and the continental socialism analyzed by such writers as Hayek. It is the reason why by-elections are watched so closely in England and why Churchill lost so much influence during the general election when he accused the Labor party of treading the path to the totalitarian state and the Gestapo.

The program which the Labor party presented to the nation in 1945, and which it was elected to carry out, placed the interests of the working classes before the interests of any other section of the community. Like other election platforms it promised to deal effectively with housing, agriculture, education, and social reform; unlike other election platforms it based its program first and foremost on a policy of "full employment." Under this heading came four points:

[First:] Production must be raised to the highest level and related to purchasing power. Over-production is not the cause of depression and unemployment; it is under-consumption that is responsible.

[Second:] A high and constant purchasing power can be maintained through good wages, social services and insurance, and taxation which bears less heavily on the lower income groups. But everyone knows that money and savings lose their value if prices rise, so rents and the prices of the necessities of life, will be controlled.

[Third:] Planned investment in essential industries and on houses, schools, hospitals and civic centres will occupy a large field of capital expenditure. . . . The location of new factories will be suitably controlled, and where necessary the government will itself build factories. There must be no depressed areas in the New Britain.

[Fourth:] The Bank of England with its financial powers must be brought under public ownership, and the operations of the other banks harmonised with industrial needs.

The second cardinal declaration of policy was nationalization. Under this heading it said:

Each industry must have applied to it the test of national service. If it serves the nation, well and good; if it is inefficient and falls down on its job, the nation must see that things are put right. . . . There are basic inlustries ripe and over-ripe for public ownership and management in the direct service of the nation. There are many smaller businesses rendering good services which can be left to go on with their useful work.

It then declared that it was the intention of the Labor party to nationalize coal, gas and electricity, rail, air, and road transport, and iron and steel.

Most governments are attacked by the opposition for not honoring their election pledges; but the Labor government is attacked for carrying them out. While the Conservatives declare hotly that it is irresponsible to experiment with Socialism when the nation is faced with an economic crisis the government stubbornly continues on its way; within the last four years it has driven through its nationalization program, it has maintained its policy of full employment, and has pressed ahead with its social reforms.

There is no doubt that the vast amount of legislation passed has accomplished what it set out to accomplish in benefiting the people in the lower income brackets. Taxation has been lifted on earned incomes and increased on unearned; subsidies have kept food within the reach of the poorest; the school-leaving age has been raised to fifteen; the qualifications for the civil service have been broadened; a complete medical service has been made available to all; necessities in short supply have been strictly rationed under the slogan "Fair shares for all"; a compulsory insurance scheme has been introduced which insures everyone, in the words of the cynics, from "the womb to the tomb."

The Conservatives cry that the country is too poor to afford the public expenditure involved in launching these schemes; the Socialists reply that it is only by providing a basic standard of life for the working classes that the production targets are likely to be reached. Which theory is right will not be proved until the government presents the nation with its balance sheet at the next election.

Party warfare has raged even more hotly, however, on the subject of controls. While the Conservatives declare that controls are strangling enterprise the Socialists declare that they are preventing inequalities. At the Gravesend by-election in 1947 the issue was fought out before the public. The situation was critical; bread had been rationed a short time before, a fuel crisis had resulted in electricity cuts, and a drought had resulted in potato rationing. The Conservative candidate made as much party capital as possible out of these events; Eden and Morrison took part in the campaign; Churchill declared that the country was sickening of Socialism and demanded a general election; and the press described Gravesend as a miniature Britain with the eyes of the world fixed upon it.

When it was announced that the Socialist candidate had carried the day, the rejoicing among Labor M.P.'s was so great it inspired one of them to tie a ribbon of Tory blue on a potato and roll it down the aisle of the House of Commons.

Today the battle continues. The Socialists tell the public that if the Conservatives were returned to power they would lift many controls, prices would rise, and only people with the most money would be able to afford the necessities of life, while the Conservatives declare that many of the controls are a Socialist plot to grasp more power. An example of this was shown at the last Conservative conference when a member introduced a motion in which it was stated that government control of newsprint was deliberately enforced to "suppress the freedom of the press."

So many accusations have been flung back and forth between the two parties that foreign visitors usually ask in bewilderment: What controls are due to Britain's economic situation and what controls are due to Socialism? It is not easy to draw a straight line between the two for it is Socialist policy to control all essential consumers' goods which are in short supply; but clothing is now free and as various articles become plentiful the rationing is lifted.

However, steel and timber are also in short supply. They too must be controlled so that firms bringing in dollars or supplying essential industries in Britain will have priority in obtaining materials. This plays into the Socialists' hands, for the control of steel and timber gives the government some of the powers of direction it has always claimed to be necessary for a planned economy. For example, by promising manufacturers allocations of materials they could not otherwise get, the government has been able to persuade many factory owners to move into depressed areas, thereby forestalling unemployment. Whether or not the government will be willing to relinquish its allocation powers once goods are no longer in short supply remains to be seen; and if so, what controls will be put in their place? At the present time no one knows the answer; not even the government.

In the face of controls and the nationalization program, which the Conservatives regard as an infringement of human liberty, the Socialists add fuel to the fire by declaring that Socialism is an "extension of democracy." They argue that from the days of tyrant kings onward the progress of civilization has been marked by restricting the actions of the few for the benefit of the many. What were the Factory Acts of the last century, limiting the hours women and children could be employed, if not restrictions of liberty? The laws that tell a man how much money he must give to the state; that send children to school; that forbid people to make public nuisances of themselves; that force men to fight for their country? To Socialists, government control over industry which affects the lives of all is a logical step in a long sequence of events. They declare that if the people decide that the limitations imposed by the state do not, in fact, expand their freedom but curtail it, they can elect another government; that under a free parliamentary system government action springs from the will of the people and is dependent on the will of the people; that an extension of this action must, therefore, be an extension of democracy itself.

Just as there are reactionaries and progressives in the Conservative party, there are extremists and moderates in the Labor party. A "right-wing" Socialist may sound like a contradiction in terms, but the majority of Labor M.P.'s fit into this category. Their leaders are Attlee, Bevin, and Morrison; their socialism is evolutionary and democratic. If you ask them what sort of Britain they would expect to see after twenty years of Socialist rule they answer that 70 percent of industry probably would still be in private hands. They are not in a hurry; and since democratic government is the basis of their creed they have no compunction in allying themselves spiritually with capitalist America against communist Russia.

Out of the four hundred Labor M.P.'s the left-wing Socialists number somewhere between twenty and thirty. Their approach is Marxist; they believe that socialist economy comes first and democracy second and that if the interests of the two ever clash it is democracy that should be jettisoned. They are dogmatic and doctrinaire and would not balk at drastic measures to achieve their aims. Their natural sympathies go to Russia; America is their bugbear.

At present they have no leader and little following; but if the social democracy of the moderates breaks down they prophesy that the working classes will turn to them. Many people believe that Aneurin Bevan or John Strachey might become their leader. But not until the wind is blowing in the right direction.

CHAPTER 11

The Conservative Party

The Conservatives have one great asset. They
believe themselves to be the natural rulers of the
country.

—JOHN PARKER, *Labour Marches On*

BEFORE the war when you thought of the Conservative
party you thought of blue ribbons and blue blood; of political talk over vintage port and titled ladies opening garden fetes;
of the Primrose League and the Carlton Club; of country
houses, conscientious landlords, and respectful tenants; of a
middle class proudly conscious of its betters; of nationalism,
imperialism, and patriotism; of an England as imperturbable
and well set in its course as the sun; of an England with its
roots deeply in the past resisting all change until that change
became inevitable, then accepting the new with enough good
grace to preserve the pattern of the old.

Although the Conservative party was greatly discredited in
the years directly preceding the war, when it went to the polls
in 1945 led by Winston Churchill at the height of his fame and
power, few people predicted its defeat. Labor's victorious landslide came as a shattering blow and for a time Conservative
ranks appeared to be demoralized and broken. The Socialists
proclaimed jubilantly that the Tories were out of power for
twenty years, and the Tories revealed the extent of their own
agitation by carrying on a heated discussion as to whether the
name "Conservative" ought not to be changed to something
with a more progressive ring. Those who had studied political
history, however, refused to become alarmed, for the long record

of Toryism is a fascinating study of defeat and revival. Time and
again the party, clinging to a defense of the *status quo*, has
been swept aside by the great waves of reform that have rolled
across the country; time and again the body has been left on
the shore for dead. But it has always risen again and oddly
enough the resuscitation has usually been accomplished by a
leader unrepresentative of the party as a whole; in the seventeenth century it was Bolingbroke and Chatham; in the eighteenth century Disraeli and Lord Randolph Churchill.

Toryism has always reflected the "right wing" of British political thought. The terms "Tory" and "Whig" came into being
in the 1680's when the party system fight began to develop,
and from that time until the Labor administrations of the present day one or other of these two divisions provided the governments of England. During the seventeenth century only a few
thousand men of property and wealth had the right to vote, and
Tory and Whig politicians were cut from the same cloth; yet
the temperaments of the two parties were distinct from the
earliest days.

The Tory party received the bulk of its support from the
stodgy, stalwart, unimaginative, and reliable landowning
"squirearchy," while the society-loving Whigs began to attract
the more adventurous merchants and financiers. "They rather
despised the Tory governors of the country as people less fashionable than themselves," wrote George Trevelyan.* "They
were so well connected that they could afford to toy with democracy. . . ."

While the Tories defended the *status* quo the Whigs reached
out for power. In the seventeenth century they took the initiative in ousting James II from the throne and establishing the
supremacy of Parliament, only enlisting Tory support when the
latter became fearful lest James turn the nation Catholic. In
the eighteenth century they stripped the King of the right to
appoint his own advisers while the Tories fought an unsuccessful battle to maintain it, becoming known as "the King's
friends." "To check as much as may be possible the spirit of

* *The History of England.*

party appears to be one of the first duties and noblest employments of a King," cried Thomas Gisborne, the Tory writer. "To countenance it is to encourage interested nobles and aspiring commoners, factious orators, needy and profligate adventurers to combine in bands and confederacies for the purpose of obtruding themselves into all the offices of Government, and under the name and garb of servants of imposing on the monarch and on the people chains too strong to be broken."

With the Crown's interference in government finally ended, the nineteenth century heralded a new era. This was the century during which Britain was transformed from an agricultural country into the greatest industrial power in the world; it was also the century in which Britain was transformed from an oligarchy into a democracy. Tories and Whigs developed into Conservatives and Liberals and a "right" and "left" began to form in the sense that we understand these terms today.

The two most powerful and uncompromising influences on the thought of the day were represented by Conservative Edmund Burke's *Thoughts on the French Revolution*, a brilliant castigation of mob rule which he believed to be the inevitable outcome of democracy, and Tom Paine's *The Rights of Man*, which declared that all power was derived from the people and that governments, therefore, should be properly representative of the people. The Conservatives accepted Burke as their philosopher while the Liberals, although not in sympathy with Paine's republicanism, were fascinated by his new conception of society. This division soon revealed itself in political legislation. The Conservatives, under the leadership of the famous soldier, the Duke of Wellington, hotly opposed the rising pressure among the population for the right to vote. When Wellington made a speech to this effect in the House of Lords, he sat down amidst a buzz of conversation and asked the reason for the excitement. "My Lord Duke," came the reply, "you have announced the fall of your government." The Liberals swept into power and two years later, in 1832, passed the first great Reform Act, extending the franchise to the middle classes. With the new vote solidly behind them the Liberals became the champions of the new democracy. The Conservatives, except for Peel's five-year ministry in 1841, did not again command a majority in the House of Commons for forty-four years.

During the first half of this fabulous century of power and riches, unrest, poverty, and even starvation, Conservative philosophy stood out in bold contrast to the early Liberalism. The Liberals believed in individualism, and they linked this individualism to an economic policy of *laissez faire*. While private enterprise was building up a great industrial empire, women and small children were slaving in the new factories and mills twelve and fourteen hours a day. They were living in conditions of appalling squalor and disease and the death rate was increasing daily. Many Conservatives were horrified by this state of affairs. The Tory squirearchy had been taught to believe in *noblesse oblige*; they lived in a world where landlords looked after their tenants and pensioned off their servants. Led by Lord Shaftesbury, the Conservatives succeeded in putting on the statute books a series of acts limiting the hours of employment for women and children which were bitterly opposed by some Liberals as "state interference."

During the second half of the century Liberalism, under the great William Gladstone, was freed from the bonds of *laissez faire* and enterprise was gradually coupled with responsibility. The Conservatives accepted democracy as inevitable and began to rebuild their party, so long in the wilderness, on these lines.

The man most responsible for the revitalizing of the Conservative party during its long years in the wilderness was the brilliant, bizarre, unorthodox Benjamin Disraeli. Disraeli first stood for Parliament several times between 1832 and 1835 as an Independent, declaring: "Toryism is worn out and I cannot condescend to become a Liberal." However, he finally joined the Conservative party announcing: "I shall withhold my support from every ministry which will not originate some great measure to ameliorate the lower classes." Although Disraeli did not become Prime Minister for the first time until he was nearly seventy, and held the office, altogether, under eight years, he initiated reforms in public health and housing and after defeating a second Reform Bill by Gladstone had been shrewd enough in 1867 to pass one of his own, in order, as Lord Derby explained, "to dish the Whigs." Disraeli's great contribution, however, was in reorienting his party to the new democracy; in teaching the upper classes "not to retire to their tents in anger at their lost privileges, but to go down into the street and appeal to the masses on grounds of patriotic sentiment and Imperial interest."*

When Disraeli died in 1881 the torch of "Tory democracy" was carried on by the brilliant, provocative Lord Randolph Churchill, son of the Duke of Marlborough and father of Winston. Lord Randolph's wit and independence made him one of the most popular orators in the country. In the 1880's when the Conservatives were once again opposing an extension of the franchise his battle cry became "Trust the people." "The Conservative Party," he insisted, "will never exercise power until it has gained the confidence of the working classes. . . . Our Interests are perfectly safe if we trust them fully, frankly and freely; but if we oppose them and endeavour to drive them and hoodwink them, our interests, our constitution and all we love and revere will go down. If you want to gain the confidence of the working classes let them have a share and a large share— a real share and not a sham share—in your party Councils and in your party government. . . ."

Lord Randolph's influence and popularity throughout the country grew by leaps and bounds; his public meetings were packed and he was booed and cheered as he exerted all the force of his intellect and high-spirited energy in selling "Tory Democracy" to the man in the street. But among many of his own party he was deeply resented. In his famous life of his father, Winston Churchill writes:

It is curious to reflect that all this time, while Lord Randolph Churchill was straining every nerve in the service of his party, he was the subject of almost passionate jealousy and dislike in high places. The world of rank and fashion had long been hostile to him. The prominent people and party officials who formed and guided opinion at the Carlton Club, on the

* G. M. Trevelyan, *History of England*.

Front Opposition Bench, and in the central Conservative offices, regarded him with aversion and alarm. They could not understand him. Still less could they explain his growing influence. He was as unwelcome and insoluble a riddle to them as ever Disraeli had been. To them he seemed an intruder, an upstart, a mutineer who flouted venerable leaders and mocked at constituted authority with a mixture of aristocratic insolence and democratic brutality. By what warrant did he pronounce in accents of command on all the controverted questions of the day, when men grey in the service of the State, long installed in the headship of the party, held their peace or dealt in platitude and ambiguity? By what strange madness of the hour had this youth who derided Radicals for abandoning their principles and preached Liberalism from Tory Platforms, gained acceptance throughout the land? . . .

In truth, at this crisis in their fortunes the Conservative party were rescued in spite of themselves. A very little and they would never have won the new democracy. But for a narrow chance they would have slipped down into the gulf of departed systems. The forces of wealth and rank, of land and Church, must always have exerted vast influence in whatever confederacy they were locked. Alliance or fusions with Whigs and moderate Liberals must from time to time have secured them spells of office. But the Tory party might easily have failed to gain any support among the masses. They might have lost their hold upon the new foundation of power; and the cleavage in British politics must have become a social, not a political division—upon a line horizontal, not oblique.

Instead, "Tory Democracy" caught the imagination of the classes enfranchised during the century, the Conservative party was triumphantly returned in 1885 and for nearly fifty out of the sixty years until 1945 either served as partners in wartime coalition governments or completely dominated the political scene.

Today, once again, the Conservative party is trying to resell itself to the nation. Under the barrage of Labor propaganda with its emphasis on social service, many Conservatives have grown self-conscious about the history of their party and, forgetting Lord Salisbury's dictum about change, have even gone so far as to try and prove that Conservatives, and not Liberals or Socialists, have always been "the party of reform." The Conservative Central Office has issued a booklet entitled *Conserva-*

tive Social and Industrial Reform, and the lengths to which
the author has been driven are illustrated by the fact that he
has found it necessary to list many reforms as "Tory" without
mentioning that they were made law by Whig administrations.
Also listed is the repeal of the Combination Act of 1825, but
no mention is made of the fact that there would have been no
need to abolish this repressive measure had it not been introduced by the Conservatives twenty-five years earlier, and that
it was only lifted when the agitation among the working classes
was bordering on rebellion.

It is impossible to separate the contribution of any one political party from the development of Britain as a whole. Ever
since the supremacy of Parliament was established, the two
great parties of the day have acted and reacted on one another
like the parts of a wonderfully co-ordinated machine. No single
party would have followed the same course without the inter-
play of the other, and in the elaborate pattern that has evolved
the threads are closely entwined. Nevertheless, it is possible to
trace a rough design and it is patently absurd to pretend that the
forces of Conservatism have been the forces of reform. Although
the Conservatives have passed much useful social legislation,
the pressure for change has always come from the movements
on the left; from Chartists, Democrats, Radicals, Liberals, or
Socialists. The great contribution of the Conservatives has been
to conserve.

It would be impossible to contemplate the history of Britain
without the influence of the Tories, for the stability for which
the nation is famous is largely due to the fact that British Conservatism has always been effective. And proof that this has
required skill and imagination is offered by a European continent strewn with the wrecks of reactionary factions. Enlightened Conservatives have been elastic enough to accept change
when change has become inevitable, and the fact that they have
lived to defend with vigor the customs and institutions handed
down to them has always had a sobering effect on the left. Indeed, it is because of Britain's genius for right-wing government

that it has been possible for the nation to make the long transition from feudal days to social democracy with so little violence and such striking continuity.

In many ways there is a parallel between the defeat of the Conservative party a hundred years ago and the defeat of the party today. Both times Toryism was swept aside by a new philosophy; then it was democracy, now it is socialism. Winston Churchill, speculating as to what his father's career might have been had he not died at an early age, wrote in 1907: "Would he, under the riddles the future had reserved for such as he, have snapped the tie of sentiment that bound him to his party, resolved at last to 'shake the yoke of inauspicious stars'; or would he by combining its Protectionist appetites with the gathering forces of labour have endeavoured to repeat as a Tory-Socialist in the new century the triumphs of the Tory-Democrat of old?"

There is no doubt that sooner or later, Tory Socialism will be sold to the British public. The difficulty of the moment is the lack of a Disraeli or a Lord Randolph Churchill to do it. And since no spirited young Tory with the force and eloquence to grip the imagination of the country has come forward, Conservative efforts are concentrated not so much on a rehabilitation of outlook as on a rehabilitation of the party machine.

Soon after the general election Lord Woolton was appointed chairman of the party and given the task of reconstruction. Woolton was not a politician, nor, for that matter, even a party man. "I am a political neuter," he announced when Churchill invited him to become Minister of Food during the war. He had rarely attended debates in the House of Lords or shown any interest in party diversions. He began life as a professional economist, then put his theories into practice by going into business and building up a successful chain of department stores.

In appearance Lord Woolton is far removed from the usual American conception of a self-made business tycoon. In his sixties, with gray hair and a pink complexion, he talks in a precise, almost old-maidish way, reminding one more of a high-school teacher than a party boss. The fact that Lewis' department stores show a profit of a million and a half pounds a year, however, should be some indication of his organizing ability.

Lord Woolton began the job of reorganizing the Conservative party by appealing for a million-pound "fighting fund." Up to date he has raised nearly two million. He has also raised the membership of the Conservative party from one to two million; he has sent "instructor-demonstrators" around the country to teach Conservatives how to canvass; he has lectured the constituency parties on the advisability of adopting candidates of ability rather than wealth; he has urged Conservatives to fight local elections on party lines; he has begged them to attend local meetings and encouraged them to heckle and cheer. He has studied Herbert Morrison's methods and announced publicly that Herbert "knows his stuff."

The Conservative Central Office itself, however, still breathes an air of amiable amateurishness. The building in which it is housed offers a marked contrast to the modern efficiency of Transport House, the headquarters of the Labor party. Transport House is full of new paint and big windows, while Abbey House has creaking wooden floors, dark corridors, an aged attendant, and an elevator that moves with all the caution of old age. The dingy offices are animated by voluntary workers, most of whom are prospective or defeated candidates, hopeful that their labors will one day be rewarded with winnable seats.

The absence of the professional note is largely due to the fact that the Conservative party, as a national organization, has never taken any part in shaping policy. This has been left exclusively in the hands of Conservative politicians, and as a result annual conferences have been poorly attended and spiritless. In the last few years Lord Woolton has succeeded in whipping up interest by encouraging members to introduce resolutions; even though they may never be acted upon he believes that the psychological effect is to the good.

Conservatives have the support of the upper classes, a large proportion of the middle classes, and a small proportion of the

working classes. When election day comes Lord Woolton will
have his goods tastefully displayed; but can he undercut the
firm across the way?

If the answer is yes, the politicians on the Conservative front
bench, the majority of whom began their ministerial careers
under Baldwin and Chamberlain, will be dusted and taken off
the shelf. They follow in the approved style of British public
men.

Most of them have been to Eton; most of them served with
distinction in World War I; most of them are men of property;
most of them are hard-working, agreeable, conscientious, and
ambitious. They view each other with a mixture of friendship
and spite bred from a long association both political and social.
But they are united in a common detestation of the Socialists
and a common belief in their own superiority.

There is little jostling among them for party position, for Anthony Eden's role as crown prince is undisputed. Except for
Winston no other Tory politician commands so great a following throughout the country. When Churchill retires the
mantle of leadership will fall on his shoulders, and a Conservative victory would make him Prime Minister.

Eden is the son of a Yorkshire squire, Sir William Eden, who
is reputed to have had such a temper that he sometimes up-
rooted the flowers in the garden, much to his wife's consternation. Eden served in the first war as an artillery captain and was
awarded the Military Cross for valor; two of his brothers were
killed. When he returned to England his mother packed him
off to Oxford, in spite of protests, where he won first-class honors in Oriental languages. In those days his bent was literary,
not political.

He went into the House of Commons largely because it was
the sort of thing a gentleman did. And from the first he was
tagged by that careless and often fatal phrase "a promising
young man." But Eden fulfilled the promise; not only did he
rise rapidly from being Parliamentary Private Secretary to the
Foreign Minister to being Foreign Minister himself, but his

good looks and well-pressed clothes excited the imagination of the public and he soon became a world figure; when he went to America in 1937 he received the adulation of a movie idol.

However, there was something more in it than that. Eden stood for the League of Nations; he was the symbol of a generation who believed in peace and when it became apparent that there was to be no peace with honor he became the symbol of a generation who also believed in integrity. In an article published in 1940 Winston Churchill wrote of him: "There is no one else of his age and experience who has a greater hold upon the sympathy and imagination of what may, in its widest sense, be called the liberal forces of England."

Today Eden is fifty-two and gray haired. As deputy leader of the opposition he spends most of his time in the House of Commons, and his public meetings are infrequent but they still draw large crowds. Many of his party seem puzzled by his success. Some of his critics accuse him of being vain, others of being weak, still others of being superficial. It is true that he rarely makes a profound remark; he has little wit and his speeches are often masterpieces in the use of the cliché. And yet even in the House of Commons he commands more respect from the Labor benches than any other Conservative.

What's the answer? "Cricket," said one of his supporters heartily. "You can always rely on Anthony to play the game!"

R. A. Butler has none of Eden's charm, none of his popularity in the country, none of his following in the Commons. Yet he has done more hard thinking on how to reorient Conservative policy to the postwar world than any other man in the party. He has come to the conclusion that a certain amount of "planning" will have to be swallowed if Toryism is to survive. "Change we are bound to face," he announces, "although all change hurts."

Butler is forty-six and looks even younger. He has an aloof, almost priggish air but is modest and friendly to talk with. The most surprising thing about him is his laugh, which is like a volcano which will not quite erupt; it shakes him savagely, but only giggles emerge. He had a brilliant career at Cambridge where he was president of the Union and took a double first in modern languages and history. There he met a Miss Courtauld who also took a first in history. He married her and shortly afterward her father, a famous silk manufacturer, died and left her a million pounds.

Butler received office after being in the House of Commons only a few months; he was Undersecretary of State for India, for Labor, and for Foreign Affairs. During the war Churchill made him Minister of Education. Save for Lord Swinton, no other politician has survived so many Prime Ministers; and unlike Swinton, Butler is still in the front rank. His political opponents make capital of this and in the *Daily Herald* Michael Foot recently wrote:

As long ago as 1931 he first appeared on the scene as the rising hope of the pliant, appeasing Tories. Thereafter he held office without interval until 1945. He was without protest a Man of Manchuria, a Man of Abyssinia, a Man of Non-Intervention, a Man of Munich, a Baldwinite and a Chamberlainite *par excellence*. Nothing in this record prevented him from also becoming a Churchillite. Indeed, while Churchill is writing his memoirs he is given the task of writing Churchill's policy.

In trying to elbow Socialism out of the way to make room for the "Tory planning" he launched in *The Conservative Industrial Charter*, he writes: "We wish to substitute for the present paralysis . . . a system of free enterprise which is on terms with authority, and which reconciles the need for central direction with the encouragement of individual effort." To confused supporters who ask Mr. Butler exactly what he means he explains: "Our aim is the humanization rather than the nationalization of industry," adding brightly, "We might call it private enterprise with public responsibility." Butler's political instinct, never to be driven into a corner, led one newspaper writer to remind the public of a classic statement he made in 1939 when, as Undersecretary for Foreign Affairs, he was called upon in the House for information: "I have every reason to hope that I shall be in a position to say something definite before very long."

Butler's hazy words may confuse his followers but his mind is clear; he knows what he is doing and where he is going; he knows a certain amount of socialism has come to stay and he intends to stay with it.

Oliver Stanley may one day be Chancellor of the Exchequer. During the last four years no other ex-minister has grown so much in stature. Before the war he was regarded as an able man but a disappointing politician; today only Churchill and Eden supersede him in the party hierarchy.

Ellen Wilkinson once wrote: "Oliver Stanley is the type England breeds for state occasions." Tall, gray-haired, and courteous, Stanley is the product of several centuries of aristocratic statesmen. His father and grandfather, both Earls of Derby, were cabinet ministers; his great-grandfather was Prime Minister. "*Sans changer*," the family motto, seemed appropriate enough when Oliver was made Minister of War in 1940, the fourth Stanley to hold the post.

Like many of his front-bench colleagues Stanley went to Eton and Oxford. He fought in the First World War and at nineteen was known as "the boy major"; he was awarded the Military Cross and the *Croix de guerre*. After that he was a barrister, a stockbroker, and finally member of Parliament for Westmoreland.

He received his first office when he was thirty-five and like Eden was hailed as a promising young man; but the promise was slow to materialize for during the ten years between 1931 and 1941 he held six ministerial appointments without distinction. He was moved from post to post in the hope that the next would command the talents which the previous one had failed to do. But in spite of a remarkably shrewd brain, indecisiveness undermined his ability and he himself once referred to "my many ministerial jobs in which I have led a transient and embarrassed existence."

When Churchill sent him to the Colonial Office in 1942 his star began to rise, but it was not until the Conservative party was defeated and he sat on the front bench no longer as a min-

ister but as a member of the opposition that his highly critical
and cynical cast of mind found its real outlet. All at once the
diffidence, the indecisiveness, the lack of conviction vanished.
He attacked and he attacked hard. And because his speeches
were masterpieces of wit and irony the House packed to hear
them. Once, much to everyone's delight, he taunted Ernest
Bevin with putting forward a "Conservative" policy, and congratulated him on understanding The Importance of Being
Anthony.

Stanley is extremely modest and inclined to exaggerate his
limitations; he pooh-poohs the idea of ever being Prime Minister, and insists that what he would like most is to return to
the Colonial Office. Although he is regarded as a progressive,
and although he is probably the only Tory about whom Harold
Laski has ever written a friendly article, there are few men more
deeply Conservative. He can understand a workingman supporting Socialism but he finds the middle-class intellectuals hard
to forgive. And nothing annoys him more than to be referred
to as an intellectual himself. "Thank heaven," he once retorted
in a debate, "I have one of the lowest brows in the House, which
enables me to still enjoy a good knock-down comedy."

Three more Etonians who sit on the Conservative front bench
and who are certain to be returned to ministerial office if their
party comes back to power are Robert Hudson, Harold Macmillan, and Oliver Lyttelton.

Hudson is big, red cheeked, and vigorous; he looks forty-three
and is sixty-three. He enjoys the distinction of having been the
first successful Minister of Agriculture. Before the war his Tory
colleagues considered him too blunt to be safe in high office;
what he lacked, they said, was tact and finesse. For this reason
he cooled his heels for nine years as a junior minister. When
Churchill became Premier, however, he put Hudson in charge
of shipping, then switched him a year later to deal with agriculture.

Hudson was enterprising; the country needed food and he
began the unheard-of process of dispossessing glaringly ineffi-

cient farmers and transferring their holdings to those who could produce it. Under his auspices county and district agricultural committees were set up whereby farmers themselves were given the task of seeing that such new measures were enforced; these committees are still functioning today.

Hudson took up farming himself to show how it should be done, and built up a herd of Frisian cows which in 1947 topped the milk records for Britain.

Macmillan is an intellectual rather than a man of action. He is a grandson of the founder of Macmillan's publishing house and took first-class honors at Oxford. Pompous, dignified, with spectacles and a walrus mustache, Macmillan is so much a caricature of the English Blimp it is difficult to reconcile his appearance with the fact that in the 1930's some of his Tory colleagues regarded him as a dangerous Liberal. He wrote a book entitled *The Middle Way* which advocated many socialist ideas.

During the war he was sent to North Africa as British minister; after that to Italy as High Commissioner. Macmillan's only taste of political power was as Air Minister in Churchill's caretaker government which remained in office no longer than two months. If the Conservatives come back Macmillan might become Foreign Minister.

Oliver Lyttelton is the large, fifty-six-year-old, boisterous, good-natured exponent of big business. He is not a professional politician. He was managing director of the British Metal Corporation at the outbreak of war; Churchill persuaded him to enter the House and invited him to run the Board of Trade. In 1942 he was made Minister of Production and given a seat in the war cabinet. Although he is a hard worker and an excellent administrator, he has never mastered the technique of debate and is seldom able to conceal the fact that he regards all those who disagree with him politically as fools. He enjoys life and puts the secret down to his favorite maxim: "Never do anything in the name of pleasure that bores you."

CHAPTER 12

Conservative Policy

Britain's greatness has been built on character
and daring, not on docility to a State machine.
—WINSTON CHURCHILL

A good Tory has never been in history afraid of
the use of the State.
—R. A. BUTLER

WINSTON CHURCHILL'S father, Lord Randolph
Churchill, once said: "Whenever by an unfortunate con-
currence of circumstance an Opposition is compelled to support the government, the support should be given with a kick
and not with a caress and withdrawn at the first available moment."

The Conservatives have faithfully followed this advice, but
the fact that their kicks of encouragement have been delivered
with unusual vigor has made it difficult to distinguish them from
their kicks of abuse, and this has led to a good deal of confusion.
Although they have excoriated the system of controls they have
promised not to free any goods while they remain in short supply; although they have demanded a cut in government expenditure they have remained silent when asked where the reductions should begin; although they have declared themselves the
champions of free enterprise they have adopted a charter of
planned economy.

What then is Conservative policy?

The division between the two parties is not so much a difference of philosophy as a difference of approach. Assuming that

160

both parties agree that the aim of society is, in the words of Bentham, "the greatest happiness for the greatest number," and interpreting the word "happiness" in a political context as "material well-being," the question is how can this best be achieved?

Whereas the Socialists believe that the prosperity of the nation depends primarily upon the exertions of the working classes, the Conservatives believe that the prosperity of the nation depends primarily on the enterprise of the capitalist class; accordingly, the Socialists emphasize full employment and the Conservatives emphasize increased incentives. The Socialists argue that full employment produces purchasing power which produces expansion of industry; the Conservatives argue that increased incentives produce the expansion of industry which produces purchasing power. Each believes that the other has the cart before the horse.

These two approaches inevitably create a division between the high and low income brackets. It is not surprising that the working classes prefer the Socialist cart and the upper classes the Conservative cart; neither is it surprising that the middle classes stand by undecided and anxious as to which will give them the best journey.

The fact, however, that the working classes represent the great mass of the electorate has put the Conservatives into a quandary. How can they solicit more third-class passengers? Eventually, of course, they believe that the Socialist cart will break down. They believe that the Socialist conception of society does not take the human element into account. The donkey must have the carrot at its nose and the stick at its tail; man must have the hope of reward and the fear of hunger. The Socialist idea of guaranteeing security at the bottom levels and curtailing rewards at the higher levels does away with these two great spurs and will result in a slackening of effort which will lower, rather than raise, the standard of life for all. To this the Socialists retort that it is the Conservatives, not they, who do not understand human nature; that the working classes will no longer tolerate insecurity and an unfair distribution of wealth, and failure to remedy these things would not only result in strikes and a general paralysis of industry but might even sound the death knell of democracy with communism taking its place.

The will of the electorate helped to impress the Conservatives with the logic of this argument. In order to guarantee a basic standard of life, planning was essential; but free enterprise was also essential. The result was "Tory Socialism," the twentieth century Conservatism that Winston Churchill had prophesied nearly forty years ago.

Tory Socialism was launched by R. A. Butler, ex-Minister of Education, in a pamphlet called *The Conservative Industrial Charter*. Henceforth not only was planning to be regarded by obedient party men as a necessity but a certain amount of nationalization was to be swallowed as well. Howls of anger arose from the die-hards, who branded it as "milk and water" Socialism, while the Beaverbrook press tried to bury it with indecent haste.

That nine-day wonder the Industrial Charter produced by the Conservative Party after strenuous labour pains is already dead [it pronounced]. No doubt the corpse will be disinterred for examination at the annual conference of the party at Brighton in October but the Coroner's verdict is: "Dead from nationalization causes." Mr. R. A. Butler still pretends that life is not extinct. And this is a very proper attitude, for Mr. Butler wrote it. Why he was selected to produce an industrial programme is not clear. Mr. Butler is not an industrialist but an academic educationalist who knows nothing of the trials and disappointments of management and control of business.

The Charter raised a storm not only in England but even across the Atlantic. News reports appeared on the front pages of the British papers declaring that Senator Arthur Vandenberg had been asked to write Mr. Butler to address a joint session of Congress. "Congressmen want him to explain," wrote the *Daily Express* reporter, "why British Tories back so many Socialist theories."

Mr. Butler has been explaining ever since. In spite of the fact that the Charter was accepted by a large majority at the

Conservative conference of 1947 he has been kept busy elaborating his ideas. In a recent propaganda pamphlet he wrote:

It is the remarks upon the need for strong central guidance in the Industrial Charter which have led to the charge that this statement of Conservative policy is but thinly veiled Socialism. This question of planning is of such importance for the country and the Party that I make no apology for devoting the greater part of the discussion to this issue. . . . The term "planning" is a new word for coherent and positive policy. The conception of strong government policy in economic matters is, I believe, in the very centre of Conservative tradition. We have never been a party of *laissez-faire*. It was we who called in the power of the State to rectify the excesses of the Industrial revolution. It was Disraeli who sought consciously to preserve that balance of agriculture and industry which the Liberals overturned. . . . Conservatives were planning before the word entered the political jargon.

In conclusion, Butler sums up:

There is, we believe, a proper sphere for the government and a proper field for industrial enterprise. It is the duty of the government to take the grand strategic decisions and to collect the information on which those decisions are based. It should exercise those general powers to which I have already referred. It should, in fact, create and maintain the atmosphere in which industry can give of its best and set the general aims to which the economy should be guided. It must concern itself with social as well as economic development and lay down, as part of the general aims, the social as well as economic standards which the community expects to be attained. That broadly is the proper field of government activity in industry. The rest must be left for industry itself in all its diverse and flexible forms of management and ownership. This is very far from *laissez-faire*, because it does not believe that the uncontrolled impulses of *laissez-faire* will inevitably produce the maximum good.

Mr. Butler has worked so hard to explain planning to his party that at times he is in danger of thinking he invented it. Recently he said: "I think we are already justified in claiming that the Conservative Political Centre has wrested from the Left the initiative in political thought."

In the House of Commons, however, there still appears to be confusion on the subject. Is a planned economy Conservative; did Mr. Butler invent it? Or is it really Socialist? And if Socialism is not a planned economy, what indeed is Socialism? In a debate on foreign affairs the following exchange took place:

MR. CROSSMAN: One may not like the word "Socialism" and I do not want to make the matter a party one, but what did the right hon. Gentleman, the member for Warwick and Leamington [Mr. Eden] mean by saying to us yesterday that we must not have Socialism in Europe? We cannot defend the freedom of Western Europe without a planned economy, and what is meant by a planned economy if not Socialism? If hon. Gentlemen opposite will say that they are in favour of the planned control of capital investment and heavy industry we shall really have national unity about how to defend freedom in Western Europe.

MR. EDEN (Warwick and Leamington): I never said that we must not have Socialism in Europe. It is for the various countries to decide the various forms of government which they want. What I said was that we could not hope to build a united Europe if this Government assumes that it can only be done on the basis of Socialism in Europe.

MR. CROSSMAN: I must say in reply that we cannot conceivably save ourselves from disaster in 1948 unless this Government knows that Western union means the planning of Western Europe, whether that be called Socialism or not.

MR. BOOTHBY (Aberdeen and Kincardine, Eastern): Why should the hon. Member go on confusing a planned economy with Socialism? He knows perfectly well that the greatest advocate in this country of a planned economy is one of the stoutest Tories in this country, Mr. Amery.

MR. CROSSMAN: I do not intend to enter into a long discussion on a planned economy. I would only say that most of us think of the planned control of heavy industry and the control of capital investment as something to do with Socialism. I shall welcome it if hon. Members opposite are glad to see that happen in Western Europe.

The truth of the matter is that planned economy, by whatever name you call it, has come to Britain to stay. Whereas the Socialists accept it enthusiastically the Conservatives accept it reluctantly, but the fact is they accept it. British economy will no longer give forty-seven million people a livelihood without capital expenditure beyond the means of private individuals and without careful management at the top.

The division between the progressive Conservatives and the moderate Socialists is, therefore, very slight; what is happening is that Tory Socialism is attempting to muscle in on the Labor party's ground. In order to make room for themselves it is a political necessity to elbow the Socialists to the left and picture them to the public as a party of extremists. Recently Rab Butler solemnly announced: "There is a line of policy alternative to State Marxist Socialism on the one hand and *laissez-faire* on the other."

Foreigners are often deceived by the heat and acrimony of Britain's party warfare. Politics has always been one of the major sports of the land and the public expects the controversy to be provocative and vigorous. But it is well to remember that the reason the parliamentary system works is because a thousand years of history have bound the English people together in a common faith; and that the field of agreement between the two opposing parties is always wider than that of disagreement.

It is not surprising, therefore, to find Conservatives as fiercely Conservative as Quintin Hogg, M.P., writing in his treatise *The Left Was Never Right*:

> Let us begin by finding something each side can praise in the other. It is not true that all Conservatives are reactionaries. It is not true that all members of the Labour Party are revolutionaries. On the contrary the great majority of each party is inspired by the same reverence for constitutional forms and parliamentary institutions based on a democratic franchise. Nothing but blind partisanship could obscure this fundamental political truth.

And even Churchill, who loves the cut and thrust of party warfare and brands the government with every epithet from sloppy to sinister, occasionally rises to its defense:

23rd January 1948
Debate on Foreign Affairs

> MR. CHURCHILL: . . . Let us try to keep the idea of a united Europe above the Party divisions which are inevitable, permissible and even tolerable in all free countries. Let us try on a basis above Party to bring the collective personalities of the anxious States and nations as a whole into the

larger harmony on which their future prosperity—aye, and indeed their life—may well depend.

Mr. Scollan (Renfrew, Western): We cannot do that in this country, never mind Europe.

Mr. Churchill: We have very great unities in this country. The vast majority of the people of this country are united on fundamentals both in regard to constitution and freedom. They are also united in resistance to continental forms of totalitarianism and also united in their pride of their past and will, I trust, become united in their hopes for the future.

PART IV: THE SOCIAL PATTERN

CHAPTER 13

How Rich Are the Rich?

You never find people labouring to convince you
that you may live very happily upon a plentiful
fortune.

—SAMUEL JOHNSON

DESPITE six years of total war and four years of a Socialist
government, English millionaires still manage to live on a
more luxurious scale than the millionaires of almost any other
country in the world. While the castles of Austria are abandoned
and the chateaux of France in sad repair, while Italian palaces
are converted into flats and Polish mansions are burnt-out ruins,
the stately homes of England which in 1940 were turned into
schools and hospitals and government offices are once again occupied by their owners. Once again guests arrive from London,
once again hounds meet and guns assemble; once again the
country-house week end is a stable institution.

The shadow of austerity has fallen lightly on the rich. Although the government bases its policy on the slogan: "Fair
shares for all," there is little that money cannot buy, and buy
legally. Flats and houses are always on the market for those who
can pay the price, and luxury foods ranging from caviar to

pheasant, from lobster to duck, from partridge to plovers' eggs
are unrationed. Most rich people have their own farms which
provide them with cream and butter and eggs; they are allowed
to kill two pigs a year, a calf every three months, and as many
sheep as they can eat.

Even the problem of clothes coupons, when rationing was in
force, could be overcome by enterprise and determination, for it
involved nothing more arduous than a trip to Dublin where
materials were free. Although gasoline difficulties can be solved
by "car-hire" services which operate in plenty, many rich men
draw extra supplies for business purposes which usually afford
some scope for pleasure; indeed, the fact that peers are given
an extra allowance for putting in an appearance at the House
of Lords has had a noticeable effect on the attendance.

Currency restrictions have probably offered the greatest an-
noyance. Those who travel for pleasure rather than business are
allowed to spend only a very limited amount of money in France
or America or any other country which lies outside the sterling
area. However, the fact that the sterling area limits people to
Australia, New Zealand, Africa, Ireland, the West Indies, Ber-
muda, Cyprus, or even India cannot be deemed a serious hardship.

That life moves more smoothly for the rich than the poor
is not surprising; what is surprising is the fact that there are any
rich left. English millionaires pay an income tax of 19/6d. in
the pound ($3.90 out of every $4.00), and Stafford Cripps announces solemnly that only 250 people in Britain have an
income of over £5,000 ($20,000) a year. The answer is that the
capital value of the millionaire is still very great. In 1937 it was
estimated that ten thousand of the population owned 10 percent
of the national wealth; and although no surveys have been made
since the war, even if property has spread to twice or even three
times the number, which is highly unlikely, it is still concentrated in very few hands.

Some of these millionaires are living on reserves while others
support themselves on capital gains, which are not taxable as

they are in the United States. They make enough money from
speculations on the stock markets and from the buying and
selling of businesses and properties outside the run of their
ordinary business interests to maintain them without drawing
on their reserves. These are the men who still live on a prewar
scale, who keep up large establishments in London as well as
the country, who entertain lavishly, and who spend the winter
on their yachts with the bow turned toward the sun. But such
men are not representative of the majority of English millionaires; most rich men have closed their London houses and retired to the country where they live comfortably but exclusively
on the land. And the land is what has saved them.

What may seem curious to Americans is the fact that so
many Englishmen own land to which to retreat. In England
the rich are more of an institution than a group of individuals.
Whereas in America rich men differ widely in their tastes and
demands, ranging all the way from Newport social leaders to
Texas cattle kings, from Hollywood producers to Chicago businessmen, in England they fit into a traditional pattern. No matter whether their money is inherited or earned most rich men
send their sons to public schools and most rich men die peers.
The effect of Eton and the House of Lords is to give them a
common background and a common culture, to shape their
tastes and interests to a common pattern. And this common
pattern is laid down by the English aristocracy, whose roots
have always been in the land, and whose social life has always
centered around their country seats. For this reason the rich
and ambitious who do not inherit country houses have a strong
tendency to acquire them.

But these houses are very different from the millionaire establishments of Long Island or Palm Beach, or the solemn row
of palaces that stand side by side at Newport. English country
houses are not in towns or suburbs but in the country; they are
not isolated residences but part of an estate.

Most rich men own farmland that ranges anywhere from a
hundred to a hundred thousand acres. Before the war much of
this land was let to tenants, but today with farm produce

fetching higher prices than ever before many landlords are taking an active interest in managing their own property. Although their incomes from investments are severely reduced, the gap is considerably narrowed by the fact that they can write off a large part of the upkeep of their houses against farm accounts.

But if the house is still too large to maintain under present conditions the millionaire has another alternative. He can give his house to the nation. This arrangement enables him to continue living in it with the National Trust paying the upkeep; when he dies it passes to the public. In the last twenty-five years many great houses have been presented to the Trust. Among them are Hatfield, owned by Lord Salisbury; Knole, the great Elizabethan mansion of Lord Sackville; and Cliveden, the home of Lord Astor.

The millionaire, however, regards himself as having fallen on dark days, and compared with former times this is true. The fact is that no other Western country has offered such an attractive life to the rich through such an unbroken succession of centuries as England. Although present-day millionaires sigh for the prewar world, the prewar world sighed enviously for the splendor of the Edwardians; and the Edwardians, no doubt, envied the Victorians; and the Victorians, the eighteenth-century nobleman who was innocently unaware of the approach of income tax.

During the two wars most Americans were brought up to believe that millionaires no longer existed outside of the United States; yet life in England was conducted on a far more magnificent scale than life in New York. Rich men not only owned large houses in the country but maintained large establishments in London as well. The brilliance of the London season, which lasted from May till August, attracted people from all over the world. Opulence was reflected by the number of Rolls Royces on the street, by the lighted windows and the sound of music in the leafy squares of Mayfair and Belgravia; by the jewels and the balls at Buckingham Palace; by Cowes and Ascot and Lords.

However, what I, as an American, found most impressive was the amount people ate. Lunch was not the hurried affair it is in America but moved from entree to fish, from fish to meat with elaborate dignity. Three hours later there was tea, which usually consisted of scones and cakes and buns, and three hours after that, dinner, which often kept people at the table until nearly midnight. And this was not all; in any well-run house a tray with whisky and soda and sandwiches always awaited the master's return so that he might not have the uncomfortable sensation of feeling faint in the night. Even more unforgettable, however, was one's first sight of a country-house breakfast with the row of shining silver dishes containing porridge, bacon and eggs, and kedgeree; and next to the silver dishes the side of ham, the partridges, and sometimes even roast beef.

Next most impressive was the number of servants people employed. Even though most of the houses were larger than New York houses the servants required to run them seemed many times as numerous. They were as well drilled as an army and appeared to be organized on the same lines, with infinite gradations in rank. The secret of their success lay in the fact that they were not under the control of the mistress of the house but under the control of each other. The butler was in charge of the footman, the cook in charge of the kitchenmaids, the nurse in charge of the nurserymaids, the head housemaid in charge of the undermaids. They were divided into departments and their functions highly specialized.

This had advantages in times of ease, but when war broke out and luxuries were severely curtailed it seemed to take the servants longer to readjust themselves than their mistresses. During the blitz of 1940 I visited a friend who had moved from London to a small house in the country. Although there was not enough work for them to do, out of loyalty she had taken seven of her staff with her. But when I arrived I found the house in commotion. My friend moaned that she had just discovered that the seven she had picked were all "head servants" and as a result nothing was being done. She had complained that the windows needed washing and had called each one in turn to find out whose job it was; finally the butler had explained gently that in London a professional window cleaner had always been called in. The scene ended with the lady getting a bucket and rag and doing it herself.

In the prewar world the standard of service was high, and the amount of it English people seemed to require often struck one as astounding. In those days it was not unusual for young men to take servants to Oxford with them; and the acme of luxury revealed itself in the sight of a valet cleaning his master's white pigskin hunting breeches with the whites of two dozen eggs. But service was not confined to a man's house; you could reserve tickets for the movies over the telephone; you could summon a messenger by merely instructing the telephone operator; you could hand parcels to a train guard to be dropped at any station along the route; you could even ask the restaurant waiter to send someone to you to make your telephone calls while you ate your lunch in peace. And as far as shopping was concerned, life seemed to be organized exclusively for the rich, for no country in the world specialized more successfully in high-priced goods; from Rolls Royce motorcars to Crown Derby china, from Tip Tree jam to Heal beds you could always be sure of getting the best.

Credit was extended on an astonishingly wide scale. One young Englishman asserted that London was the only great city in the world where it was possible to operate successfully all day long "without a bean in your pocket." Most expensive hotels and restaurants allowed even strangers to pay for meals by check and West End tailors waited for years for their accounts to be settled. Indeed, prompt payment was so rare it was usual to reward it by deducting 10 percent from the bill.

Even the banks extended wide credit. To have a check returned marked insufficient funds as it is in America is unknown in Britain. Almost all clients are allowed overdrafts, but how high these are allowed to rise depends on the security behind them. Indeed, overdrafts are so much a part of life that someone once defined bankruptcy as "the state arrived at when the interest on a man's overdraft exceeded the interest on his income."

But what made life so attractive was not only the background of luxury but the fact that the wealthy were bound together by a common interest in the affairs of the day. Society was a mixture of politicians, bankers, landowners, barristers, and writers, and the fact that so many of them had known each other since childhood gave it an intimacy which added rather than detracted from its variety. Conversation was witty and intelligent and the fact that people entertained in their houses rather than in restaurants or hotels gave it a chance to flower to its fullest.

It was distinguished from the society of Paris, Rome, or New York by its function as the governing class. Rich men not only enjoyed the luxury money brought them but enjoyed the comfortable feeling that this luxury was fully justified by their contribution to the nation. Today that comfortable feeling has gone.

What measures has the Socialist government taken against the rich? The answer is, very few, for the simple reason that the wartime government had already raised taxation to a peak beyond which it would not have been economically sound to go. Income tax began to rise when rearmament became necessary in 1937 and continued to rise until 1941 when it reached its all-time peak of ten shillings in the pound, or 50 percent of a man's income. Added to this, surtax began at £2,000 ($8,000) a year and rose to 19/6 on incomes over £20,000 ($80,000), which meant that all very rich men were paying a total of 19/6 in the pound thus leveling the highest incomes to about £5,000 ($20,000) a year.

During the last few years the Socialists have reduced income tax a shilling and increased supertax a shilling which, incidentally, works out at a slight benefit for the millionaire. They have also introduced a profits tax, increased death duties, and taken a small capital levy. But although these last three measures have touched the rich man's pocket they have not seriously affected his standard of living.

What the rich man blames the Socialists for is not so much what they have done as what they have left undone. He believes that if the government cut public expenditure it could drastically reduce income tax. Instead it is continuing to impose on him sacrifices and penalties which he hoped were only wartime measures. However, even though the Conservative party claims that high taxation is destroying incentive, it has been careful not to commit itself to any specific reductions and politically many people doubt whether it could alter the scale to make an appreciable difference to high incomes. What a Conservative government could do, however, is to give the rich sympathy.

Today most rich men are isolated from the political life of the country. And not only is their power broken, not only do they seldom meet cabinet ministers and Socialist M.P.'s, but even the prestige of being rich is diminishing. The fact that so many of them have inherited rather than earned their money is constantly brought to the attention of the public by Socialist propaganda; and instead of being honored for their wealth many of them are now being regarded as parasites. Psychologically this has been disturbing and rich men no longer derive the same enjoyment from their possessions as they once did.

What is the future of the English millionaire? Although death duties were first introduced in 1894, and even in 1930 these were as high as 30 percent on estates valued at £1,000,000, today they are nearly double that amount. If a man's property is worth £1,000,000 he pays £700,000; if it's worth £250,000 ($1,000,000) he pays the equivalent of $450,000. However, there is a loophole. There is no gift tax such as exists in America. So long as a man gives away his property seven years before he dies it escapes taxation. Many fathers therefore turn their properties over to their sons and thus manage to keep their inheritance intact. But this is not always foolproof. Lord Derby, for example, assigned his vast estate to a son who died shortly afterward, which meant that the property became liable to death duties not once, but twice.

The millionaires of England will probably exist for many years to come. Today the great palace of Blenheim where Churchill was born is still occupied by the Duke of Marlborough; Chatsworth is still occupied by the Duke of Devonshire; Melbury by the Earl of Ilchester; Alnwick by the Duke of Northumberland; Drumlawing Castle by the Duke of Buccleuch; Grimthorpe by the Earl of Ancaster; Hatfield by the Marquis of Salisbury; Belvoir by the Duke of Rutland; Dunrobin by the Duke of Sutherland; Arundel by the Duke of Norfolk; Petworth by the Earl of Leconfield.

Recently someone complained that the slow but persistent decline of the rich man's fortunes would soon reduce the English millionaire to the same scale of living as the American millionaire; that, no doubt, is the change the next twenty years will bring.

CHAPTER 14

Socialism in the Countryside

> We have to return to history and look there for
> the origin of the complexes which gave birth, not
> to the English gentleman, but to the conception
> which made the English gentleman the ideal of
> the nation.
>
> —G. J. RENIER

THE SCENE is an English village on a summer evening.
The setting follows a traditional pattern with a church on
a hill, a vicarage behind a brick wall, and a squire's house
guarded by a pair of wrought-iron gates. Thatched cottages stand
at either side of the road and when they come to an end there
is a small green which faces a pub with a splendid red and gold
sign bearing the squire's coat of arms.

It is seven o'clock in the evening and most of the men are in
the fields gathering the harvest. The only people in sight are
two women pushing a pram, a man on a ladder painting a sec-
ond-story window, and a boy on a bicycle carrying some groceries.
Suddenly the quiet is broken by the sound of a loud-speaker,
and a dilapidated motorcar covered with posters comes noisily
through the village. "Hello everybody," a mechanical voice is
saying. "Hello everybody. Your member of Parliament is holding a meeting on the village green. Your member of Parliament
will be here in a few minutes, everybody, and will welcome any
questions or problems you would like to put to him. Come out
everybody, don't miss this opportunity of hearing your member
of Parliament. . . ."

The voice continues along the village, penetrating every wall
and door and window. The women giggle but the man painting

176

the house does not even look around and the fellow on the bicycle soon passes out of sight. The car turns around and pulls up alongside the green. A man jumps out and adjusts the loud-speaker. This at once attracts a boy of seven and two girls under five. Then an old man moves across from the general store to the iron bench on the green, and a woman comes out of a house and begins to sweep her doorstep. A few minutes later the member of Parliament arrives driving an Austin. He is a man in his thirties and is dressed in gray flannels and a tweed coat. He jumps out and goes over to the two men standing by the dilapidated car. They talk, and glance around, and talk some more. A big chap in overalls comes out of the pub with a glass of beer in his hand and sits on the step, three girls stop a discreet distance away, and a window in one of the cottages opens.

The member evidently takes these gestures as signs of en-couragement, for he grasps the microphone and begins to talk. Four children appear from nowhere and organize a game of hopscotch directly in front of him, but the game is soon inter-rupted by a tractor, which not only sends them off the road but drowns the member's voice.

By this time two more old men have joined the first one on the bench, a farmer with a pitchfork is leaning over a fence, and an elderly woman with an armful of parcels is standing at the side of the road. The children have resumed their game but they are scattered out of the way by a motorcycle, then another tractor, then a farm cart. The member's words are lost but his lips keep on moving and suddenly he is saying: "If there are any questions anyone would like to ask I will do my best to answer them."

There is a silence, then the farmer leaning over the fence says what he would like to know sir is when he is going to get more cake for his cows; we'll produce the food if you fellows will produce the feeding stuffs he says. One of the girls moves closer and asks how much longer she must go on waiting for a house; she lives in one of the thatched cottages with her husband and in-laws and two other relatives sir, and there isn't any water or electricity and the roof leaks and she's been waiting for a new house for three years now; it really isn't fair she says; the man with the beer says a lot of things aren't fair; it isn't fair for instance that people in towns should be able to get meals in restaurants and people in the country should have to live on their rations and he thinks blacksmiths like himself should get the same cheese ration as agricultural laborers sir. Then one of the old men on the bench speaks up and says if the young fellows remembered what things were like after the last war they wouldn't complain; after the last war men were walking the streets looking for jobs and food prices were soaring and wages were low; everyone has something to complain about says the old man; he for one would like to see the price of tobacco come down but the country's got to pay its way, and anyone can understand the position and it's time people stopped complaining and did some work. The old man next to him chuckles and says, "Ask your dad," and the girl who is still waiting for a house flings back: "Ask your mum, too." Then the woman with the parcels breaks in and says she isn't the girl's mum but she's old enough to be, and she thinks no one around here has much to grumble about what with the health scheme and there's plenty to eat no matter what people say sir, and besides that free milk for the children. The blacksmith has been in the pub for the last few minutes but now he is returning with half a pint of beer in each hand. Free milk is fine but free beer would be even finer he says and everybody laughs. He hands the member one of the glasses and adds: "Here's to the day when it's double the strength and half the price."

The dilapidated car moves off but everyone is talking and the M.P. is hemmed into a group. Soon he shakes hands and promises to come again; then he moves off to another village and another meeting.

The fact that today the political battle is being carried into every hamlet in the land is something new for Britain. Before the war most country areas were regarded as safe Conservative seats and few politicians bothered to woo the villagers. An M.P. was thought to have done adequately if he confined his efforts to the towns, and one Conservative who was returned to Parliament consistently for twenty-five years is reputed never to have answered a single letter or held a single meeting. But in 1945 when many country seats swung to the Socialists the atmosphere livened in shocked surprise; and ever since that time the village green has been steadily gaining prestige as a rostrum.

Today this village green probably offers a more striking view of the changes taking place under Socialism than any other vantage point, for the village has always been the great respecter of custom and tradition; indeed, the village is the very foundation of the class system on which the English way of life is based, a system which although it has evolved through the years nevertheless has its roots in feudalism. But change never comes abruptly to England; it comes as slowly and cautiously as a reconnaissance patrol. And the incursion of Socialism upon the conventional pattern is therefore a curious infusion of new ideas into old-established ways.

Before the war the countryside was ruled, as it had been for centuries, by the landed gentry. The gentry were the upper class; it was composed of both peers and commoners and distinguished from other classes not only by superior wealth and breeding but by the superior education that wealth could buy at famous and expensive public schools. At the other end of the scale came the working classes and lumped in between were the farmers and shopkeepers, the doctors, teachers, and local officials who made up the middle class. The middle class was riddled with snobbish distinctions of its own, all of which tended to strengthen the prestige of the gentry.

The rule of the gentry expressed itself through the squirearchy. Every village had a squire, who was one of the largest landowners in the neighborhood. Sometimes he owned most of the cottages in the village and employed most of the people on his own estate. But he was much more than a landlord. He looked after his tenants when they were ill or in trouble and often pensioned them off when they were old. He gave much of his time to the affairs of local government and served as a magistrate as well.

He was a firm supporter of the church and had the gift of the parish, which means that in consultation with the church he appointed the vicar.

The squire's personal life followed the accepted pattern of an English gentleman. He hunted in the winter and went fishing and shooting in the summer. He had guests from London every week end and once a year probably gave a ball to which other members of the gentry were bidden. But he also played a large part in the social life of the village. Every summer he organized a cricket team to play against the village eleven and opened his grounds for a garden fete to raise money for the school; he donated clothes to the rummage sale, trees for the Christmas party, prizes for the whist drive. And his wife was always on tap to open church bazaars.

Most squires were hard-working and conscientious. Deeply conservative, they have long been the delight of cartoonists and before the war acquired new distinction as the inspiration for Colonel Blimp. Although in the nineteenth century their authority was unchallenged owing to the fact that only men of property had the right to vote, the advance of democracy diminished their influence surprisingly little. They were not merely cogs in the Conservative party machine; they were the machine itself. And all went well with the machine until 1945 when the agricultural laborer, the forgotten man of the countryside, went quietly to the polls and sold the pass.

The squire still lives in a big house; he still hunts in the winter and fishes and shoots in the summer. He is still active in local government, but his prestige has diminished because the life of the village no longer revolves mainly around his estate.

Today many village workingmen are not dependent on the squire for their job, their house, or their pension. They enjoy greater economic independence than ever before. This is due partly to postwar conditions, partly to legislation prepared by the coalition government, and partly to Socialism.

For the first time the villager lives in a world of full employment. He pays for an insurance scheme which protects him financially against sickness and old age and gives him free medical care. Food prices are kept down by subsidies, and three houses out of every four are built for rent and not for sale, which places them within the reach of the lowest incomes. Village schools which do not reach required standards are closed down and busses provided to take the children into towns; and the school-leaving age has been raised to fifteen. Besides all this the agricultural laborer has been granted a minimum wage which is nearly 200 percent greater than it was before the war.

But the effect of Socialism is not only economic. The psychological factor plays an important part in the worker's outlook. For the first time his member of Parliament is not a man who moves in an entirely different world, but who makes himself known to the ordinary folk of the village and comes to hear their complaints and answer their questions.

Because of this, the villager has a new independence and a new sense of responsibility. He knows it is up to him to run the machinery and raise the money to keep his party in power; he is learning how to take the chair at his own meetings, to organize his own entertainments, and to take a lead in social life.

But although the squire's status has altered, in many areas he still has considerable influence. For one thing, he still rules the world of society which commands the following of many members of the middle classes on the basis of snobbery alone. And old people who have been brought up not only to know but to respect their betters still accept his word without question.

There are also people who remember the days of unemployment and still have the fear that if they show themselves to be politically opposed to the men they work for they may be risking their jobs. On two occasions a carpenter and an electrician have told me that although they vote Labor at the polls they do not attend political meetings for fear "the gentry" on whom they are dependent for their work might discriminate against them. And on another occasion I accompanied a Socialist M. P. to a meeting on a village green at which only half a dozen people were present. "You won't get people coming out," explained an old man, "but talk loud, because they'll be listening behind the windows." When the M. P. asked him why he said: "Oh, it don't do to be Labor in this village."

On still another occasion, at a village "brains trust" when a Socialist M. P. made reference to bad housing conditions there was a loud burst of clapping at the back of the hall which stopped almost as suddenly as it had started. After the meeting was over the squire's wife provided coffee and sandwiches at her house and when the M.P. was leaving the butler helped him on with his coat. "Did you hear that clapping tonight?" he whispered. "That was me. But I suddenly thought it wasn't quite discreet, if you know what I mean, sir."

The squire is probably more opposed to Socialism than any other member of the Conservative community. His attitude is one not only of bitter opposition but of resentment. If he has been conscientious he resents the Socialists' publicizing the fact that many of the cottages on his estate have neither water nor electricity, claiming that it was beyond his financial means to make the necessary improvements.

Even more than this, however, he resents the Socialists' portraying him as a man whose public spirit was largely inspired to serve his own propertied interests. He protected a system and a way of life in which he believed and still believes; and the fact that these beliefs happened to coincide with benefits to himself appears to him as purely incidental. In one village where I accompanied an M.P. the squire was so angry that a Socialist should dare to intrude on what he evidently considered his private domain that he came stalking up to the green and ordered the M.P. away. When the latter pointed out that he was standing on the King's Highway and reminded him that freedom of speech was one of the tenets of the land, the squire strode angrily away stopping every now and then to hurl abuse over his shoulder.

The clash between Socialism and Conservatism in the countryside springs from a fundamental difference in philosophical outlook; and that outlook has always characterized the difference between the British and the American way of life.

The squire has been brought up to believe in the patriarchal system. In feudal days he fulfilled the role of lord of the manor; he gave his protection to serfs in return for their services. As land capitalism slowly emerged from feudalism the lord of the manor no longer had the power to rule without public support.

But the squire's sense of responsibility toward those of inferior station continued; and his belief that protection should command loyalty also persisted. Once I heard an Englishwoman criticizing Americans because, she said, they rarely "look after" the people they employ. She went on to say that they never pensioned off their servants or seemed to feel any responsibility toward those they fired. I tried to explain the difference in outlook; that Americans believe all men are equal, and that given equal opportunities in life, it was each man's individual responsibility to look after himself and not to be dependent on others.

But the English attitude does not limit itself to economic help. Many English people believe that it is proper and right for the masses to be guided by men of superior education and breeding. Thomas Carlyle long ago expressed this feeling by stating: "Surely of all 'rights of man' this right of the ignorant man to be guided by the wiser, to be gently or forcibly helped in the true course by him, is the indisputablest."

The effect of this system in the past should not be underestimated, for in many respects it brought great benefits with it. The fact that the squirearchy maintained close contact with the people spread the culture of the country evenly and instilled in all classes a rigid sense of moral values which has served the nation well.

The Socialist, however, argues that all men are entitled to equality as well as liberty. He believes that men should not be beholden to any single individual for the economic protection to which they are naturally entitled, and that it is only right and proper that the state should guarantee all its people a minimum standard of life.

Today many of the landlords' functions are being taken over by M.P.'s, councilors, and civil servants. Slowly self-government is supplanting the squirearchy.

CHAPTER 15

Oxford University

Among other achievements Oxford becomes a
nursery of statesmen.

—HERBERT MORRAH

MANY great men have paid homage to Oxford in their
memoirs and many writers have used it as a background
for novels on undergraduate life; yet not a single comprehensive
book has ever been written about it, and the university itself
has no publicity, or even information, department. When I remarked on this to an Oxford man he replied in a shocked voice:
"Publicity department? Why, even Buckingham Palace is more
in need of a publicity department than Oxford!"

Oxford is famous for many things: for its age and its dignity,
for the beauty of its buildings, the freedom of its intellectual
thought, the illustrious men who have been its scholars. But
it is also famous for the powerful influence it exerts on the
political life of the nation. It has produced more politicians than
all the other universities of Britain put together, and probably
more than any other single university in the world. In this field
it leaves its distinguished rival, Cambridge, far behind, for
Cambridge has always specialized in science rather than the
humanities; or, as someone put it, Cambridge studies Nature
while Oxford studies Man.

The fact that Oxford supplies the country with such a high
proportion of its cabinet ministers, bishops, field marshals,
judges, ambassadors, admirals, civil servants, lawyers, and M.P.'s
has had a marked effect upon English public life; for these men
are bound together not only by a common attachment to Oxford

184

but by a common method of approach to intellectual problems. Because of this it can easily be argued that Oxford is largely responsible for the characteristics that stamp English public men; an ability to compromise which has always meant an ability to submerge party differences in time of crisis.

But first, what is the fascination of Oxford? To the casual visitor it lies in the wonderful centuries-old buildings with their cloistered velvet-green quadrangles; in the narrow crooked streets where the students lodge; in the chestnut trees and the almond blossoms of the spring and the soft murmur of the river running through country fields. Wherever you walk you are reminded of the past, and the great men of the past; at Trinity you think of Pembroke's Dr. Johnson working on his dictionary; at University College of the girlish, pink-and-white Shelley who was expelled for being an atheist; at Merton of the high-spirited Lord Randolph Churchill; at Exeter of Burne-Jones and William Morris; at Magdalen of Addison, Gibbon, Charles Reade, and Oscar Wilde. You think of Walter Pater, Charles James Fox, Lawrence of Arabia, Christopher Wren, Matthew Arnold, and Cecil Rhodes. And you think of a long, dignified procession of Prime Ministers: Pitt, North, Shelburne, Addington, Canning, Peel, Derby, Gladstone, Asquith, Rosebery, Salisbury, and today Clement Attlee.

But great men are not the source of Oxford's magic. Its spell lies in the freedom it offers both spirit and intellect. Americans are often surprised by the latitude students are allowed: first, that Oxford is only in session six months of the year; second, that "classes" in the American sense do not exist; third, that undergraduates are not compelled to attend lectures; and fourth, if they do not wish to live in college they can take rooms in a boardinghouse in the town.

Each student has the opportunity to see his "tutor" at least an hour a week. The tutor exchanges ideas with him, recommends books for him to read, and suggests essays for him to write. If the undergraduate "cuts" too many appointments with his tutor the latter may upbraid him but disciplinary action is seldom taken. So long as he passes an examination at the end of his first year and persuades his tutor he is using his time advantageously he can do as he sees fit.

Oxford has a great number of clubs, but membership is seldom based on "popularity"; anyone can join, which means there is none of the intense social competition that mars the lives of so many students at American universities. There are worlds for all sorts and all temperaments; for intellectuals or socialites, athletes or aesthetes. In 1890 Andrew Lang contrasted the lives undergraduates led in prose which today has a quaintly Victorian flavor:

> There are very many varieties of undergraduates who have very many various ways of occupying and amusing themselves. A steady man, that reads his five or six hours a day, and takes his pastime chiefly on the river, finds that his path scarcely ever crosses that of him who belongs to the Bullingdon Club, hunts thrice a week, and rarely dines in hall. Then the "pale student" who is hard at work in his rooms or in the Bodleian all day, and who has only two friends, out-college men, with whom he takes walks and tea,—he sees existence in a very different aspect. The Union politician who is for ever hanging around his club, dividing the house on questions of blotting paper and quill pens, discussing its affairs at breakfast, intriguing for the place of Librarian, writing rubbish in the suggestion book, to whom Oxford is only a soil carefully prepared for the growth of that fine flower, the Union. He never encounters the undergraduate who haunts billiard rooms and taverns, who buys jewellery for barmaids and is admired for the audacity with which he smuggled a fox-terrier into college in a brown paper parcel.

Much of Oxford's charm remains rooted in its reluctance to force itself upon its students. It is generous to those who wish to take advantage of it and superbly indifferent to those who do not. Its structure resembles a system of states grouped under a federal government, for the university is a central authority which binds together twenty-one independent colleges. There are two categories of "dons": professors who are chosen by the university, and tutors who are chosen by the college. But what distinguishes Oxford and Cambridge from most other universities in the world is the fact that they are designed for students to study rather than teachers to teach.

It may seem a curious distinction but it amounts to this: Almost all Oxford and Cambridge professors are eminent scholars who are engaged on original research work or important writing of their own. Every year they give a series of lectures on their particular subject which students have the privilege, but not the obligation, of attending. For example, G. D. H. Cole, the professor of political theory, is the most prolific and authoritative writer on the history of trade unionism and the labor movement in Britain today; Lord Cherwell, the professor of experimental philosophy, has made important contributions to science and during the war served as Churchill's chief scientific adviser; Lord David Cecil, brother of the Marquis of Salisbury, who leads the Conservative opposition in the Lords, is a professor of English literature, has written books on Melbourne, Cowper, and Gray and often is heard over the air on the Third Program; Sir Walter Howard Florey, professor of pathology, was one of the team that discovered penicillin; Gilbert Murray, ex-professor of Greek, was one of the leading supporters of the League of Nations and is the author of translations of Euripides which are regarded as standard works; Lord Lindsay, the Master of Balliol, is a writer and politician who sits on the Labor benches in the Lords. Some of the Cambridge professors of the last twenty-five years have won even greater fame: George Trevelyan, Bertrand Russell, and the late Maynard Keynes.

Tutors as well as professors are active in the outside world. Most of them are men who won first-class academic honors as students for which they were offered "fellowships" at the various colleges. Tutors are expected to give about twenty hours a week to undergraduates and to take their share in the administration of the university and colleges; otherwise their time is their own. Some of them do research work, others are writers and lecturers, travelers and journalists, and even aspiring politicians. Roy Harrod, a tutor in economics at Christ Church, stood as a Liberal candidate in the last election and is now writing a life of Keynes; Trevor-Roper, a history tutor at Christ Church, went to Germany at the end of the war and collected material for an official record entitled *The Last Days of Hitler*; C. S. Lewis, an English tutor at Magdalen, is the author of some widely read books on theology and several books of literary criticism, the most important of which is *The Allegory of Love*; Isaiah Berlin, a tutor in philosophy at New College, worked in the British Embassy in Washington and sent weekly political reports which won the admiration of Mr. Churchill; A. L. Rowse, a history tutor at All Souls, wrote a brilliant study of *The Reign of Queen Elizabeth* as well as many other books on the Tudor period; Hugh Seaton Watson and Alan Taylor are well-known journalists and broadcasters.

The fact that Oxford and Cambridge students are taught by men who are making a valuable contribution to the thought of the day, and often to the thought of the future, links them automatically with the outside world. Knowledge for knowledge's sake gives way to knowledge for the sake of arriving objectively and logically as near to the truth as possible, which means that students are taught not only the art of thinking but the purpose of thinking. But aside from the influence of the university as a whole, there are two institutions in particular designed to keep the students bound to the world of action. One is the Oxford Union and the other is All Souls.

The Oxford Union is the most famous undergraduate debating society in the world. It is housed in a long oblong room with a gallery running along three sides of it, modeled on the House of Commons. It has about two thousand members which represents nearly 30 percent of the student body. Debates are held every week, and several times a term distinguished visitors ranging from cabinet ministers to foreign officials, from scientists to writers and M.P.'s, are invited to take part. Almost all the famous British politicians of the last twenty-five years have spoken at the Union: Lloyd George, Birkenhead, Churchill, Morrison, Cripps, and Attlee. Thus the students have the opportunity of coming into contact with the best minds of the day.

Although debates take place on political party lines, Oxford has always displayed a fine indifference to the national temperature. Before the war, when Britain was Conservative, the largest party in the Union was Socialist; today when a Labor government is in power the Conservatives have almost as much strength as Socialists and Liberals combined. The Union is usually regarded as a training ground for Parliament which is borne out by the fact that of the sixty-one presidents of the Union in the twenty years between the two wars, twenty-one became M.P.'s. Yet the Union is not just a forgotten stepping-stone. It continues to have a curious fascination for many men long after they have left Oxford. The late Lord Birkenhead, the famous Lord Chancellor, once wrote of it nostalgically:

> On many occasions I have been able to pass through Oxford and spend a few hours there. I often go to the Union and spend some minutes in the Victorian Debating-Hall. The room is empty and the place is silent, but yet these walls have listened to nearly all the great masters of rhetoric . . . the walls might seem to exude the very savour of oratory. But the portraits on the walls forbid the idea that Oxford depends in any way on the imported orator.
>
> There the portraits hang, row on row, a pictorial constellation of the past and present. . . . Here are Salisbury, Gladstone and Asquith standing on their enduring pedestals . . . Manning and Mandell Creighton, E. T. Cook, York Powell, the Cecils and the Asquiths, the Mowbrays and the Talbots, and on the living roll of fame, Milner and Curzon, Antony Hope and A. E. W. Mason. Here within a single chamber lies the sifted ability of Oxford. The pictures, the photographs, the etchings, and the busts possess all the charm and demand all the reverence which we might give to some Gothic cathedral raised by the piety of our ancestors to commemorate a belief in the joy and the high destiny of our successors.

According to Oxford lights, the Union is a young society because it is only 126 years old. It was started by undergraduates and its first debate took place in 1823: "Was the Revolution under Cromwell to be attributed to the tyrannical conduct of Charles, or to the democratic spirit of the times?"

Its most notorious debate, however, was in 1933, when British pacifism was at its height. A motion was put down "That this House will not fight for King and country." The fact that it was carried by a vote of 275 to 153 made headlines all over the world; and in spite of a spirited attempt on the part of a group of indignant graduates to get it expunged from the records, it remains there still. Churchill refers to the debate in *The Gathering Storm:* "In 1933, the students of the Oxford Union, under the inspiration of a Mr. Joad, passed their ever-shameful resolution, 'That this House refuses to fight for King and country.' It was easy to laugh off such an episode in England, but in Germany, in Russia, in Japan, the idea of a decadent, degenerate Britain took deep root and swayed many calculations. Little did the foolish boys who passed the resolution dream that they were destined quite soon to conquer or fall gloriously in the ensuing war, and prove themselves the finest generation ever bred in Britain."

Today the Union remains as provocative as ever. Here are some of the motions which have been debated since the war:

That in the opinion of this House Socialism forms the only effective barrier to Totalitarianism.

That in the opinion of this House British Propaganda and British Censorship lead the British Public by the nose.

That this House deplores the tyranny of convention.

That in the opinion of this House the Liberal Party is dead and damned.

That this House deplores the growing menace of Trade Union activity.

That this House is sure that to be a politician is a sin.

That this House welcomes the Coal Industry Nationalisation Bill.

That this House believes that the separation of the American Colonies had better not have occurred.

That this House agrees with Clive Bell that the maintenance of a high standard of civilisation depends on the existence of a leisured class.

That this House deplores the fact that although Woman tempted Man to eat he took up drinking by himself.

That in the opinion of this House State interference has gone far enough.

That this House considers His Majesty's Government's proposals concerning the House of Lords to be both ill-timed and ill-advised.

That this House would rather be a Dustman than a Don.

That this House would support a further reduction in British food consumption in the interests of feeding the German people.

That this House is of the opinion that British civilisation is on the wane.

Another institution which links Oxford with the world of politics is All Souls. This college is unique for it is composed exclusively of graduates who have won high academic honors.

Dr. Samuel Johnson once remarked: "Sir, if a man has a mind to prance, he must study at Christ Church and All Souls."

The college is limited to forty members who are selected by competitive scholastic examination. Anyone can sit for All Souls but usually only two men are admitted each year. Successful candidates are appointed "fellows" for seven years, after which their names come up for re-election. If they live in the college they receive a stipend of £350 ($1,400) a year, which rises according to the amount of teaching they wish to do.

But fellows are not compelled to remain at Oxford. Many of them become civil servants or barristers or politicians. They can always have rooms at the college for short periods, and the fact that many of them visit Oxford regularly gives All Souls a lively and cosmopolitan atmosphere. A. L. Rowse, the well-known historian, who is a fellow of long standing, wrote:

> There are two elements in All Souls, the strictly University element and those whose work lies mainly outside. And yet they are not two colleges but one college. The division is less rigid than you might suppose—as with everything that is truly English; for the most academic of its members are imbued with ideas of public duty and are not averse to playing some part in public affairs, while the most eminent of its Fellows in the outside world, whether Archbishop or Lord Chancellor, Viceroy of India or editor of the *Times*, takes a responsible interest in the affairs of the University and would resent being regarded as not an academic person in the widest sense.

Famous men of the past who were fellows of All Souls include Linacre, "the father of modern medicine"; Christopher Wren, the architect; and Sir William Blackstone, whose summing up of English law in his commentaries served as a basis for American law and influenced the making of the constitution. Today, to be an "All Souls man" is regarded as a great distinction and gives a young politician immediate recognition. Those in the present House of Commons are Quintin Hogg and John Foster, Conservatives, and Douglas Jay, Socialist, who is Financial Secretary to the Treasury. Among the All Souls men in the Lords are Lord Simon and Lord Halifax, both former Foreign Secretaries.

What is curious about All Souls, however, is the fact that its dignified scholastic reputation appears to be of fairly recent standing. All Souls is over five hundred years old, having been founded by Archbishop Chichele in 1437 to pray for the souls of King Henry V and all the lords and lieges "whom the havoc of that warfare between the two realms have drenched with the bowl of bitter death." The purpose of the founder was to endow study rather than teaching but because the fellows had no one to keep them in order they soon trod paths far removed from what was originally intended. Official records of the seventeenth century show that the Warden of All Souls was asked to "punish such of your society as do spend their time in taverns and ale-houses to the scandal of the House," and that one of the Fellows was reprimanded for "beating the under-butler."

The college became more subdued as the years went on but its scholastic reputation did not improve. As recently as 1910 Francis Gribble wrote: "Well born, well dressed and moderately educated is the hackneyed description of a Fellow of All Souls." He went on to add: "The candidates for Fellowships, it used to be said, instead of being put through an examination were invited to dinner and given cherry tart to eat; their fate depended on the manner in which they disposed of the cherry stones. The story is told of the Fellow who was rewarded for his delicacy in swallowing the stones. It is not to be supposed that the story is literally true; but no doubt a certain symbolic truth is enshrined in it. The unmannerly bookworm has never been wanted at All Souls." About the same period a story circulated of a visitor who, when taken into Codrington Library, asked the college porter whether the fellows read all the books. "Lord bless you, sir," replied the porter, "they don't need to read books. They're gentlemen."

Today Oxford can claim about 50 percent of Britain's civil service officials and nearly 40 percent of the university graduates in the House of Commons. The fact that so many men of all parties share a common intellectual background has had a profound effect in narrowing contentions between the various leaders of political thought. And for this reason Oxford must take large credit for the civilized way in which Britain's social revolution is being carried out. Oxford is more than a bond; it is a bridge.

CHAPTER 16

Social Security

Benefits in return for contributions, rather than
free allowances from the State, is what the people
of Britain desire.

—Beveridge Report

IN 1948 two great, history-making schemes were launched in
Britain which gave every man, woman, and child in the country one of Roosevelt's four freedoms: freedom from want. These
measures were the National Insurance Scheme and the National
Health Service. They entitled every individual to free medical
and dental care, and every worker to financial protection against
unemployment, sickness, and old age, and many other benefits
ranging from maternity to burial grants.

Neither of these schemes is a "gift"; they are paid for first by
taxation and second by compulsory weekly contributions. They
represent the effort of all for the benefit of each. Next, neither
of these schemes is a "party" measure. They were drawn up
during the war by Churchill's coalition government. However,
when the time came to introduce them the country had returned
to party politics and the Socialists were in power. Many changes
were made in the original drafts, and the Conservative opposition attacked various clauses in the bills. Some Conservatives
were severely critical of the amount of government expenditure
involved and some even hinted that because of Britain's financial
position the introduction of the bills should be delayed; and for
this reason a large number of people have the idea that the two
schemes are purely Socialist measures. Nevertheless, in appreciating the changes taking place in Britain today it is important

to realize that these enlightened and far-reaching measures were the subject of common agreement by men of all political parties.

The Health Service offers free medical and dental care to every individual in Great Britain. It is not an insurance scheme. It costs about £350,000,000 ($1,400,000,000) a year, £260,000,-000 of which is met by the Exchequer which represents one-fourteenth of the total receipts from taxation.

The Service was launched in a storm of protest and recrimination agitated by the doctors' understandable fear of a loss of freedom and further aggravated by the Minister of Health's antagonistic personality. Protection of the doctors' freedom was a serious consideration. It was agreed (a) that no doctor should be compelled to enter the scheme if he did not wish to and (b) that doctors entering the scheme should be allowed to continue a private practice as well. In other words, like most British innovations, a public health service was gently grafted on to the existing pattern.

Even so many people predicted failure. They prophesied that not enough doctors would co-operate to make the scheme feasible and that the public would become so exasperated at not receiving the care to which it was entitled that the Service would eventually break down. However, at the end of the first year it was shown that over five-sixths of all the doctors in England, Wales, and Scotland (about 20,000 out of 23,500) had joined the service; and that 45,000,000 people, or 90 percent of the population, had registered with them as public patients.

From the patient's point of view how does the Service work? You can choose any doctor you wish as your "family doctor." The doctor, however, is not automatically obliged to accept you as a patient and if he declines you must find someone else. However, once you are registered with a doctor you are not obliged to continue with him. If you are dissatisfied, you can change to another doctor, and equally, if he is dissatisfied with you, he can drop you as a patient. Your doctor will visit you at home when you are really ill; otherwise he will expect you to come to his office. You have the right to see a specialist—the specialist of your choice whenever it can be arranged. In other words, your relationship with your physician is precisely the same as it was before the Health Service, except (a) that you receive no bills and do not even pay for prescriptions and (b) that you must visit your doctor's office for minor ailments.

Even though you are registered as a public patient, you can use the services of a private doctor as well, so long as you are prepared to pay his fee. For instance, if you have a carbuncle and do not want to bother to go to a clinic, you can ring a physician and ask him to come and see you privately.

The same procedure applies to specialists. Although almost all of Britain's leading specialists are in the scheme, if you are dissatisfied with the treatment you are receiving there is nothing to prevent your calling any specialist you like and asking him to treat you privately.

A large number of people with money are continuing as private patients because they can ask the doctor to visit them at their convenience and thus have a certain priority over public patients. This is criticized by many Socialists, who believe that priority should depend upon the gravity of the illness, not the ability to pay. However, Ministry of Health officials argue that as time goes on and more doctors come into the scheme there will not be the same pressure of work and things will sort themselves out.

And how does the scheme work from the doctor's point of view? If a doctor is a general practitioner (not a specialist) his list of patients will range anywhere from a few hundred to four thousand* patients, depending on his area. General practitioners are paid "capitation fees" or, in other words, a fixed amount per year for each person on their list. This amount comes to nearly a pound (about $4.00) per head. Therefore, the doctor with a thousand patients earns just under £1,000 ($4,000) and the doctor with four thousand about £3,500 ($14,000) a year. These rates are exclusive of maternity work, emergency cases, and, of course, a doctor's private practice.

Specialists fall into a different category. They can join the

---

* Because of the present shortage of doctors, some have as many as ten thousand patients on their lists, although four thousand is supposed to be the maximum.

Service on either a part- or a full-time basis. If they are part-time workers they receive a proportion of the full-time salary and carry on with their private work as well. In some ways, this is financially beneficial for instead of giving free time to the hospitals they are paid for what they do.

Specialists working full time receive salaries (according to their age and training) which begin at £1,400 ($5,600) a year and rise to £2,750 ($11,000). As they obtain distinction they qualify for added awards ranging from £500 ($2,000) to £2,500 ($10,000) a year, thus bringing the most eminent members of the profession into the £5,000-a-year ($20,000) class.

The two criticisms most frequently leveled at state medicine are (a) how to get rid of inefficient doctors and (b) how to guarantee that enterprising specialists will not be frustrated by prejudice among the older men in the profession. The answer to the first of these problems is that even in private medicine there is no way to get rid of inefficient doctors; and since patients have the right to choose their own physicians, the bad doctor will not be "guaranteed" patients but will have just as difficult a time to prosper under state medicine as under private medicine.

As to the second problem, a committee has recently been formed to select the doctors who will receive financial awards. This committee consists of eleven members nominated by the Royal Colleges and the Scottish Royal Corporations; one by the Medical Research Council; and one by the Universities Committee of Vice-Chancellors and Principals. Although it is mainly composed of physicians and surgeons it includes a number of professors and eminent laymen in an effort to achieve strict impartiality.

Free dentistry is available under the Health Service. A patient is not required to "register" with a dentist but merely to make an appointment and take his identity card with him. Up to the present time nine thousand out of the ten thousand dentists in England and Wales, and an even higher percentage in Scotland, have joined the scheme.

Dentists are not paid by "capitation fees" but according to a scale of fixed charges. For instance, a dentist receives 5 shillings

($1.00) for examining a patient's mouth; 7/- to 15/- ($1.40-$3.00) for a filling; 7/- to 37/- ($1.40-$7.40) for extractions. When the scheme was first introduced the scale of payments was 20 per cent higher. But when an analysis of the earnings of 5,078 dentists from October to May showed that 1,066 were earning much more than £6,000 ($24,000) a year gross and of these 333 were earning exceeding £8,400 ($33,600) the scale was hastily revised. At the present time a committee set up by the Minister of Health and the British Dental Association is reviewing the situation.

Such high earnings are due not only to "over payment" but indicate the great need of the public for dental treatment. To most Americans English indifference has always been difficult to understand. In many parts of the country preventive dentistry is still practically unknown and even today thousands of people visit a dentist only when they are in actual pain. This attitude was reflected by a group of working-class women with whom I recently discussed the subject. I asked them which they regarded as the most important, free medicine or free dentistry. "Medicine," they cried in unison. "After all," one of them explained, "you go to the doctor often but you only go to the dentist once to have your teeth pulled out."

The next generation is expected to develop a different outlook.

The National Insurance scheme which went into operation in July, 1948, was the result of the Beveridge Report issued during the war. This report showed that out of the millions of pounds paid privately to insurance companies each year 60 percent went into the cost of administration and only 40 percent into benefits.

The government scheme is based on Beveridge's insurance plan and is compulsory for all employed or self-employed wage earners (other than married women). It costs the employee 4/7d. (94 cents) a week and the employer 3/10d. (78 cents) a week (slightly less for women). Although £122,000,000 ($488,000,000) a year is raised by these contributions, the Exchequer has to find another £320,000,000, for the total costs come to over £450,000,000 ($1,800,000,000) a year, some of which is paid for by the interest on reserves. This cost will continue to rise for the next thirty years, after which the scheme will gradually carry itself.

The benefits provided include sickness and injury benefits, maternity and burial grants, child allowances, unemployed payments, old-age pensions that are large enough for people to exist on, and a superannuation fund to supplement them in cases of hardship.

Is security a good thing? Or will it destroy initiative? And will people work as hard without the threat of unemployment? Today production is 15 percent higher than it was in 1938 and Thomas Finletter, administrator of the Marshall Plan in England, describes British strides toward recovery as magnificent. These facts should serve as an answer and yet in England the subject still arouses heated controversy. Many Conservatives argue that security protects the mediocre and therefore frustrates the enterprising, while Socialists claim that on the contrary only by freeing people from basic financial worries will you give them opportunity to develop their talents.

It is interesting that people most opposed to security are usually those who have had a good deal of it themselves. Recently I had lunch with an old lady who is one of the largest landowners in the southeast of England. "All this talk of security," she scoffed, "is making people soft and destroying the character of the nation. What if I had brought up my sons to value security? What sort of men would they be today?" Someone gently reminded her that whether or not she had brought them up to value it, they had always had it. The old lady was astonished by this idea; she thought of security as an attitude of mind curiously unrelated to hard currency.

Whether or not security will alter the character of the nation, it has already altered the character of the working class. Not only are their clothes and shoes and curtains and furniture and houses better, but their attitude is buoyant and independent. "We don't have to fuss so much about putting money aside," a brick-layer explained to me. "Every week we can buy something for the kids like shoes or a coat or whatever they need."

But whereas the insurance scheme is a boon, the Health Service is a miracle. I visited a woman's club in the East End of London and asked them what benefits were proving the most valuable. They were unanimous about the Health Service. "We couldn't afford to call the doctor unless we were really ill. This way it's going to put years on our lives. What I mean is by the worry it saves us alone!" The fact that the Health Service is costing nearly £58,000,000 ($232,000,000) more this year than was originally estimated is some indication of the pressing need there was for medical attention.

It is ironical that although most doctors are Conservatives they will probably be the most important single factor in returning the Socialists to power.

CHAPTER 17

By-elections

Politics is the first sport of the land.
—G. K. CHESTERTON

SUPPOSE America had the same parliamentary system as Britain; and suppose one of the congressmen from New Jersey died. An election would be fought on the spot which would soon assume the importance of a miniature Presidential campaign. If politics were a national pastime to the same extent as in England, the whole weight of the national Democratic and Republican machines would be thrown into the fray and the isolated contest would become a national one.

Overnight Hackensack or Orange or Englewood would become the political focus of the country. Party headquarters would be set up on the main street, press and photographers would take over the local hotel, hundreds of voluntary party workers would move in from neighboring states to take part in the canvass and senators and congressmen would journey from Washington to tour the district and make speeches.

Both parties would have to state their policies, and the issues would become front-page headlines all the way from California to New York. Newspapers would carry feature articles ranging from economic summaries to how the candidate's wife managed her weekly budget and still kept herself in nylons. And whichever side was victorious would declare ecstatically that New Jersey was the true reflection of the nation as a whole.

In Britain thirty-three Labor members of Parliament have died or resigned their seats since the general election in 1945,

201

which has meant that the government has defended its policy in thirty-three contests in the last four years; and the fact that it has established an unprecedented record by retaining every one of the seats is the reason many people believe it will be returned to power in the approaching national elections.

Of the contests which were fought, Hammersmith was the most exciting. Hammersmith might be Brooklyn. Although it is part of the London area, and only half an hour from Piccadilly, it is a large, noisy metropolis with its own crowded shopping district, its own theater and movies, its own parks and restaurants and dance halls. And like most thickly populated city areas it has a representative cross section of rich, poor, and in-betweens.

Before the war Hammersmith was a safe Conservative seat, but with the Socialist swing in 1945 it returned a Labor member to Parliament with the slim majority of 3,458 votes out of a poll of about 40,000. The Conservatives, therefore, had to "turn over" only 1,800 votes to recapture it. In view of the dissatisfaction any government incurs after being in office four years it seemed an easy thing to do and Conservative newspapers began preparing for victory by building it into a "prestige election." Hammersmith, they declared, would show the nation the way the wind was blowing. The Labor party accepted the challenge and the fight was on. Over a hundred M.P.'s took part in the campaign and a total of nearly two thousand party workers volunteered their services. And in the national press, predictions about the outcome even drew forth statements from professional astrologers.

Forty-eight hours before the voting I went to Hammersmith to see what was happening. First I visited Labor party headquarters. They were in a small two-roomed shop on a quiet side street well away from the center of the town. In the window were jovial photographs of the candidate surrounded by workingmen and a bulletin board covered with telegrams of encouragement from loyal supporters.

There seemed to be little going on. In the far room the agent and three or four men were locked in earnest discussion and in the outer room a man stood behind a desk to answer inquiries. When I asked him if I could go around with a canvasser for an hour he pointed to a chair and told me to wait until someone came along. A few people drifted in and out, but no one seemed in a hurry, and the atmosphere reminded me more of a doctor's waiting room than a campaign headquarters. A driver came in and asked if he could get a cup of tea; an M.P. asked what district he could cover with the loud-speaker truck; an elderly gentleman from New Zealand called to wish the candidate success; and a workman explained that he was one of the men in the photograph in the window and could he take it home after the election?

Finally the man behind the desk said to me: "Here, miss. You can go around with this gentleman if you like." He introduced me to a small man with a thin lined face and a timid smile, and told one of the drivers to take us over to another district where we would receive our instructions.

When we got into the car the small man said apologetically: "I'm afraid I'm not a very good person for you to go with. I've never canvassed before. In fact, I don't even live in Hammersmith."

I was curious to know how he happened to offer his services. "It's my wife," he explained. "She said it wasn't enough to just sit around and cheer every time the government won a by-election. This looked like a close fight, she said, and we ought to help. So we drew lots which should stay at home and look after the baby and which should canvass. And here I am."

The car drew up in front of a house with a Labor party banner over the window. When we went in a woman with spectacles welcomed us and handed us a small stack of yellow cards with names and addresses under which were printed "For, Against, Doubtful." She gave us our instructions crisply: "Because this election is close we are canvassing every individual rather than every family. So please ask for each person by name."

She loaded us with pamphlets and posters, and as we were leaving added: "Another thing. We don't want any more cards marked 'Doubtful.' It's too late for that now. So judge as best you can whether they are for or against and mark the spaces accordingly."

The street we were to canvass ran down to the Thames. It was now 6:30 and beginning to get dark, and when I saw the little man shiver I couldn't tell whether it was from cold or apprehension. "I've never canvassed before," he repeated. "I hope people won't be rude."

I wondered how so timid a man had steeled himself to so purposeful an act and asked him if he had been a Labor supporter for long. "Ten years," he replied. "I'm a commercial artist, but before the war I was unemployed for three years. That's because the Conservatives didn't create the right economic conditions and that's why I'm a Socialist." There was no bitterness in his voice, only a note of patient explanation. "Here's No. 4," he said, taking a deep breath. "Well, here we go."

The houses on the street were ordinary three-story brownstone houses, each exactly like the other. Many of them had party stickers on the windows and at first we were confused by the fact that the same houses were displaying both Labor and Conservative signs; then we discovered that most of them were converted into flats with a different family on each floor.

"There are five Browns," said the little man, knocking on the door. Soon the light in the hall went on, and a tall thin man in shirt sleeves was staring at us suspiciously. We had a glimpse of a shabby hall with worn linoleum and a dilapidated pram standing in the corner.

"We're from Labor party headquarters," said my friend. "We wondered whether you were going to vote tomorrow and-er-well-er-what we really wondered was how you feel about the Labor party."

"I never tell anyone how I'm voting," said Mr. Brown. "I don't believe in it."

"Oh, of course not," said the little man in a stricken voice.

"I wasn't trying to pry into your affairs. I'm afraid I'm not very good at canvassing. I've never done it before. But I just thought I'd step around to see if you'd like to have any of our literature."

The man shook his head, then tapped his forehead with his finger. "Everything I need to know is right up here. But don't let me discourage you," he added, his voice softening. "I don't mind saying I've been friendly to Labor all my life."

I could feel the little man's relief. "I'm so glad to hear you say that. I hate breaking in on people, but up at headquarters they think the canvass is important. I suppose it's really to get at people who haven't made up their minds."

It was obvious that Mr. Brown was enjoying himself and would talk indefinitely if we let him. "I've made up my mind all right. In fact I never voted Tory in my life. But I don't like being asked, if you know what I mean."

"Of course I do. After all, the ballot's secret, isn't it? Now can you tell us about Mrs. Brown and another Mr. Brown and two Miss Browns?"

"That's the wife and kids. And we all vote alike if it's any help to you."

"Indeed it is. Thank you, Mr. Brown. We won't keep you any longer."

When the door closed the little man said: "I'm feeling better."

Next came Mrs. Gebb. We had to wait some time for her to answer, and when she did she was young, pretty, with an apron on and a bandanna tied around her head. Beyond was the same dull, brown hall with the same ugly, dark-brown flowered wallpaper. At the end we saw a kitchen with a man sitting in a chair tipped back at a perilous angle, his feet on the table.

"Sorry, I can't talk, but supper's on," said the girl.

"I thought you might like to take some of our pamphlets."

"For God's sake don't leave any more literature. We've had tons of stuff around here. But I'm going to vote Labor if that's what you want to know."

"Good. And what about Mr. Stanway?"

"He's a Tory. Lives on the next floor. Look at his windows. He's got so many stickers on them he can't see out of them."

"And Mrs. Mason?"

"Wouldn't like to say about her. We hardly know her. She's new here. She lives on the top floor but if you knock three times she might come down."

We did as we were told and soon we heard footsteps. We saw a tall woman in a tea gown coming down the stairs. She must have been about fifty. She had gray hair brushed back from her ears and a stiff, almost regal carriage. Her tea gown had obviously seen better days and when she talked it was in the educated accents of the upper class. "I never take part in politics," she smiled. "I don't believe it's the sort of thing women should meddle in. I was very much opposed to woman suffrage; in fact, I think that ever since women got the vote the world has been rapidly deteriorating. But I'd like to see your pamphlets. I have some Conservative pamphlets as well and it amuses me to compare them."

"But you ought to vote," protested the little man. "An intelligent woman like you . . . "

There was something unreal about Mrs. Mason. She had a far-away look in her eyes and spoke her lines as though she were acting a part in a play. She lifted her hands in a helpless little flutter. "Perhaps because I *am* intelligent I leave political matters to the men. Oh no, I'm afraid you'll never get me to a polling booth. But it's charming of you to take the trouble to call."

When we left my companion said: "Did she seem a little balmy or is it me?"

Down the street we went knocking at door after door. Although the houses were all alike the people we talked to and the glimpses we had into the lighted halls reminded me of movie previews, brief and tantalizing, with the suggestion of human drama behind each one. There was the young man who looked liked a bank clerk who was going to vote Conservative, the old lady with a cane who said she was a Communist, the family of four who were divided among themselves. Then there was the old gentleman in the black velvet smoking jacket and the black velvet cap who seemed as agitated as a character from *Alice in Wonderland.*

"Oh my goodness! My goodness me!" he cried in obvious distress. "If you knew how many times I have opened this door! If you knew how many pamphlets have been pushed under it! If you knew how many people have called! And all I want is to be left alone to read my books in peace. I don't care *who* wins the election. Not the least little jot. So long as people don't keep knocking on this door. . . . "

At the end of the canvass we counted up our cards. We had seen twenty-two people; six were "Against" and sixteen were "For." "Not bad," said the little man. "Not bad at all. If things keep on like this, we're in." It was colder now and the wind was beginning to rise. He pulled up his collar. "So long," he said cheerfully. "Perhaps we'll meet at another election. Now I'm beginning to get the hang of things."

The next afternoon I visited Hammersmith again to canvass with the Conservatives. This was the last day before the poll and the party was playing its trump card in the form of Churchill's tour of the constituency. Hundreds of Union Jacks were flying and people were in a holiday mood. Extra police were on duty and school children with red, white, and blue badges were being shepherded to take up positions along the route.

Far from being daunted by the arrival of the great man, politicians were busy trying to capitalize on the crowds. There must have been twenty meetings taking place along the main street. One Socialist M.P. was stationed near the market, and while women shoppers went from stall to stall buying fish and vegetables and shoestrings and kitchenware, he talked through a microphone of the benefits the Labor government had brought by the insurance scheme and the Health Service. When a Salvation Army band chose the same moment to make its way through the market one almost wondered if it had been sent by the Conservative M.P., a little farther along, who was emphasizing the fact that the insurance scheme and the Health Service had been prepared by Churchill's coalition government. The

Conservative went on to claim that Socialist extravagances would soon bring the country to ruin. "Aw, change your record," grunted a young man. "Shut up," retorted someone. "We come to 'ear 'im, not you." Political argument even spread to a line waiting for a bus. As I passed I saw an old man shake his fist at someone and caught the words "Tory" and "that Bevan" in a heated exchange.

I had a list of the places at which Churchill was speaking and walked to a side street away from the main thoroughfare. By a coincidence, it happened to be at the foot of the street I had canvassed the night before. A wind was still blowing from the river and several hundred people were waiting, stamping their feet to keep warm. Soon two police cars arrived followed by a car with a loud-speaker. A man announced that Churchill was on his way, then took the opportunity to declare that Conservatives would *not* allow food prices to rise, would *not* abandon controls, would *not* cut down pensions or any of the other allegations Socialists were making. But no one seemed to be listening and presently his voice was drowned by cheers as Churchill's car came into sight. The old man was sitting on the back hood; his chest was covered with Tory blue ribbons; he was wearing a black silk top hat and smoking a cigar. His face was so round and pink and white, he looked exactly like the china mugs that were sold of him during the war. "Isn't 'e rosy," I heard the woman behind me saying. " 'E looks like a baby, 'e does."

Crowds surged around the car and although Churchill talked for only a few minutes he lacked none of his characteristic fire. He attacked the government's building program and declared that one of his greatest regrets when he was "dismissed from office" was not to be able to mobilize the vast organization at his command to tackle the housing problem. "And no one can say our organization was not capable," he added, "for in those days we were used to handling pretty big business." Then he went on to deride the Socialists for claiming a monopoly in the field of social service, reminding his audience that he himself had introduced major reforms with Lloyd George over forty years ago. "Why, these Socialists are the very product of our reform!" he cried. Then his voice grew serious. "If my excellent friend, Mr. Fell, is returned tomorrow the whole world will cry, 'Aha! The old country is coming back into her own again!' "

The crowds surged around cheering wildly. "Isn't he lovely," I heard a woman say. "And don't he enjoy himself though." Behind, a man commented: "Good old Winnie, if he'd only drop the Tories maybe we'd vote for him." If looks could kill this remark drew a death blow from two old ladies next to him. As Churchill's car drove away hundreds of people ran after it, one little boy making a noise like a machine gun pretending that they were fleeing before his attack.

I walked over to Conservative headquarters and when I asked if I could canvass with someone I was directed to a district office a mile away. I arrived to find three men and a girl hard at work checking returns between sips of tea. A businesslike man, about thirty, was in charge of the office. He handed me a cup of tea and told me to wait until someone came along. "We're expecting fifty M.P.'s," said the girl brightly. "Well, perhaps not quite so many as that," interjected the young man, a little embarrassed. "We're never sure until they turn up."

Although the house was the same sort of semi-detached villa that Labor headquarters were in, the atmosphere was different. There were no shabby clothes, no loud voices, no middle-class accents; one was back in the polite, educated world of ladies and gentlemen, and because of it for some curious reason one had a feeling of amateurishness.

The young man and the girl continued checking returns and I saw that their charts showed a preponderance of Conservative votes just as the Labor charts showed a majority the other way. Suddenly the door opened and a boy of nineteen came hurrying in and placed a stack of cards on the desk. "I've covered this street pretty thoroughly," he said breathlessly. "About 70 percent have promised to vote for us. And that's all the canvassing I can do now. I want to go to some of the meetings and heckle." Ten minutes later another canvasser came in. This time it was a lady of fifty, well dressed and with the look of the aristocrat. "Such a dreadful street," she expostulated. "And what houses. I asked if the local council couldn't do something about it. Four or five in a room. And outside, my dear, a Communist making a speech telling everyone it's the fault of the Tories. Oh, I could have wrung his neck! And when I asked people to put up our posters they said if they did they'd have their windows broken. It's monstrous. I don't know what England's coming to."

The young man did his best to pacify her. "I'm sure it's only small boys. Have a cup of tea?"

"No thank you, I must run along. But I think it's a scandal . . . " She left, shaking her head sadly.

Soon after this two men arrived and volunteered to canvass. Both were in their twenties; one was studying at Oxford and the other, whom I had met before, had recently graduated from Cambridge. They agreed that I should accompany them and when we were walking down the street the Cambridge man told me that he now had a permanent job at Conservative headquarters and was hoping to go into Parliament himself one day. He had spent the afternoon in one of the cars following Churchill.

"How do you think it's going?" he asked.

"After the American elections I wouldn't like to prophesy," I said.

"The American elections must have been a shock to a lot of people. But I thought it was ridiculous the way the Socialists here tried to pretend that a vote for Truman was a vote for them. The Americans aren't Socialists. They stand for what *we* stand for—Tory Radicalism."

"Is there much difference between Socialism and Tory Radicalism?" I asked. "Long ago Winston described the Tories of the last century as Tory Democrats and suggested that the Tories of this century might be Tory Socialists."

"Winston doesn't know anything about the Conservative

party," said the Cambridge man scornfully. "He's an old-fashioned Whig."

We were now at Mrs. Rawlin's house. He stepped up to the door and knocked boldly while the Oxford man, who had not spoken at all, drew well back into the protection of the darkness. When the door opened and a frowzy woman in a soiled dress and bedroom slippers peered out at us, he did not mince his words. "We're from Conservative party headquarters, and I hope you're going to vote for us tomorrow." Suddenly I was embarrassed by his voice and his self-assured manner, and the fact that he so obviously came from another and a protected world. But I might have spared myself, for the woman smiled and opened the door wider.

"Did you see Mr. Churchill today?"

She nodded. "Didn't 'e look young, though?"

"And he made a jolly good speech, didn't he?"

She nodded again. By now a pale boy with an expressionless face was standing behind her. His coat was shabby and he was in his stocking feet.

"Then you'll vote for us tomorrow?"

"Don't see why I shouldn't," said the woman thoughtfully.

"And that gentleman there?"

"That's Ronnie. You'll vote for Mr. Churchill, won't you Ronnie?"

Ronnie didn't reply, but the woman said: "I'll see 'e does. Ronnie don't follow politics too close but I'm sure 'e'll do like I say."

We stopped at four more houses, and the Cambridge man's confident manner appeared to be successful, for all the people we saw promised to vote Conservative. The first rebuff we had was when we rang a bell in a large block of flats. A young woman announced briskly: "I never disclose the way I'm going to vote." And the door shut.

"Labor," said the Oxford man gloomily.

We tried another flat and a big man grinned cheerfully at us: "I'm from Texas," he said. "I've just borrowed this apartment from a friend. I'm afraid I'm no use to anyone in this election."

Next came a man and his wife. The wife was middle-aged, tall, and smartly dressed. "Oh, do come in," she said warmly. "I've been a Conservative all my life and I simply adore Mr. Churchill. Of course I'm going to vote for you but I'm having trouble with my husband." Her voice dropped. "He's the other way."

"But that won't do at all," protested the Cambridge man. "That means you cancel each other out."

"We certainly don't," said the woman. "I lock Henry up. I say to him: 'If you can't vote my way you won't vote at all.' "

Henry suddenly appeared in the doorway. He was in shirt sleeves. He had a mop of thick, untidy hair and a determined chin.

"What's my wife telling you?"

"Just that you promised to stay at home tomorrow so my vote will count," said the wife in a sudden purring tone.

"Can't we persuade you to change your mind and vote for us?" asked the Cambridge man.

"Not me. I'm not backing either side. Personally I think they both stink."

"Oh Henry!"

Out in the street once more we counted up. We had seen twelve people and ten had promised to vote Conservative.

"Not bad," said the Cambridge man. "If things keep on like this, we're home."

The following night when the poll was announced Labor had retained the seat by a majority of 1,600.

The three things that interested me about the election were: the anomaly of Churchill's position, the result of the canvass, the political issues involved. Ever since the general election it has frequently been alleged that Churchill is appreciated by everyone except the British. Yet with the exception of the King no Briton enjoys greater popularity. Margaret Cole sums it up this way: "During the war people wanted a Father-Protector and they turned to Churchill. After the war they still wanted a Father-Protector but the fact that Churchill allied himself to the Tory party, which to the mass of people represented the antithesis of protection, destroyed the image."

The British have never followed their heroes blindly. No nation accords its great men more enduring respect but no nation is more independent in its political judgments. Because a man is great does not also mean he is infallible. Such hard-headed logic has always been a British characteristic and is probably the reason that dictatorships strike the English as slightly comical, and in the last analysis is probably the reason the English are wedded to a system in which no man is indispensable.

The canvass revealed another well-known British characteristic: politeness. I was fascinated by the fact that no matter whether I was in the company of Conservatives or Socialists the reception was equally sympathetic; and I came to the conclusion that it takes a wise man to read a canvass return correctly. When I remarked on this to Morgan Phillips, secretary of the Labor party, he told me that his method was to chalk up all "doubtfuls" as "against." "Then add 25 percent of the people who promised to support you and you'll get somewhere near the truth," he said. However, the politeness indicated something more than manners. Not only did it serve to refute the statement frequently heard in sophisticated London circles that "class hatred is sweeping the country," but it seemed to me to indicate a Britain more united and good-natured than at any time since the war.

I was also interested in the fact that although both Socialists and Conservatives regard the canvass as the most important feature of a by-election the people we called upon showed no inclination to discuss politics on the doorstep. Their minds appeared to be made up. On this point Phillips commented: "The value of the canvass is not in converting people, but in finding out where your strength lies and getting people to the polls."

Lastly, the political tactics involved in the campaign showed a significant change in the political scene. Instead of attacking, the Conservatives were on the defensive. While the Socialists plugged national insurance, the Health Service, subsidized food, and the old cry "Fair shares for all," the Conservatives were left hotly denying that they would lift subsidies, abolish controls, or cut pensions.

This rear-guard worried many Conservatives, and Mr. Churchill at once became a target of criticism for not committing the party to a clear-cut policy. Tory M.P.'s hurriedly called a conference where, the press rumored, "Winston would be taken to task." However, I was in the gallery of the House of Commons when the old man appeared after his meeting. His face was wreathed in smiles, which left little doubt as to who had been triumphant.

Nevertheless, the criticism continued. *Picture Post* came out with an article entitled: "Is Churchill a Liability to the Tories?" while the *Sunday Express* championed him stanchly: "When Mr. Churchill is in his seat, the Opposition breathes fire. When he is not, the Tory Front Bench has the venom of a bunch of daffodils."

However, the truth is that most Conservatives realize that with or without Churchill their dilemma is the same; and their dilemma is the lack of a common, agreed policy. Robert Boothby, a Conservative M.P., summed up the position in an outspoken letter to the *Times*:

> The Tory party will not recapture the confidence of the public until it is in a position to put forward a precise policy, in simple terms, based not on dogma but on certain clearly defined principles; and it will not be able to do this until it makes up its mind whether it is going to accept the advent of the managerial society as an established fact, or whether it wishes to make yet another attempt to return to the *laissez-faire* economy of the nineteenth century. . . . What we have to do is to convince the public that our programme amounts to something more than the dole, the quinquennial vote, and recurrent world war. In order to do this we must first of all convince ourselves that the defeat of Hitler will no more restore *laissez-faire* capitalism to Europe than the defeat of Napoleon restored feudalism.

CHAPTER 18

The Press: Private Enterprise

Every now and then the question of the ownership of newspapers becomes a topic of public
discussion. . . .

—Lord Northcliffe, 1922

NEWSPAPERS which constitute 80 percent of the circulation of the entire British press are in the hands of ten men.
Five of these men are chairmen of the controlling companies
by virtue of appointment, and five by virtue of ownership. They
are known as the press lords. Six of them are peers (four of the
first creation) and six of them are multimillionaires. Before the
war the latter lived in ducal splendor and were famous for their
hospitality. They owned yachts and race horses and entertained
the most fashionable and influential people in the land. They
were courted assiduously by politicians, who believed their power
to be very great, and frequently consulted by the government,
which was always eager to enlist and retain their support. They
accepted the deference paid to them as a natural right and often
adopted a patronizing air toward the men who ruled the country. Once a newspaper owner remarked to me airily: "These
political chaps come and go but we remain forever."

As far as political influence was concerned this was not strictly true for the Conservative defeat in 1945 did more than oust the Conservative party. The fact that the most famous press lords, Beaverbrook, Camrose, Rothermere, and Kemsley all threw their weight behind the Tory campaign, and their weight proved ineffective, destroyed the myth of their power. Their prestige suffered a severe loss with the public and today you frequently hear people remark: "Oh, no one pays any attention to what the newspapers say." Added to this, most of them are no longer consulted by cabinet ministers and are less well informed of the inner workings of the government than the average back-bench Labor M.P.

Nevertheless the press lords are still supreme in their own sphere. They control newspapers that boast the highest circulations in the world. While only two morning papers in America have a sale of over a million, seven out of the eight London morning papers sell anywhere from one to four million copies a day. Their combined circulation comes to about fifteen millions whereas in the whole of the United States the total circulation of morning papers is only 21,000,000 and is made up of 334 separate journals.

The explanation for this is that London newspapers circulate nationally. They are read not merely in London but in every part of the country. Although all the major cities in Britain have their own local papers as well, known as the "provincial press," they do not attempt to compete with the big London dailies but merely to supplement them. With few notable exceptions such as the *Manchester Guardian* they run very little parliamentary or foreign news and content themselves mainly with local affairs. Their relationship to the national press is shown by the fact that even though they number over a hundred daily and Sunday papers their total circulation is only fourteen millions while the seventeen morning and Sunday papers published in the capital have sales of over forty millions. When people refer to the British press, therefore, they usually mean the London press.

These huge national circulations have molded British journalism into a pattern of its own and given it a very different character and outlook from the American press. First, the "press lord" has no real equivalent in America; second, British journalism is concentrated in the capital city which means that newspaper proprietors live not only in close touch with politicians and foreign diplomats but in close touch with each other and, both socially and professionally, in even closer competition; third, as peers they are members of Parliament.

All these things have had a profound effect. The fact that any newspaper proprietor who uses his influence on behalf of a political party will be sent to the upper house if, and when, his party comes to power has introduced a partisanship unknown in America. Few owners have remained independent but have thrown their weight into one camp or the other. And because they are directly embroiled in political life, and political life means power, opinion has a tendency to overshadow news. None of those who openly support political parties, with the exception of Lord Beaverbrook, will consistently tolerate the expression of views contrary to their own. And whereas newspaper owners in Spokane or St. Paul or Cleveland must rely on their Washington correspondents for inside news of government activity, British owners are in a position to decide questions of policy themselves; for this reason there are no independent political columnists in Britain.

This lack of independence has done great harm to British journalism. Because editors and reporters are often regarded as "stooges" the profession holds little appeal for the ablest young men. University graduates who win high honors seldom take up journalism; they prefer to go to the bar, or into the civil service or the House of Commons. Foreigners are sometimes shocked by the servility of certain newspaper editors who address their proprietors as "my lord," a manner of speech which is usually confined to servants; and the fact that reporters often call their superiors "sir" strikes a strangely incongruous note, at least to Americans.

Despite the effect on journalistic standards, press lords of all political shades consider it perfectly natural to use their papers to promote their own policies; and it is so much the rule that no particular discredit is attached to them by public opinion. I remember the owner of a paper once telling me that Low was the best political cartoonist in the world. When I asked why in that case he had never tried to employ him he looked at me in shocked surprise. "Because we're a Conservative paper," he protested. The only politically-minded papers which circulate nationally and yet do not support any one political party are the *Times*, the *Manchester Guardian*, and the *Sunday Observer*. The *Daily Telegraph* and the *Sunday Times* are admirable papers but their stanch Conservative views are often reflected on the front page in the reports of their political correspondents. When Lord Beaverbrook gave evidence before the Royal Press Commission he stated bluntly:

A. When more actively engaged in the conduct of the papers, I ran the paper purely for the purposes of making propaganda on my own issues. . . . I have only an interest in a paper so long as propaganda is going on.

Q. How do you allow your mind to be known by those who actually have the putting of it [policy] into effect?

A. I am not now concerned in direction . . . like I used to be, but I have got this young lot growing up in control of the papers.

Q. I suppose they know by now the opinions and themes to which you attach importance.

A. They would not have been asked to join the Board of Control of the paper if they had not views like I have.

The press lords are a creation of the last fifty-five years. Lord Glenesk, the owner of the now extinct *Morning Post*, was the first newspaper proprietor to be raised to the peerage. He was sent to the upper house in 1895, and followed there in 1903 by Lord Burnham, the owner of the *Daily Telegraph*. But it was not until Alfred Harmsworth was made the first Baron Northcliffe in 1906 that the custom became firmly established. Northcliffe revolutionized British journalism by introducing "popular" newspapers whose circulations had to be reckoned, not in the thousands, but in the hundreds of thousands. And in doing so he made newspaper proprietors powers in the land.

Northcliffe is undoubtedly the most fabulous figure in the history of British journalism. In the first half of the hundred years before the founding of his morning newspaper in 1896, the British press had had a long hard struggle. Until 1855 the government imposed savage newspaper taxes which for many years made it difficult for newspapers to survive without becoming the paid servants of politicians. After they won their freedom they moved into an era of great respectability which soon congealed into even greater dullness. For although circulations began to rise in the 1880's newspapers were still largely written for the educated few. The language was stilted and elaborate; editorials were usually three columns long; and often there were whole pages of close type unbroken by a single subtitle.

Several attempts were made to provide the lower and lower middle classes with a readable paper but none succeeded until 1881 when George Newnes, the proprietor of a vegetarian restaurant, conceived the idea of publishing a weekly paper filled with human-interest stories. The paper was named *Titbits* and had an instantaneous success. One of its avid readers was sixteen-year-old Alfred Harmsworth, the son of a middle-class English barrister and an Irish mother, who had recently moved from Ireland to Hampstead, a suburb of London. Seven years later Alfred published a variation of *Titbits* called *Answers*. The circulation did not rise as rapidly as he had hoped and the future Lord Northcliffe went from door to door pushing free copies into letter boxes. Then he had the idea of offering £1 ($4.00) a week for life to the reader who could give the most accurate estimate of the holdings of the Bank of England at a given date. In order to spread the name of the magazine he insisted that everyone who competed must have his signature witnessed by three or four people. The idea was epoch-making; within eighteen months *Answers* had a circulation of 200,000; and when it was established Alfred's younger brother Harold, later Lord Rothermere, joined him in the business.

In 1896 when Northcliffe was only thirty-one he launched the *Daily Mail*, which became the model for all the popular London papers that exist today. Gone were the three-column

editorials, the close unbroken print, the long-winded phrase-
ology. In their place were short pithy news accounts, headlines,
heavy and light print, features, human-interest stories, cartoons,
pictures, and all the things that go to make up the modern
newspaper.

Northcliffe was hard-working and ruthless and possessed all
the drive and imagination of the born journalist. He had an
uncanny instinct of what the public wanted and as he moved
from success to success he became known as "the Napoleon of
Fleet Street." This pleased him for Napoleon was his hero; he
kept the latter's picture on his desk and when he went to France
and tried on Napoleon's hat he was said to have remarked
proudly: "It fits me."

Northcliffe had the reputation of driving his men and yet
no proprietor did more to raise the status of his employees. He
paid the highest wages in Fleet Street, increased the expense accounts of his reporters, and introduced modern canteens; and
when he died he left his workmen and staff £500,000 ($2,000,-
000).

Although he was first and foremost a journalist, Northcliffe
took a passionate interest in the affairs of the day, and his newspapers always adopted a strong but independent political line.
During World War I the *Daily Mail* burned with patriotic
fervor. Northcliffe did not hesitate to criticize public figures
whom he believed were inept and called for the dismissals of
great generals and statesmen with an imperious authority that
was summed up by the current quip: "The Cabinet has resigned and Northcliffe has sent for the King." However, he was
bitterly disappointed when Lloyd George refused to give him a
seat at the Peace Conference.

The *réclame* and power Northcliffe won from his newspapers began to attract millionaire businessmen to Fleet Street
who decided that newspaper ownership offered a quick cut to
fame. Northcliffe resented these "amateur journalists" and before he died in 1922 attacked them in a pamphlet entitled
Newspapers and Their Millionaires. Beatrice and Sidney Webb
commented on the pamphlet in the *New Statesman*:

Lord Northcliffe claims to be one of the very few newspaper proprietors who has made his money out of newspapers and the rest he regards as interlopers. He is not prepared, he declares, to accept in his own business of producing newspapers the dictation of Shipping Kings and Cotton Kings and Coal and Cocoa and Oil Kings. The argument as he states it is perhaps a little over-strained, but it is one which will arouse a sympathetic echo in the heart of many a professional journalist who has no reason to entertain a tender regard either for Lord Northcliffe or for his views. . . . The outstanding merit of Lord Northcliffe is that he is himself a journalist, and he has proved that he knows his business. He is a millionaire, but since he has made his millions out of newspapers directly controlled by himself, he has acquired a moral right to bully or sack his employees which no ironmaster or soapmaster who has purchased a newspaper can ever possess. That, from the journalist's point of view, is a matter of infinite importance, for in it is involved the whole question of the status of the profession. . . . The curse of journalism is the absentee proprietor behind whose edicts there is no authority save that of the purse, and who more often than not appoints as his mouthpiece someone whose claims upon the respect of the profession are scarcely greater than his own.

Today most of the "amateur millionaires" to whom Lord Northcliffe objected have faded away. Some have been squeezed out by ineptitude, others have been transformed into professionals through long years of experience, others have died and left their properties to their sons. Today the ten men who control eighteen of the twenty* newspapers published in London, as well as a group of provincial papers that constitute half the total circulation of the provincial press, are as follows: Lord Beaverbrook, Lord Camrose, Lord Kemsley, Lord Rothermere, Lord Astor, Lord Layton, Guy Bartholomew, Harold Aldridge, A. G. Cousins, and Colonel the Honorable J. J. Astor.

If Lord Northcliffe's mantle has fallen on anyone, the spiritual inheritor is Lord Beaverbrook. Of all the press lords Beaverbrook is the journalist par excellence and the most fascinating and provocative of personalities. A small, gnomelike man, with

* The *Daily Herald* is owned by Odhams Ltd., with the agreement that the T.U.C. shall direct its policy, and *Reynolds News* is the property of the Co-operative Society. I have not included financial or trade papers or the Communist *Daily Worker*, which is not a British newspaper in the true sense of the word.

THE LONDON OR NATIONAL PRESS*

Type of Paper	Name	Politics	Owner or Controller	Circulation	Associate Papers
	(The following are morning papers.)				
Serious	Times	Independent	Col. Astor	240,096	
Serious	Daily Telegraph	Conservative	Lord Camrose	996,792	
Popular	Daily Express	Conservative	Lord Beaverbrook	4,027,290	*Evening Standard* Circ: 815,959 *Sunday Express* Circ: 2,566,391
Popular	Daily Mail	Conservative	Lord Rothermere	2,197,000	*Evening News* Circ: 1,773,472 *Sunday Dispatch* Circ: 2,044,410
Popular	News Chronicle	Liberal	Lord Layton	1,617,420	*Star* Circ: 1,084,679

					People Circ: 4,632,671
Popular	Daily Herald	Socialist	A. G. Cousins	2,109,916	Sunday Pictorial Circ: 4,004,572
Tabloid	Daily Mirror	Socialist	G. Bartholomew	4,319,000	Sunday Graphic Circ: 1,185,485
Tabloid	Daily Graphic	Conservative	Lord Kemsley	771,744	Sunday Times Circ: 529,689
	(The following are Sunday papers unattached to any other paper.)				
Serious Popular	Observer	Independent	Lord Astor	383,460	
	Reynolds News	Socialist	Co-operative Society	720,339	
Popular	News of the World	Nonpolitical	H. Aldridge	Over 8,000,000	

an impish smile, who always wears a dark-blue suit and a bat-
tered black Homburg hat, he probably has more friends and
bitterer enemies than any other single man in England. Lord
Camrose wrote of him: "He is no ordinary man and he takes
care not to act in any ordinary way." Beaverbrook raised the circulation of the *Daily Express* from under 400,000 to over 4,000,-
000; until the *Daily Mirror* recently nosed ahead it was the
largest daily newspaper in the world.

Beaverbrook was born in northern Ontario seventy years
ago, one of nine children of a poor Scotch Presbyterian minister. By the time he was nineteen he had sold newspapers, run
a bowling alley, peddled washing machines, cleaned bottles in
a chemist's shop, and worked as a law clerk in the offices of
R. B. Bennett, who afterwards became Prime Minister of Canada. But he soon turned his attention from law to business and
before he was thirty had made a fortune as a company promoter.

He burst upon London several years before World War I, entered Parliament, and soon became the friend of the three most
brilliant men in England: Lloyd George, Winston Churchill,
and F. E. Smith. In 1917 he was created a baron as a reward for
arranging the series of meetings that resulted in Lloyd George's
becoming Prime Minister. But he likes to pretend that he regrets his peerage. He often holds up his short, square hands and
cries: "See. I am a son of the soil. I am no nobleman."

Beaverbrook bought the *Express* in 1913 but he did not pay
much attention to it until 1918. Then he flung himself into journalism with all the force of his personality. He hired and fired
ruthlessly; he took a passionate interest in every department; he
surrounded himself with his writers and editors and dinned
into their heads exactly what he wanted the paper to be. Dullness was the unforgivable sin. Whereas newspapers usually insist that the "lead," or the first paragraph of the news account,
shall contain the meat of the story Beaverbrook encouraged his
reporters to write news messages as though they were short stories with a beginning, a middle, and an end.

The originality of the *Daily Express* is a reflection of Beaverbrook's own unexpected and complicated nature. He has an almost feminine love of intrigue coupled with an uncontrollable urge to prick all bubbles of complacency. Before the war he lived in a large house near St. James's Palace where he worked in a room strewn with papers, often with a dictaphone in one hand and a telephone in the other. There were rarely less than eight or ten people to dinner and Beaverbrook always dominated the scene, bullying and jeering at his terrified employees with merciless pleasure. And yet no man has been more generous as far as money is concerned; he has helped innumerable people out of financial troubles and given away to his friends literally thousands of pounds. Besides this he is immensely religious. He quotes the Bible at length and when, many years ago, he bought an airplane, he promptly named it *John Knox*.

These strange contradictions make Beaverbrook's character perplexing even to his closest friends. Because it amuses him to surprise people he often allows uncomplimentary paragraphs about himself to appear in his papers just for the astonishment they cause. Once I picked up the *Sunday Express* and read the following extract from Peter Howard's column:

Strange, is it not, that so few newspaper peers have lifted up their voices in the House of Lords? So far as I can discover, my Lords Camrose, Kemsley, Iliffe, and Southwood have yet to make their maiden speeches in the Upper Chamber. Lord Rothermere has spoken there, Lord Beaverbrook also is maiden no more, so far as the House of Lords is concerned. He is the only newspaper peer who has engaged in prolonged political controversy on the debating floor of the House of Lords. Lord Beaverbrook is always complaining about others that they want their palm without the dust. This is exactly his own condition. He wants power without working for it. He imagines himself to be ill. He walks out of the arena and takes his place in the grandstand. From there he wishes to continue to take part in the game. Lord Baldwin once said of him that he desired to exercise power without responsibility, the prerogative of the harlot throughout the ages. . . .

Where Beaverbrook differs from the late Lord Northcliffe is that although he is one of the greatest journalists in the world, journalism comes second and politics first. During the last thirty years Beaverbrook has wielded great political power. He was the *éminence grise* behind Bonar Law's prime ministership in the 1920's, and during World War II he was Winston Churchill's closest adviser. Although today his newspapers, the *Daily Express*, the *Sunday Express*, and the *Evening Standard*, run a consistent anti-Labor policy, when the Conservatives are in power Beaverbrook plays his hand as an independent. This gives him far greater opportunity to command attention than if he were docile and obedient. The fact that he allows Low, the brilliant left-wing cartoonist, to jeer at the policies he supports in his editorials has always aroused the indignation of stanch Tories. His own particular policies have been "Empire Preference" and "Splendid Isolation," which, before the war, took the form of appeasement and after the war the form of violent opposition to the American loan.

In 1938 when the clouds were darkening Beaverbrook perversely slapped a banner at the top of his paper declaring emphatically: "This newspaper says there will be no war this year or next." Once when I asked him why he had done this he replied: "Other people can be wrong many times, but I can be wrong only once." Shortly after the war broke out I went to call on him at his house in the country and found him in the garden, in a black coat and hat, cutting roses. "It's a terrible mistake," he said solemnly. "If it were in my power to stop this war I would."

It is some tribute to both Beaverbrook's personality and ability that Churchill, who so deeply resented anyone who had not seen eye to eye with him, was able to forgive Beaverbrook and make him Minister of Aircraft Production in 1941. But Beaverbrook had no reason to thank Winston for in doing the job as magnificently as he did he performed a great national service. Indeed when history is written it will probably be for this, and not his journalism, that he will be remembered.

Beaverbrook has always suffered from asthma and two years ago announced that he was retiring and leaving England for a sunnier climate. But he has announced his retirement before and always returns. Since his farewell he has been back several times, and those who know him best say he will be back again. Beaverbrook's motto is: "Things for me, not me for things."

Like Lord Beaverbrook, the Berry Brothers, Lord Camrose and Lord Kemsley, are self-made men. Shortly before Lord Northcliffe died in 1922 he wrote: "The Berrys are buying up Fleet Street and its environs. . . . There are alarming rumours of a tremendously rich Berry somewhere down in Wales. Perhaps he is the gentleman who is constantly offering, through a firm of well-known lawyers, ten million pounds to buy my control of certain newspapers. I wonder!"

The "rich Berry" was Seymour, later Lord Buckland, who made a fortune out of coal and steel and died when he was only fifty. But he never attempted to buy Lord Northcliffe's newspapers or, for that matter, was never interested in his brothers' newspapers. His activities were confined to industry, while his two brothers built up independently what the *Encyclopaedia Britannica* described as the largest newspaper holding in the world. Together they controlled three national newspapers, eleven provincial papers, and over a hundred obscure but profitable magazines.

The Berrys were born in a coal-mining town in Wales of lower-middle-class parents. Their father, John Mathias Berry, was a strong nonconformist who regarded public service as a duty. For many years he was an alderman and once mayor of Merthyr Tydfyl. He followed national affairs closely and was such a stanch admirer of the great Gladstone that he named Camrose "William Ewart." He must have been a man of unusual quality to send three sons into the world all of whom won fame and fortune before the age of forty.

Although Camrose was associated with many of Buckland's enterprises he was not, as his detractors like to pretend, a rich man who took up newspapers as a hobby. He has been interested in newspapers all his life, and his success is due not only to his shrewd business sense but to his talent and perspicacity as a journalist. He began as a reporter on the local Merthyr *Times* when he was only fourteen. The paper was edited by W. W. Hadley, whom he later repaid by appointing editor of the *Sunday Times*.

Camrose came to London when he was eighteen and after working for three years on various newspapers founded his own publication, the *Advertising World*. He took his younger brother Kemsley into partnership and in 1915 they purchased their first important newspaper, the *Sunday Times*.

This marked the beginning of the Berrys' rise. During the next thirteen years they "bought up Fleet Street," acquiring most of their newspapers from Lord Rothermere, and the prize, the *Daily Telegraph*, from Lord Burnham. They jointly ran the controlling company, Allied Newspapers, until 1937 when they decided to divide their property. Camrose took the *Telegraph*, the *Financial Times*, and the *Amalgamated Press*, with its group of magazines, while Kemsley retained the *Sunday Times*, the *Daily* and *Sunday Graphic*, and the provincial papers.

Lord Camrose is undoubtedly the most respected of all newspaper proprietors. He has the reputation of treating his employees better than any man on Fleet Street as far as high wages, secure jobs, and good pensions are concerned. He is a strange mixture of reserve and sociability, for although few people know him intimately many people have enjoyed his hospitality, which has always been generous. He lives in a house an hour from London which was occupied for many years by the late Lord Curzon. Although he is nearly seventy he considers a ten-mile walk normal exercise.

Hard-working and hardheaded, he has made a success of every newspaper he has touched. He raised the circulation of the *Sunday Times* from 30,000 to 263,000, and at the present time the *Daily Telegraph*, with a sale of nearly a million copies a day, has the largest circulation of any quality paper in the world. It is immensely respectable, immensely conservative, and the favorite of the upper middle classes. Although its prestige is not so great as that of the *Times* and the *Manchester Guar-*

dian, its circulation is almost three times as large as both put together.

While Lord Camrose has concentrated on quality Lord Kemsley has gone in for quantity. He controls more newspapers than any other man in Britain, but except for the *Sunday Times*, which was built up by Camrose and edited by William Hadley, a charming old man who at the age of eighty-three still goes to the office, none of his papers exercise much influence or are particularly distinguished. The answer is that Kemsley is a businessman and not a journalist. His political views are so strongly conservative he often makes Camrose look like a Liberal. His London papers are the tabloid *Daily* and *Sunday Graphic* and the *Sunday Times*, which although it has a circulation in excess of its rival the *Sunday Observer* has not the same reputation for impartiality.

Kemsley is kindhearted and generous. He gave me my first job, for which I will always be grateful and during the three years I worked for him allowed me the widest scope as a roving correspondent. Some of his colleagues, however, consider it unfortunate that he decided to introduce a personal note into his newspaper ownership by slapping a banner at the top of his many papers saying: "A Kemsley Newspaper." This contributed more than any other single act in raising a cry against press monopolies. Today he has the dubious distinction of being the most criticized of all the lords of Fleet Street.

Lord Rothermere, Lord Layton, and Lord Astor have certain qualities in common; they are amiable, modest, philosophic, and liberal-minded. This may seem a strange assertion in view of the fact that Rothermere's *Daily Mail*, *Evening News*, and *Sunday Dispatch* are all highly conservative papers. But the truth is that if it were not for the goadings of his friends, Rothermere would probably adopt a far less partisan attitude, for he has no political aspirations himself and is less interested in the editorial than the financial side of his papers. As a businessman he is astute and enterprising. Since the war he has succeeded in strengthening his control of the *Daily Mail*, which was left in a somewhat fluid financial state upon his father's death in 1940. Although Rothermere is the youngest of the press lords he has been chairman of the Newspaper Proprietors Association since 1934.

Lord Layton is not the owner of the *News Chronicle* but he controls the policy. The paper belongs to the Cadbury family, who made a fortune out of cocoa, and is the only Liberal paper to circulate nationally. During a long life it has swallowed up three other Liberal dailies: the *Daily News*, which began its life under the editorship of Charles Dickens, the *Morning Leader*, and the *Westminster Gazette*. After the general election of 1945 British Liberals were in a strange predicament for they had only a skeleton of a party and a skeleton of a policy. They were divided as to which direction they should throw their support and some gave it to the Conservatives and others to the Socialists. The *News Chronicle* was one of the latter, and during the last four years has backed up many Labor measures. As a result Lord Layton, who represents the Cadburys as business and editorial chief, is the only newspaper controller to be raised to the peerage under the present government.

Lord Astor, a brother of Colonel J. J. Astor and the husband of Lady Astor, owns the Sunday *Observer*, which has less circulation but more prestige than any other Sunday paper. His son David, a Liberal, is the working editor and is allowed a free hand.

Three more newspaper controllers who are often referred to as the "future press lords" are H. G. Bartholomew, Harold Aldridge, and A. G. Cousins. All of them have become chairmen of the controlling companies since the end of the war, and the papers they run boast the largest circulation of any three newspapers in the world. Bartholomew, a man of sixty-eight, is responsible for the sensational, provocative, pro-Labor tabloid, the *Daily Mirror*, whose circulation of over four million is a few hundred thousand higher than the *Daily Express*. Aldridge is chairman of the Sunday *News of the World*, which even leaves some of America's top-selling magazines such as *Life* far behind with a circulation estimated at well over eight million a week. This paper is nonpolitical and highly sensational, specializing in police-court cases. The mechanics of printing so many copies is no small feat for it works out at an average of ten thousand copies every minute of every hour of every day of the week. Although Cousins' Sunday paper, the *People*, is a long way behind the *News of the World*, its circulation of over four and a half million is the second largest in the world. It is owned by Odhams Ltd., of which Cousins became chairman when Lord Southwood died in 1946. This company also prints the Labor party's *Daily Herald* with the understanding that the trade unions shall control the policy.

The most modest and unassuming of all newspaper proprietors, Colonel the Honorable J. J. Astor, is the owner of the most powerful and respected of all newspapers, the *Times*. It is the only daily paper to cost threepence, to devote its front page to advertisements, to keep its news reports and articles unsigned, to be directed by an independent working editor. It has less circulation and more influence than any other national paper in Britain, and more national prestige than any other paper in the world. It is, in fact, an institution.

The *Times* thinks of itself as the Voice of Britain and as a result has worked itself into a curious position vis-à-vis political affairs. It tends to support the government of the day as the expression of the people's will, but at the same time manages to remain aloof from party politics in the narrow sense. For instance, it refused to take sides in the critical general election of 1945 but viewed the struggle with an Olympian detachment; and although today it favors many government measures it is highly critical of many others, including the Iron and Steel Bill. It is in the enviable position of having its cake and eating it too, and with this unique advantage delivers its pronouncements with the authority of an oracle.

The prestige of the *Times* has been built up by detail and reliability. It carries fuller parliamentary, law, and foreign reports than any other paper, and so great is its reputation for accuracy a wit once remarked: "A *Times* report is considered correct until the opposite is proved." The *Times* is never in a hurry; it would rather be a day late with the news than report the news wrongly. Every fact and place name is carefully checked and great efforts are made to achieve impartiality. Even though it pays its correspondents and special writers far less generously than the *Daily Telegraph* does, the distinction of working for the *Times* consistently attracts men of the highest academic honors.

Because of its virtues the *Times* has easier access to government departments than any other paper. Indeed, few politicians from the Prime Minister down would deny its editor an appointment if he urgently requested it, and as a result it is so well informed its pronouncements are carefully studied by foreign governments and often interpreted as "official." In Britain itself it is read not only by every man and woman who takes an interest in world affairs but by most members of the upper class; a census taken before the war revealed that half its subscribers had incomes of over £5,000 ($20,000) a year.

But the *Times* is not only famous for its news coverage. The front page, that often astonishes Americans with its columns of closely printed notices, is almost indispensable to the smooth working of the nation. It covers everything from announcements of bankruptcy to reunion dinners, vacant posts for university professors to stamp collection sales, naturalization statements to pleas for charity donations. It also includes announcements of Births, Deaths and Marriages, sometimes referred to as the "Hatches, Matches and Despatches column." This institution saves people endless time and trouble; instead of having to write hundreds of personal letters, an insertion in the *Times*, at a cost of 5 guineas (about $21), serves the same purpose and is socially acceptable.*

In an inside page the *Times* publishes a Court Circular with a number of paragraphs reporting the doings of the royal family from christening ships to attending divine service. Beneath this a small space is reserved for people of social or political prom-

---

* The *Daily Telegraph* runs even more classified advertisements than the *Times*.

inence. Although the language is tremendously dignified they are also often surprisingly intimate. You may see an announcement that Lord X is recovering from his operation and wishes to thank people for their flowers, or that Lady Z has sold her house and is now at such an address with such a telephone number. The *Times* is even famous for its Domestic Help column and its crossword puzzle, but above all else for its correspondence.

"Letters to the *Times*" are written by the most illustrious people in the land. They range in subject from criticisms of Conservative policy to discussions on Pain in Childbirth. And since everybody of importance reads this column these letters are often as effective in stirring up public opinion as a speech in the House of Commons.

During its long life, the *Times* has had only six owners, four of whom were members of the same family, and nine editors. It was founded in 1785 by a coal merchant named John Walter who took up printing as a hobby and wished to demonstrate a new process. However, in the eighteenth century journalism was faced with both economic and legal hazards. The government feared the press and controlled it by severe libel laws and an almost prohibitive newspaper tax. Although John Walter declared that in the *Times* there would be "no concealing the native deformity of vice" he was soon obliged, like most other papers, to either become a political hireling or go out of business. When the Pitt administration offered him £300 ($1,200) a year to oppose the Prince of Wales's claim to unlimited power as Regent, he accepted it. But he performed his obligations so zealously he brought the wrath of the royal dukes upon his head and was sentenced to a fine of £250 ($1,000), an hour in the pillory at Charing Cross, and two years at the felons' prison at Newgate, a sentence of which he served sixteen months.

This dimmed his enthusiasm for journalism, and the paper's rise to eminence did not begin until John Walter II took control in 1803, followed in the middle of the century by John Walter III. Under this ownership and under the editorships of Barnes, Delane, Chenery, and Buckle, the distinguished biographer of

Disraeli, the *Times* became a power. It boasted the fastest communications and the most modern presses; it was the first paper to introduce war correspondence and to devote space to book reviews, art, music, and dramatic criticism. In 1877 Bulwer-Lytton wrote that if he were asked to leave a memorial to contemporary civilization he would choose not docks, railways, or public buildings, but a file of the *Times*.

In the beginning of the present century, however, the paper fell into difficult straits. Bad management resulted in a lack of capital necessary for re-equipment in the face of the rising competition of the popular papers with their huge revenues, and an unfortunate law suit between members of the Walter family finally brought it on the market a few years before World War I. In 1912 the people of Britain learned with shocked dismay that the czar of the penny press, Lord Northcliffe, was the owner. But even under the impact of this powerful personality the policy changed little, and when Northcliffe died in 1922 and it was again for sale, it possessed modern machinery and was a thoroughly sound financial proposition. This time nine-tenths of the shares were acquired by Colonel Astor while the other tenth went to John Walter, a great-grandson of the original founder. These two are the present owners. And to protect the *Times* from ever again falling into undesirable hands a committee of five trustees has been set up without whose consent none of the controlling shares may be transferred. They are: the Lord Chief Justice of England, the Warden of All Souls College, Oxford, the President of the Royal Society, the President of the Institute of Chartered Accountants, and the Governor of the Bank of England.

Today in spite of the small salaries the *Times* pays it is as big a money-maker as the *Daily Telegraph*. It is edited by a charming Irishman, W. F. Casey, a graduate of Trinity College, Dublin, who has been on the paper for over thirty years. Colonel Astor never interferes with the policy. He is a shy, retiring man who lost a leg in the First World War and for many years was a Conservative M.P. Although he is a member of the Newspaper Proprietors Association, he rarely appears at public functions and spends most of his time at his country house, Heber Castle. He controls the *Times* as a public duty and guards it as a great institution.

Americans who visit Britain often complain that the newspapers do not print any news. Even though their size is limited to six pages because imported newsprint requires foreign currency which the government cannot afford, a high percentage of space is devoted to crime, sports, features, comic strips, and special articles. The only three daily papers which make an effort to be truly informative on current affairs are the *Times*, the *Daily Telegraph*, and the *Manchester Guardian*, which, although a provincial paper in the strict sense of the word, has a national reputation and circulates in London.

Despite the fact that Conservative proprietors have persistently attacked the government for not allowing the importation of more newsprint, accusing it of attempting to suppress freedom of speech, the dearth of news is not merely due to a paper shortage. It lies fundamentally in the character and function of the British press. Because newspapers circulate nationally and on a huge scale they are unsurpassable as an advertising medium and as such have monopolized the field; and for this reason weekly and monthly magazines, which in America are the only national medium aside from the radio, have never been able to gain a real footing. This is illustrated by the fact that whereas in America there are dozens of magazines with a circulation of over a million in Britain there are only six. The popular press therefore tends to fulfill the role of both newspaper and magazine. The importance attached to providing the public with light material was recently shown when papers were allowed to expand from four to six pages three times a week, and most editors devoted the increased space to features rather than news; the steadily rising sales of the popular papers can leave no doubt that this is what their readers want.

While the Conservatives are busy attacking the Socialists over newsprint, the Socialists are busy attacking the Conservatives over their presentation of news. Ever since the Labor government came into office there has been an agitation against the press led by Socialist M.P.'s who claim that few papers make any attempt to achieve impartiality. No one will deny that there is truth in this charge, but the Socialists are scarcely in a position to make it since the Labor paper, the *Daily Herald*, is perhaps the most partisan of all. Nevertheless, because of the insistence of back-benchers, in 1946 Mr. Attlee appointed a Royal Commission to investigate the matter. It consisted of twenty-one members and included a professor, a businessman, an accountant, an editor, a politician, a novelist, a trade-union leader, a lawyer, an economist, and a historian. They sat for two years and took several volumes of evidence but were not able to unearth any great scandals, or even any information that was not already public knowledge.

The truth is that, although British newspapers are partisan and opinionated, freedom of expression is not in the least endangered for between them they reflect every shade and almost every nuance of political feeling. And although today most Conservative papers are united in attacking the Labor government, it must be remembered that before the war most of them ran their own independent and often disastrous lines. Beaverbrook favored Splendid Isolation, Rothermere favored an alliance with the Axis, Kemsley favored appeasement, and Camrose favored Churchill.

What it amounts to is this: If you want to be well informed read the *Times*; if you want to be amused read the popular press; if you want a well-informed Conservative slant read the *Daily Telegraph*, a Socialist slant, the *Herald*. But if you want to know what people as a whole are thinking subscribe to three or four. This is what a great many British families do; and as a practice it is not discouraged by the lords of the press.

CHAPTER 19

The Radio: Public Enterprise

The written requirement upon the B.B.C. to be a
means of entertaining, informing and educating
the public is no stronger than the unwritten one
to be a means of raising public taste.

—SIR WILLIAM HALEY

THE British Broadcasting Corporation has its headquarters
in a large, bald, egg-shaped building at the end of Regent
Street. Once on a bus I overheard two American tourists arguing
as to whether it was a temple or a fortress, and I wondered
whether Val Myer, the architect who designed it, had tried deliberately to give it a mysterious look; for to most foreigners the
inner workings of the B.B.C are just as perplexing as its façade.
Although the B.B.C. is a public monopoly it is also an independent corporation; although it is responsible to Parliament it
is free from government interference; although its board of
overseers is appointed by the Prime Minister it is politically
nonpartisan.

The B.B.C. is a fascinating product of the British character.
It could not happen anywhere but in England. To begin with,
its finances depend on the honesty of the people. Each person
who owns a radio is on his honor to send £1 ($4.00) to the Post-
master General every year for a license.* There is no way to
enforce this regulation and yet it appears to work; it is estimated
that there are twelve million families in Britain and £11,000,000
($44,000,000) flow into the Post Office annually.

* Occasionally the Post Office sends a man around to check whether people have
licenses, but if there were widespread evasion compliance could not possibly be enforced.

Secondly, the B.B.C.'s independence is real, not mythical; it operates, undisturbed by the absence of written constitutional protection, under that famous British arrangement known as a "tacit understanding" which happily relies upon the integrity of British public men.

English broadcasting did not begin as a monopoly. It began shortly after World War I as a commercial venture on the part of manufacturers to sell radio equipment. As it became apparent that it was likely to become one of the twentieth century's greatest forces for good or evil Parliament set up a committee to study the question; and the committee advised that because of radio's "potential power over public opinion and the life of the nation" it ought to take the form of a public monopoly. At once a cry was raised. Could such a monopoly be preserved from becoming an instrument of the government? Would it be allowed the independence vital to its development? Would it remain politically impartial?

In 1925 the government appointed the Crawford Committee, of which Rudyard Kipling was a member, to study the problem and present a formula. After due deliberation, the group recommended that the B.B.C. should operate by royal charter, under the control of a Board of Commissioners appointed by the Prime Minister. "This Commission," said the report, "should enjoy the fullest liberty, wide enough to mark the serious duties laid upon it, and elastic enough to permit variation according to technical developments and changes in public taste. It would discourage enterprise and initiative, both as regards experiments and the intricate problem of programmes were the authority subject to too much control. . . . The Commissioners therefore, should be invested with the maximum freedom which Parliament is prepared to concede."

Their recommendations were acted upon and a Board of Commissioners, styled "governors," were appointed for five-year terms. Most foreigners seize upon this as conclusive proof that the B.B.C. is "government-run." You have to live in England to understand, first, that no Prime Minister would dare outrage public opinion by "loading" the Board with members of his own party and that he deliberately selects governors of mixed political views; and second, that once the governors are appointed they neither owe nor display allegiance to any one political faction.

Of the seven men and women who rule the B.B.C. today the most forceful personality is gray-haired, statuesque Lady Reading, whose dynamic energy is reputed to be second only to that of Mrs. Roosevelt. Lady Reading is the widow of the Marquis of Reading, who went to India first as a cabin boy and second as Viceroy. She is head of the Women's Voluntary Services, which during the war had over a million members; although she is not a member of any political party she is usually described as a Liberal. Another governor is thirty-five-year-old Barbara Ward, assistant editor of one of England's most famous weeklies, the *Economist*. Then there is Air Marshal Sir Geoffrey Peck, who served as chief Public Relations Officer to the Air Ministry during the war and politically is an Independent; Geoffrey Lloyd, an ex-Conservative M.P. and Minister of Fuel under Churchill; E. Whitfield, a blind musician and a Socialist; John Adamson, a chartered accountant and a Conservative; and Lord Simon, chairman of the Board, a one-time businessman, Lord Mayor of Manchester, and ex-Liberal M.P. who is now a member of the Labor party.

The governors meet at least once a fortnight and are paid £600 ($2,400) a year, except for the chairman, who receives £3,000 ($12,000). They are responsible for hiring and firing the top directors of the B.B.C. and for all decisions on policy. Although the charter lays down that it is the duty of the Corporation to run a full and impartial news service and that daily accounts of the proceedings in Parliament must be given, it leaves the arrangement of political broadcasting to the governors, merely stating that controversial subjects may be handled provided they are "distributed with scrupulous fairness." This problem has been solved by allotting a given number of hours every year for party political broadcasting, then asking the leaders of the parties to decide among themselves, on a basis of numerical representation, how much time each should have. The independence af the B.B.C. was illustrated a short while ago when it refused requests from both Attlee and Morrison for extra time on the air.

Although the B.B.C.'s instructions to broadcast strictly impartial news bulletins may seem an easy task, the public listens with supersensitive vigilance. Before the war, the slightest intonation in a news announcer's voice was sufficient to draw a flood of indignant letters accusing him of "sneering" or "rejoicing" at some event or other and revealing a left- or right-wing bias. Because of this, the B.B.C. trained its announcers to give the news in a flat, dead-pan voice that Continentals often mistake for British lack of feeling and Americans find highly comical. However, the fact that these flat voices relayed reliable and uncolored news throughout the war was what won the B.B.C. its greatest fame.

The differences that divide British and American radio stem from the fact, not that the B.B.C. is a monopoly or public-owned, but that it is noncommercial. In America the success of a program is usually measured by a single yardstick: the number of people who listen to it. In Britain the emphasis is put on quality, with the result that its lighter features suffer in comparison with those in America while its serious entertainment is undoubtedly the best in the world.

As a public service the B.B.C. is instructed to provide entertainment and information for every section of the community. It must heed the tastes of the minority as well as the majority, to appeal to the *Times* audience as well as the *Daily Mirror* audience. And it is supposed not only to entertain but to raise the level of taste. On this subject the Crawford Report commented: "We are, of course, familiar with the inevitable criticism of current propaganda. Classical music depresses one section of listeners; the jazz band exasperates a second; and a third desires greater immunity from each. . . . The listener is entitled to latitude. He must not be pressed to assimilate too much of what he calls 'highbrow' broadcast, and the Commissioners would not be wise in transmitting more educational matter than licensees are prepared to accept. At the same time every effort must be made to raise the style of performances."

At the present time the B.B.C. produces three programs: the Light Program for the masses, the Home Program for the thinking public, and the Third Program for the intellectuals. And it is this last program which has given the B.B.C. claim as a pioneer and brought a new dimension into broadcasting.

The Third Program is a university of the air, open every night from six to twelve. When it was launched in 1946 it was hailed by editorials and letters to the *Times*, and Edward Sackville-West wrote in the *New Statesman*: "The Third Programme may well become the greatest educative and civilizing force England has known since the secularization of the theatre in the 16th century," while the *Observer* declared: "The Third Programme has left the Philistine speechless, for even in those newspapers which delight to deride our serious pleasures, he has not yet uttered his barbaric yawp."

Half the program is given to music both classical and modern. During the last two and a half years it has broadcast nearly 150 complete operas, some of them relays from Milan, Vienna, Brussels, Stockholm, and Amsterdam. In the field of drama it has given plays by Shakespeare, Racine, Strindberg, Shaw, Euripides, and Aeschylus as well as modern plays including *Huis Clos* by Sartre, *The Family Reunion* by T. S. Eliot, *The Bronze Horse* by James Forsyth, *The World of Light* by Aldous Huxley, *The Devil's General* by Carl Zuckmayer.

And yet, to my mind, its most important contribution has been in its lectures and discussions, for it has not only aroused the interest of intellectuals but succeeded in making use of them. T. S. Eliot has lectured on Milton; E. M. Forster on music and criticism; G. M. Trevelyan on Roman Britain; Roy Harrod on Keynes; and America's Professor R. B. Perry on philosophy and religion. Recently Professor Butterfield of Cambridge broadcast Saturday night talks on "Christianity and History" which were the longest sustained series of lectures ever given on the radio.

The Third Program's most ambitious effort was "The Ideas

and Beliefs of the Victorians," a group of talks by eminent
people which took a year to prepare and provided the material
for eighty-three programs stretching over four months. The
explorative nature of the Third Program's work is revealed in an
account of how the idea was born, given by Harman Grisewood,
the present director.

It was some time in February 1947 that Mr. Barnes, then head of the
Programme, at an informal meeting of the talks division somewhat startled
his hearers by the unexpected announcement that he would like all the
talks in the next few months to be about the Victorians. With a view to
bringing this intention closer to a practical result he engaged the services
of a research assistant, Miss Jean Rowntree. She started work in May of
that year. Her written instructions began thus:

"We plan a number of broadcasts to take place this autumn in which
we intend to examine the assumptions of the Victorian Age, those sup
positions which were unquestionably accepted and therefore determined
action, and to appraise its ideals and reassess its controversies in view to
shedding some light on matters which puzzle us today."

The work was then divided into five headings:

1. Man's Relation to God.
2. Man's Relation to Nature.
3. Man's Relation to his Fellow Man.
4. Man's Relation to Woman.
5. Man's Relation to The State.

The talks ranged from "Evolution and Human Progress" to
"The Victorian Family," and from "The Aristocratic Idea" to
"Victorian Ideas of Sex." The men and women who took part
in the broadcasts included most of the famous names of the
intellectual world: Bertrand Russell, Lord Lindsay of Birker
G. M. Young, George Trevelyan, Lord David Cecil, G. D. H
Cole, Graham Hutton, Douglas Woodruff, Julian Huxley, Har
old Laski, E. L. Woodward, and Richard Crossman.

Among the controversial broadcasts which have aroused great
interest were a debate between the editors of a Catholic weekly
and a left-wing weekly as to whether General Franco is a force
for good or evil, and a discussion between a war correspondent

and a general as to whether General Eisenhower's *Crusade in Europe* had been fair to the British effort. The most sensational broadcast, however, was the debate between Bertrand Russell, the famous atheistic philosopher, and Father Copleston, a Catholic priest, on "The Existence of God." The controversy lasted an hour and the sensation it caused in the intellectual world is comparable to the debate in 1860 between Huxley and Wilberforce on evolution. Here was Russell, the accepted leader of progressive thought, being brought to grips by a brilliant Jesuit representing a faith which has retained its power for two thousand years. The two minds met on the common ground of logic and wrestled with each other with merciless precision, giving the listener dazzling flashes of insight as each unfolded the chain of reasoning that represented the quintessence of a lifetime of study. Several times Copleston backed Russell into a corner; and this was what made the debate so memorable, for modern doubters suddenly became acutely aware of the chinks in their armor.

The Third Program has its critics as well as its fans. Some of the newspapers have attacked it for being too "Bloomsburyish" with particular scorn heaped upon the poetry readings. But most protests have been directed at the length of its programs. Marsland Gander wrote in *Picture Post:*

It gives broadcasting a third dimension—length. But what of the fourth dimension—time? Who has the time to listen to these events in a continuum? The best thing about the Third Programme is its originality; there is nothing quite like it in the world. The worst thing is the reception which makes it available to little more than fifty percent of the country and, for many, gives Chaucer a background like frying sausages.

The not-so-bad things are its honest appeal to a minority and complete disregard for "popular taste." The not-so-good things are insincere posturing discernible in such features as "The Critic on the Air" and the heavy emphasis on academic intellectualism. . . . The leisurely presentation makes a change from the headlong breathlessness which the B.B.C. has unsuccessfully copied from America on other wave-lengths. But there is sometimes an air of sheer cussedness about it when there are gaps of five to ten minutes in the programme.

The Home and the Light programs are the regular daily service which command the bulk of Britain's listeners. The Home Program produces a good deal of music both popular and classical; a feature called "Twenty Questions"; a Saturday night theater which presents current hits; a Friday night forum which is a controversial discussion of some topic in the news. It carries the royal broadcasts, an educational series to the schools, reports on Britain's economic position, and a regular feature entitled "Window in Europe." It is a hodgepodge of entertainment and information which is designed to reflect the life of the nation.

The Light Program is the lightest and the most popular of the B.B.C.'s efforts, and the nearest thing to American radio. It began after the war as a huge nonstop music hall with jazz bands and variety shows from morning to night. However, when Britain was caught in the grip of her economic crisis in 1947, the governors decided that a serious note must be interjected. Talks were given on economics, and features entitled "The Plain Man's Guide to Music," "The Curtain-Up" series of midweek plays, and "The Woman's Hour" were introduced. A series of discussions were given by eminent men on "Atomic Energy" which consistently commanded an audience of eight million. Indeed, at the end of the year Sir William Haley, the director-general, announced triumphantly that although the variety programs had been reduced by a quarter the audiences had continued to increase.

Although no such high-powered research as America's "Hooper Ratings" exist, the B.B.C. makes a serious effort to check the success of its programs. The Listener's Research Department tests (a) the size of the audience and (b) the quality of enjoyment. It employs five hundred part-time workers each of whom interviews twelve people picked at random every day and marks down what programs they listened to the day before. These sheets are mailed in to the B.B.C. every night, which gives the Department material from which to compile a daily "Listening Barometer." Charts on the "quality of enjoyment" are prepared from weekly reports sent in by 3,600 people who volunteer to serve on the listening panel for several months at a time.

But British radio is far from perfection. There is no doubt that the public has suffered because the B.B.C. is a monopoly. Before the war the B.B.C. was slow and nonconciliatory and to many people had an unbearable air of refinement. It was under constant fire and the "fraightfully naice" young man of the B.B.C. became the delight of caricaturists. In those days dour, six-foot-seven, bushy-eyebrowed Sir John Reith was the director-general. Although Reith fiercely guarded the independence of the Corporation and clung stubbornly to the conception that the B.B.C. must remain mindful of its Artistic Purpose, he was astonishingly indifferent to public opinion. He refused to allow programs to start before ten o'clock in the morning; he refused to institute a research department to test public reaction; and because of his Scotch Presbyterian background he refused to allow popular entertainment on Sundays. Maurice Gorham, an official of the B.B.C. for twenty-one years, wrote: "Personally, I believe Reith suffered increasingly from a subconscious horror lest the listener should have too good a time. Giving pleasure to the ungodly was not amongst his objectives for the B.B.C. If they liked it too much it could not be doing its job." However, when it became apparent that millions of British people were tuning in to Radio Normandie, Luxembourg, and Athlone, the B.B.C. was forced to take stock of itself and make concessions. And this, of course, was a victory for the power of free competition.

The drawbacks of a monopoly not only are felt by the public but affect employees as well. The B.B.C. is like a large and rather mysterious club with an undercurrent of intrigue, enthusiasm, sycophancy, jealousy, earnestness, and imagination. B.B.C. officials receive salaries that correspond roughly to the civil service and are usually promoted on length of service rather than merit. All jobs are advertised and a preference is shown for university graduates. Because employees have no alternative to the B.B.C. there is always an air of frustration. After twenty years' service it takes a courageous man to resign since it means starting life anew. For the same reason officials are seldom fired, which means it is difficult not only to make the best use of talent but to get rid of incompetents as well.

These are the disadvantages of monopoly; but most British people believe they are outweighed by the advantages of being noncommercial; and since it is impossible to be noncommercial without being a monopoly the choice is the lesser of two evils. First of all, they argue, the listener is free from the tedium of advertising interruptions, and secondly he is offered a wider range of choice. In spite of the fact that commercial competition is supposed to produce variety the American program designer is tied down to providing a single mass type of entertainment that often has little appeal for a more critical if less numerous audience. And because the programs are sponsored by firms who naturally do not wish to raise any antagonism, many controversial subjects, such as arguments on religion, are banned.

Americans claim that they give the people what they want while the British give them what they think they ought to have. The British answer is that it is possible to make people want something better. In a recent lecture Sir William Haley described the three main programs as "broadly overlapping in levels and interest, each Programme leading on to the other, the listener being induced through the years increasingly to discriminate in favour of the things that are more worth-while. Each Programme at any given moment must be ahead of its public, but not so much as to lose their confidence. The listener must be led from good to better by curiosity, liking, and a growth of understanding. As the standards of the education and culture of the community rise so should the programme pyramid rise as a whole."

Great Britain is the largest overseas broadcaster in the world. It broadcasts in forty-five languages to almost every country in the world. Overseas broadcasting is paid for by a grant-in-aid sum from the government which costs about £4,000,000 ($16,-000,000) a year.

All these activities have developed within the last eleven years. The first British broadcasts in a foreign language were made in Arabic in 1938 to counter Mussolini's propaganda to the eastern Mediterranean. After Munich more services were introduced.

The clandestine role the B.B.C. played during the war has not yet been written. The hush-hush department at Bush House was in touch with agents all over the world, with prisoner-of-war camps, with leaders of the Maquis. News bulletins often contained code messages giving the time supplies were being dropped or an airplane would land to pick up an agent.

But even more important was radio's ability to project the truth beyond the barriers set up against it. All members of the governments of occupied countries and leaders of Resistance factions who were in London had free access to broadcast to their people; they were encouraged to set up their own departments inside the B.B.C. Léon Blum, a captive in Germany, described the B.B.C.: "as beautiful as a Beethoven symphony—because Frenchmen were allowed to express disagreement with the British Government."

The B.B.C. concentrated mainly on broadcasting straight, unvarnished news bulletins. No one had any idea what the size of the audience was until in 1941 a Belgian, Victor de Laveleye, decided to try and test it by suggesting to his listeners the secret marking up of the V sign. Hundreds of V's appeared in Belgium, and soon in other countries, until the sign had spread all over Europe. It was chalked up on walls, tapped out in wireless messages, flashed in lights. It was a signal not only that the audience was there but that the audience believed in victory. Indeed, B.B.C. announcers became so well known to the mass of people in Europe that when one of them, a Colonel Stevens, entered Rome with the army he was astonished to hear people shout: "Viva Roosevelt, viva Churchill, viva Colonel Stevens."

Today the B.B.C. overseas service still specializes in the news;

it also attempts to give a reflection of Britain by broadcasting comment and reaction to daily events taken from newspapers and speeches. Its policy remains the same: to inform as truthfully as possible.

The argument as to the relative merits of private and public radio will continue. Americans believe that radio should be first and foremost a means of entertainment, while the British believe that entertainment should not sacrifice quality. Whatever the answer, in the words of H. G. Wells: "Broadcasting will draw a dividing line across the whole of history."

PART VI: INDUSTRY

CHAPTER 20

The Trade Unions

Trade Union traditions are a part of the British heritage.

—VINCENT TEWSON

IT is dramatic enough that men whose childhood ended at the factory benches at the age of twelve should hold the future of an old, proud, and aristocratic country in their hands. It is even more dramatic that men who have spent their lives fighting to improve the lot of the working class should now sternly remind that class of its duty to the nation. For years the function of British trade-union leaders has been to persuade employers to pay more for their work; today it is to persuade workers to work more for their pay. Said one of these leaders: "We are in the delicate position of poacher turned gamekeeper."

Someone once complained that socialism was a creed for rich countries but only poor countries tried it. In the days when trade-union leaders were forecasting the blessings a Labor government would bring, they did not envisage that it would be called upon to steer the country through the worst economic crisis in its history. Instead of the promised millennium they had to turn around and ask their members to work longer hours, to abandon the protection of many of their restrictive practices, to accept a modified direction of labor, and in the very face of full employment, which for the first time placed trump cards in the workers' hands, to resist the temptation of pressing for higher wages. The fact that the rank and file have accepted this sweeping reversal of policy is a remarkable tribute to organized labor. But it is also a tribute to the national character, for few institutions are more British than British trade unionism. It is steeped in tradition; it is constitutional, slow, patient, and persistent.

Its history stretches back to the trade clubs of the eighteenth century composed of craftsmen who called each other "worthy brother" and held regular meetings at the local pub. Hence such names as "The Blacksmiths Arms" and "The Colliers Rest" which still decorate the English scene. Although according to old records the chief expenditure of these clubs was "cash pade for ale," unemployment benefit was instituted in the form of "tramp money" paid to members to tramp to another town in search of work.

However, it was not until the great industrial revolution began, bringing in its wake riches and poverty and booms and slumps, that the movement started to develop as a serious force. The severity of the common law reinforced by the Combination Acts which were passed at the turn of the century declaring it illegal for workers to "combine" make the early struggle sound like a modern resistance movement. The London tailors, for example, established a network of communication based on twenty houses of call which Francis Place, a member of the Parliament of the day, described as "all but a military system."

Eighty years after the Combination Acts were finally repealed in 1825 trade-union membership rose to over a million. But this was a short-lived boom which collapsed in the face of severe and unabating unemployment. In 1851 a new movement began and this time, with the improvement of economic conditions, trade unionism increased steadily in strength, reaching the million mark once again in the 1890's and continuing upward.

However, the fact that union development was always framed

by a background of chronic unemployment had an important effect on the character of the movement. It became protective rather than defiant, cautious rather than impulsive, persistent rather than revolutionary. Union leaders were always on the defensive; their only strength lay in numbers, and numbers depended on cohesion.

As a result, loyalty became the great password of British trade unionism. Men were allowed to default on other qualities but not on loyalty. And loyalty consisted not merely of supporting a leader by strike action but of accepting the outcome of his negotiations even when that outcome left much to be desired. The fact that employers knew that union representatives could, and would, keep their bargains not only added strength to the movement but gave it increasing prestige.

Today, trade-union membership is eight million strong, or two out of every five wage earners in the country. The loyalty of the rank and file to their leaders remains deep-rooted and instinctive; in many industries they are working longer hours and wages are comparatively steady. No government, whether left or right, could govern effectively without the good will of the men and women who rule this world.

These rulers control Britain's Trades Union Congress, known as the T.U.C. Although every union is autonomous most of them are voluntarily affiliated to the Congress and send delegates, one for every five thousand members, to its yearly conferences.

The T.U.C. has no direct power; it is like a federal government over a group of independent states. Its rules state vaguely and all-embracingly that its object is: "To do anything to promote the interests of all or any of its affiliated organisations or anything beneficial to the interests of past and present members of such organisations. . . . " But the fact that the T.U.C. is governed by a General Council which is elected annually by the delegates and comprises the leading trade unionists in the country means, in fact, that its authority is unquestioned; no resolution put forward by the Council has ever been defeated on the floor of the Congress, and individual unions seldom repudiate a policy acceptable to the majority.

Because of this, next to the British cabinet itself, the General Council is probably the most important body in the land. It is composed of thirty-one men and two women; all are general secretaries or presidents of their unions; together they represent 7,750,000 organized workers by hand and brain, and every industry in the country. They sit on dozens of consultative committees; they nominate representatives among themselves to serve on arbitration tribunals; they thresh out production problems with employers and labor problems with the government.

So important is their position that it is curious to reflect that most of them left school before the age of fourteen; that all of them have risen from factory benches; that many of them were on relief during the depression; that some were even imprisoned for trade-union activity. Today it would be difficult to assemble a more respectable group of citizens. When you look over the list of General Councilors for the last five years you find that many of the names carry honors awarded by the King for public service; and you even find among them a sprinkling of barons and knights.

And yet trade unionism remains more a cause than a career. Before the war Sir Walter Citrine (now Lord Citrine), the General Secretary of the Council, dominated the movement by his decisive personality, but there have never been "bosses" in the American sense. Each union is run by an elected executive committee which controls its funds. No union leader has ever accumulated more power than that given him by a voluntary following; and no union leader has ever been paid a larger salary than the equivalent of $5,000 a year, with $4,000 the average. The added work of serving on the General Council is unpaid.

Most of the Councilors live in modest houses; their wives do the cooking and their children go to the state schools. Their offices are dingy, their clothes are shabby, and they talk in the dialects of their native counties. They do not strike you as exciting or even unusual personalities; staid, sensible, hard-working are the adjectives that spring to mind. But you are impressed by the fact that they are as British as the soil they spring from; that they work as a team rather than as individuals; that character is what matters in the trade-union world.

Probably the two union leaders most in the public eye are Will Lawther and Arthur Horner, president and general secretary, respectively, of the Miners' Union. Lawther is a member of the General Council and Horner is not; Lawther is a supporter of the Labor government and Horner is not. Horner is a Communist. Although these men have offices in the same building and together control nearly three-quarters of a million miners, they do not speak to each other except on business.

Relations have been strained ever since Horner went to Paris in September 1948 as fraternal representative of the British miners; he denounced Marshall Aid as a capitalist plot and informed the Communist-led French miners, who were on strike, that they had the support and backing of their British brothers. Lawther sat in London fuming. "It is tragic," he announced to the press, "that the secretary of the mineworkers should go to France at this time to voice opinions contrary to every decision British miners have taken on policy."

But that was not all. When Horner returned Lawther called a meeting of the Executive Committee, which passed a vote of censure on Horner and issued a formal statement repudiating his attitude. It ended severely: "The Executive in disassociating itself from the unauthorised action of Mr. Horner wishes to make it plain that a recurrence of such conduct will not be tolerated." It was a humiliating rebuff but Horner did not resign; he is too valuable to the Communists where he is.

Sir Will Lawther is the first miner to become a knight, an honor he received in the 1949 New Year's List. He is big, bluff, and jolly and talks with a broad Northumbrian accent; but he is also a shrewd negotiator and can be a formidable opponent, as he demonstrated to Horner. The eldest in a miner's family of fifteen children, he started work in the pits at the age of twelve. When he was fifteen the wife of a coal manager put a

copy of Blatchford's *Merrie England* in his hands which converted him to socialism. During the national coal stoppage in
the twenties he was sent to jail for six weeks for refusing police
orders to withdraw pickets; during the depression in the thirties
he tramped the streets for eighteen months looking for a job
He educated himself at night school and possesses a surprising
collection of high-brow books ranging from Voltaire to Milton
Ruskin to Shaw, Tolstoy to the Webbs.

Lawther is proud of the fact that the miners have always been
keenly political. "Remember," he says, "that it was the miners
who took the lead over the years by their propaganda, their
money, and their sacrifices to make the Labor government pos
sible." He reminds you that they have always had more M.P.'s
in Parliament than any other union, and that he himself was
an M.P. from 1929 to 1931.

Although for twenty-two of the last twenty-five years the
miners have had more disputes per year than all other industries
put together and Lawther has led countless strikes, now that
the Labor government is in office no trade-union leader is more
opposed to stoppages than he. "Unofficial strikes? They're trea
son . . . that's what they are today," he declares.

When the mines were nationalized in 1946 Lawther turned
down a £5,000-a-year job ($20,000) as a member of the Coal
Board because he thought the salary was too high. He also
turned down a knighthood. But in 1949 when there were rumors
that the honor had been offered to him again, a friend asked him
if he was prepared to change his mind. "Perhaps," grinned Law
ther. "After all, I wouldn't like to miss the chance of making
the missis a lady. . . . "

In spite of his horn-rimmed spectacles, Arthur Horner bears
a remarkable resemblance to Lord Beaverbrook, and he has the
same puckish charm. He is unique among trade-union leaders
because he does not fit into the pattern. He is neither staid
orthodox, nor dependable. In his office there is a bust of Lenin
"I have always been a Communist," he announces flatly, "and
I shall remain a Communist until I die."

When Horner was elected in 1946 to the life position of general secretary to the Miners' Union, the press ran the news in headlines. Was this a Kremlin plot to strangle British recovery and spread communism through the usual channels of disaffection? People waited for Horner to strike but they waited in vain, for the T.U.C. took action first. By a series of skillful maneuvers it has driven him into a corner which allows him little elbow room. First, there was the rebuff from Lawther over his Paris expedition; second, the rebuff from the Congress over his attempt to gain a place on the Council; third, the rebuff from the Council itself, which made a public statement castigating Communist activities inside the movement and promised to investigate and take suitable action against culprits.

Arthur Horner was born in Wales, the son of a railwayman and grandson of a miner who was killed in the Merthyr Tydvil pits. Before he was twenty he had been a baker's assistant, a boxer, a Baptist lay preacher, and a member of the Irish Republican Army. Then he became a miner and a Marxist.

During World War I he was imprisoned twice, once for refusing to wear the King's uniform and once for inciting volunteers to rebel against taking part in the counterrevolution against Russia. And when the 1926 general strike took place he was imprisoned a third time for "riotous assembly."

Horner has all the Celtic fire and eloquence associated with the Welsh and an admirer once described him as possessing "the oratorical ability of a K.C. and the organizing ability of a general." But during the last four years the British workers' attitude toward Russia has hardened and consequently Horner's influence has declined. Would his miners back him up if it came to a showdown with the T.U.C.? Horner evidently thinks not, for a short while ago the *Times* quoted him as saying: "If I lose my position, well, I don't care. There are other things more important. . . . "

There are only two women on the General Council and both were factory workers at twelve and orphans at sixteen. One of them, Dame Anne Laughlin, is the only woman in the world to lead a big trade union. She stood as candidate for the general secretaryship of the Garment Workers in 1948 and polled nearly as many votes as her five male competitors put together. She was described sentimentally by one paper as "five-foot-one of laughing seriousness."

An attractive woman in her fifties, well groomed with varnished fingernails and carefully brushed hair, Dame Anne might be the editor of a successful woman's magazine or a high-salaried dress buyer. Instead she has spent the last thirty years of her life organizing, agitating, and negotiating on behalf of low-paid workers. She grew up in a dull, gray Yorkshire town with rows of factory houses exactly alike and led a strike before she was sixteen. She believes workers must be given more participation in the management of industry but must also be made to realize that rights carry with them responsibilities. When you ask her why she stood for the general secretaryship of her union on only a few weeks' notice she replies bluntly: "Because I was afraid the Communists might get it."

She was the first woman to serve as chairman of a T.U.C. conference and the first factory worker to be made a dame. She hesitated before accepting the honor because it was "a title" but finally said: "Somebody has to be the first in something. I shall not be the last."

Florence Hancock, the chief woman officer of the world's largest union, the Transport and General Workers, is a pleasant woman in her fifties who looks as though she ought to be baking cakes and scrubbing children's faces. But her skill in steering the Trades Union Congress of 1948 through the conference that accepted the government's wages policy left no doubt as to her ability. And she did not mince her words about communism. "We must rid our movement of these mischief mongers," she stated sharply.

She began work nearly forty-five years ago as a kitchenmaid for three shillings a week, then went into a condensed-milk factory where, by working overtime, she trebled the amount. One of fourteen children, she was desperately poor and recalls the sensation in the family circle when she suggested keeping three-pence a week for pocket money. Her father was a woolen weaver and once took her twenty miles to hear Lloyd George address a meeting. She remembers the latter saying: "To deceive is always contemptible, but to deceive the poor is the meanest trick of all."

Although as a trade unionist she has led strikes, been victimized and fired, "agitator" is almost the last word you would apply to her. Karl Marx shocks her. Her socialism is mixed up with Sunday school and doing good deeds, and she believes the emphasis should be on how much the individual can give the state, not on how much the state can give the individual.

There are many other important trade unionists; gray-haired Lincoln Evans, leader of the iron and steel workers, and heavy-built Arthur Deakin, leader of the Transport and General Workers; Sir Mark Hodson, boilermaker, and Jack Tanner, engineer; ship's steward Yates, tailor Conley, postman Geddes, ticket collector Figgins, shop assistant Burrows, and the Cockney ex-bus driver, Communist Bert Papworth, who is known as "the man everybody likes but no one follows."

These are the men and women who make the T.U.C. what it is. And what it is, according to cartoonist Low, is a nice old horse. A writer in the Sunday *Observer* recently described this animal as "the horse which has never grown up and is always pulling the cart before itself or taking a quiet nap between the shafts. Certainly the T.U.C. can be exasperating to the unsympathetic outsider: it takes its time and never does today what it may not have to do tomorrow. But there is an answer. The T.U.C. has been traveling the same road for a long time now and has found that it always leads to the stable . . . and a little more hay."

Today the horse sense of the T.U.C. has led it away from the exclusive pasture marked "Wage Negotiation" into the wider field of national recovery. No postwar British government could overcome its complicated economic difficulties without a joint effort on the part of management and labor. Although as far back as the days of Lloyd George in the First World War trade-union leaders were called in to advise the government, consultations were not regular and there were no permanent channels of approach until the beginning of World War II.

The consultative machinery that was set up then has grown today into a network of boards and committees which almost constitute a world within a world; trade unionists now meet both employers and government officials regularly and are pledged (a) to actively assist in raising production and (b) to smooth labor relations so that production will not suffer through strikes.

The central committee which deals with industrial output meets every month under the chairmanship of Sir Stafford Cripps and is known as the "N.P.A.C.I."* It is composed of seven employers and seven trade-union leaders and often attended by as many as ten ministers of the Crown. It first came into being in 1940 to co-ordinate the government's industrial war effort; and as in those days it was feared that a German invasion might succeed in cutting off the central government from various parts of the country, Britain was divided into autonomous regions capable of operating on their own. Local industrial boards, again composed of employers and trade unionists, were established in these defense regions, functioning under the central authority of the N.P.A.C.I.

Today these eleven regional boards still exist. Although some of their authority has been curtailed they wield a good deal of power. For instance, they were in charge of allocating all coal supplies during the crisis of 1947; and today they deal with anything from staggering factory hours to take the electricity load off the peak, to speeding up the turn-around of railway cars. They explain government policy to the workers and management policy to the government. And the fact that the chairmen of the boards have direct access to Sir Stafford Cripps, as well

* National Production Advisory Council of Industry.

as serving as members of the N.J.A.C.,* gives them the opportunity of making their views known at the highest level.

The N.J.A.C. was set up as a wartime institution but its work proved so valuable it has continued ever since. And it was this committee that urged the government to keep the Arbitration Order of 1940 in operation.

The order is an interesting example of the elasticity of British methods; it is one of those arrangements which do not strike the English as odd but perplex outsiders. It makes arbitration compulsory. It declares that if the negotiating machinery of a union is unable to settle a dispute, it must be referred to the Minister of Labor, and if the Minister of Labor is unable to settle it he must refer it, within twenty-one days, to the Arbitration Tribunal. After hearing both sides of the case, the Tribunal gives a decision which must be accepted as binding.

Here is where the complications set in. By law, workers who disregard the order and persist in striking can be prosecuted; but since, in actual fact, it is impossible to take action against them, they never are. Strikes, therefore, are merely branded as "unofficial"; yet the outcry from both union officials and the general public is usually loud enough to insure that the workers at least suffer a guilty conscience. A further curiosity is the fact that the order remains in operation not by the primary wish of the government but by the express desire of both employers and trade unionists; if either side asks for its withdrawal the Minister of Labor will rescind it at once. Or, in other words, it exists by that popular British arrangement known as "a tacit understanding."

During the last eight years the tribunal has settled over twelve hundred disputes. One day I attended a hearing of a wage claim put forward by the workers of the tobacco industry. The session was held in a large modern room with a U-shaped table. At the top sat the five judges, on one side the twenty or thirty men representing the tobacco employers, and on the other side an equal number of trade unionists.

* National Joint Advisory Council.

The judges were men of distinction. Lord Terrington, a former barrister, was in the chair. Sir Francis Floud, a retired civil servant, and Professor Shimmin, the professor of industrial relations at Leeds University, were on either side of him, and next to them Mr. Cockcroft, a businessman, and Mr. Conley, a trade unionist.

The hearing took only an hour. A professional lawyer argued the employers' case, claiming that the minimum wage in the tobacco industry compared favorably with the minimum wage in other industries, and insisting that any increase would be incompatible with the government's policy of keeping wages steady. Then a trade unionist rose and gave the workers' case. He was not so fluent as the lawyer but spoke with greater force. He insisted that when the tobacco workers had negotiated a wage increase the previous year the employers had promised that if the cost of living continued to rise the position would be reviewed in six months' time. He put forward statistics showing that the present wage was insufficient to meet present-day costs.

As one sat in the room listening to the immensely polite, quiet and dignified proceedings one felt that here was the pattern of sanity that might one day prevail over a world torn to pieces by the conflict between labor and ownership.

When the hearing was over the judges went into conference but their findings were not published for several weeks. In this instance they awarded the workers a five-shilling weekly increase, which amounted to about 25 percent of the total claim put forward. As in most things, the solution was a compromise.

When English people describe their trade unions as "conservative" they do not mean what most Americans think they mean. Before the war A. J. Cummings wrote in the *News-Chronicle* that he would rather rely on Sir Walter Citrine, "arch-priest of British Trade Unionism, than on Mr. Baldwin, the Conservative Prime Minister, to keep the present system intact." He went on to say: "There is today no Toryism more fearful and immovable than that which is enshrined in the ideals and practices of trade union leadership." In *Inside Eu-*

rope John Gunther quoted this remark, describing the unions
as a "great conservative force" and adding that the last thing
most of them wanted was "socialism in our time."

It is easy to see how he fell into this error for the English
use of "conservative" in connection with the unions would be
more aptly replaced by "constitutional." Trade-union leaders
are stanch supporters of church, crown, and state; they subscribe
to evolution, not revolution; they believe in democratic means
and democratic ends. But the fact remains that they also believe
in social change; that most of them are leaders of unions actively pledged to further socialism; that no British union has
ever officially supported the Tory party.

This is a striking contrast to the partisanship of the American
unions, which equally endorse Republican and Democratic candidates depending on their immediate policies. This difference
has arisen in the last fifty years. Before 1900 British unions were
not committed to changing a system but, like the American
unions today, were concerned solely with securing better wages
and conditions. During the latter part of the nineteenth century
they backed the Liberal party to further their aims. But when
the Liberals refused to accept workingmen as parliamentary
candidates they formed their own party to secure representatives
in the Commons; the Labor party did not embrace socialism
until 1918.

Each union decides independently whether or not it wishes
to support the party. Under an act passed in 1913 political
funds may not be collected unless a ballot is taken among the
members and 75 percent of the votes are in favor of it. Today
nearly all the unions affiliated with the T.U.C. are also affiliated
with the Labor party. But this does not mean that all the union
members necessarily vote the Labor ticket. Even though a union
has committed itself by a large majority, individuals who do
not want to pay the political levy have the right to "contract
out." Out of the 7,500,000 members in unions affiliated to the
Labor party, 4,500,000 pay the levy.

It is a curious fact that although the Labor party is the child
of the trade unions only four unions out of those who are po-

litically active pledge their allegiance to it in their "Rules." The rest emphasize socialism in a variety of forms: co-operativism, nationalization, syndicalism—all methods of giving the worker more participation and control of industry. When I pointed this out to a trade-union leader he replied that the unions were more interested in principles than parties. "If the Labor party failed to carry out its nationalization pledges we could not continue to support it," he said.

This remark presents a thoroughly English paradox since the Labor party is dominated by trade-union membership and is largely dependent upon trade-union finance. The explanation is that the majority of Labor members of Parliament are not workingmen but from the middle class. Although it may be difficult to convince Americans that those who hold the purse strings do not always call the tune, in this case it is true. Intellectually the unions are dominated by such men as Cripps, Morrison, and Attlee. However, it would be foolish to pretend that the T.U.C. does not carry great influence. It is likely, for instance, that the nationalization of steel might have been postponed if the unions had not urged it for so many years.

The fact that British trade unions believe in nationalization would not incline most Americans to describe them as "conservative." But in the Labor party "conservative" is used to imply an attitude of mind rather than a declaration of policy. Trade unionists want change but they want it to be slow and sure; they believe that means are as important as ends, and above all that democracy comes first.

The Communists, therefore, regard the unions as the archpriests of reaction. Because they support the government in the present economic crisis and are asking the workers to work longer hours and not to press for higher wages which will only cause inflation while goods are in short supply, the Communists denounce them as "disloyal wreckers." After the T.U.C. conference in 1948 Communist leaders declared that the General Council's analysis of the economic position was a "criminal deception of the movement," adding that it stood for "the sanctity of profits, the forgoing of wage demands, war on militant trade unionists, disruption of international unity and dependence on the American colossus of Big Business."

The General Council listened to the Communist attacks in silence, then five months later declared open war on them. They sent out a circular warning the unions of the dangers of infiltration and asking them to consider the problems of routing out Communists from committees which they were using purely for subversive activities. They announced that a thorough investigation would take place and information on Communist methods would be sent to all unions. The statement declared: "Interference by the Communist Party in the domestic affairs of affiliated unions has been constant for many years, and that conspirational work has grown. Their presumption to shape policy outside the machinery by which the Communist Party seeks to direct the policy and activities of their Unions. The General Council propose to issue material which will give further information on the working of this machinery and the evil consequences of Communist interference in Trade Union affairs. . . . They are determined that notwithstanding the smoke screen of falsehood and vilification directed against them and members of Union Executives and delegates to Congress, this issue will be fought out. . . ."

If the Conservatives returned to office, the trade-union consultative committees would continue to operate as they do under the Labor government. But psychologically there would be a change. The present harmonious relationship would undoubtedly harden into the old bargain-driving atmosphere of labor versus management. Some union leaders declare this would make their position easier than it is now. "At least," they say, "we would know where we were." And that, of course, would be back to the prewar role of negotiating for workers' improvements through the traditional channels of union machinery.

Today, with their own Labor government in power, many trade unionists feel uncertain of their ground. And as socialism

develops, the future role of union leaders becomes a complicated speculation. Can they support the Labor government on
the one hand and lead strikes against government-controlled industries on the other? And what will remain of their protective
function under a government which is carrying out a policy of
full employment and has guaranteed a minimum standard of
living by its social insurance scheme?

Under Socialism the role of the union leader as the old-fashioned, tub-thumping revolutionary is finished. But even though
he has achieved many of his aims through the legislation of the
Labor government he will always serve as the worker's spokesman and even in nationalized industries fight for wage increases
whenever he thinks them justified.

Nevertheless, his scope is widening and now he is confronted
with the new and fascinating problem of bridging the gap which
has always existed between British management and British
labor, or in other words of educating the worker to the responsibility of ownership. In America there is always a continuous
flow of workers moving up into managerial positions, but in
England if a workman is outstanding he usually achieves eminence as a trade unionist. Indeed there is such a sharp division
between the two worlds that most workers regard it almost as
"betrayal" to move into the managerial camp; this has been frequently illustrated in the last few years by the fact that so
many union leaders have refused to accept jobs on the government's nationalized boards.

But there is still another and even more important task to
be faced. As the federation of Europe develops in the next fifty
years, union leaders all over the world will have to overcome
strong prejudices and educate their people to work on equal and
friendly terms with foreigners. If the British trade-union movement takes the lead in breaking down the barriers and succeeds
in extending its own honest, sensible, and thoroughly democratic organization to other countries, it will have done the most
important work of its history.

Big Business

Well, fancy giving money to the Government!
Might as well have put it down the drain
Fancy giving money to the Government!
Nobody will see the stuff again
Well, they've no idea what money's for—
Ten to one they'll start another war
I've heard a lot of silly things, but Lor'
Fancy giving money to the Government.
                                    —A. P. HERBERT

Shortly before his death in 1944 Samuel Courtauld, the head of the great rayon firm, wrote: "An industrial career is now a *métier* and not merely a road to private acquisition." At the time, people were not sure what he was talking about but today the meaning has become clearer. Because of taxation, no British industrialist has an income over £5,000 ($20,000) a year, and yet industry is set at high pressure and Britain is producing more goods than she did before the war. The explanation may be straight patriotism but one is tempted to draw the conclusion that businessmen, like scientists, writers, professors, and other people do work not only for money but partly because they like it.

This is an idea which most industrialists would repudiate indignantly. Britain is working at full capacity, they say, because of a sellers' market; the trouble will come when business begins to slack off, for men will not take the risks involved in starting new enterprises unless they are offered greater incentives. Oliver Lyttelton, the chairman of the Associated Electrical Industries,

265

who sits on the Conservative front bench in the House of Commons, recently stressed this point of view:

"We have a number of engineers in our company who, by their brilliance and technical skill, have earned the maximum income which they are allowed to retain by the age of 35. There are higher responsibilities and greater anxieties in front of them, but not a penny more pay. We are bringing up a generation who are going to say when offered promotion. "Promotion! Move from Rugby or Warwickshire up to London, with a higher scale of living and wider responsibilities, and nearer the boss, without any extra pay? Promotion! Thank you for nothing. I will stay where I am." I only ask hon. members whether they think that is the way of carrying out the rather bombast sentence in the Economic Survey—

"Our recovery will never be complete unless we can develop a keen and adventurous spirit in management. . . ."

In the meantime many Americans regard the English businessmen's plight with a mixture of self-satisfaction and pity. In 1947 *Fortune* wrote:

In the U.S. the game is played in much the same old way, the stakes and rewards as high as ever, and plenty of chance for a skilled loser to rise again. Outside in the gloomy world of reality, the game has been shackled by controls, hamstrung by shortages, and has degenerated into little more than a struggle with umpires. . . . Lever Brothers and Unilever, the largest corporations outside the U.S. and one of the half-dozen largest in the world, knows the difference very well. One of its hundreds of subsidiaries is Lever Brothers of Boston, and the difference between the way business can be run and rewarded in the U.S. and most places is hinted by the fact that Charles Luckman the U.S. Company's President is paid more than a third as much as the twenty top men in London's Unilever House together.

And yet, despite the controls and despite the rigid curtailment of profits, industry has done well, a fact which has surprised no section of the country more than the industrialists themselves. When the Labor government came into office the businessmen were its loudest critics and most formidable opponents. Although they were well represented on the Conservative benches they did not leave it to the politicians to express their disapproval. At almost every public function they proclaimed that the government was leading the country to ruin, in words that had the familiar ring of Wall Street's opposition to the New

Deal. High taxation, they said, was destroying initiative, and restrictions and interference were stifling production; and both together would bring the nation to bankruptcy.

However, Britain's position was so dangerous there was no alternative but to co-operate. They went to work and worked hard. "Whether we agree or disagree with the policies being pursued," said Hanbury-Williams, the chairman of Courtauld's, "our ultimate salvation can be achieved only by hard plodding work on the part of all, by continuing to deny ourselves many of the things we would like to have and, above all, by collaborating with the spirit of good will and the understanding of other people's problems." But at the same time that they co-operated, their annual company reports went on prophesying disaster.

The fact that these prophecies have been proved wholly wrong has crystallized a change of attitude which has been evolving for some time. Today, government control is no longer regarded as Socialist dogma but has gradually become accepted throughout the business world as vital necessity. Even Conservative politicians have repeatedly emphasized that if they return to power strong central direction must stay.

Although this new conception is almost as much a revolution in the thinking of the businessman as what has taken place in the minds of the workers, it does not spring from socialism but from the fact that Britain has the oldest industrial history in the world. And it explains the fundamental difference in the outlook between Britain and the United States. Whereas America is still expanding and there is still room for the pioneer, Britain has been fully developed for many years. This means that there are a large number of monopolies or semimonopolies on which everyone is dependent. It is not possible, therefore, to allow business to operate without regard for the social consequences of its actions. Samuel Courtauld foretold the course of events in a booklet entitled *Future Relations Between Government and Industry* published in 1942:

The English genius for social evolution and for compromise can find a middle way between pure individualism and pure socialism which will bring the greatest obtainable good to the nation. The road will shift progressively in a direction which will leave more and more vested interests out in the cold. Unless the men in possession are prepared to adapt themselves and compromise there is no alternative to a complete socialist revolution. . . . Government control has come to stay. With the growth and progressive combination of industries until their boundaries are coterminous with those of the nation, it is the duty of the Government to take power to control them, for no Government can tolerate the existence within its borders of an organized and completely independent power with a radius of action as wide as its own. The same over-riding principle should apply to Trade Unions as developed today. It follows from this that the Government must also "plan" further industrial growth. . . .

Another great change which has taken place is in the industrialists' attitude toward labor. Before the war the average weekly wage throughout the country was £2 ($8.00) a week. There was a growing sense of injustice among workers, who believed that they should be given a higher proportion of the rewards of industry and a larger share in its management. This feeling was brought to a head during the war when labor moved rapidly forward and union leaders announced emphatically that workers would never again return to their old conditions.

Businessmen who remembered the strikes that had taken place after World War I were worried, and feared in their bones that this time things might be even worse. Before the general election you frequently heard the remark: "Perhaps it wouldn't be a bad thing if the Socialists got in for a bit, just to tide us over the worst period. Then when they make a mess of things people will be glad to have us back."

With the advent of a Socialist government the emphasis remained on labor. Employers knew that the workingman was in no mood to be deprived of his new status and most of them made concessions. In almost all big businesses the consultative committees set up during the war have remained; in other industries new ones have been established; educational facilities and extension courses have been introduced; and the doors leading to promotion have been opened wider than ever before.

Because of these changes and because of the protection and

advantages labor has received from the government, it has not pressed for higher wages in the last two years, and has made sacrifices which a Conservative administration could not have hoped to secure.

Today most business leaders admit that labor relations have never been better; and most of them admit that they are the direct result of the government's policy. Not only have employers been spared the loss of production through strikes but many of them have been able to accelerate production through the reorganization of their plants. Increased efficiency has very largely depended on two things: first, new machinery, and second, a more economic use of skilled labor. Before the war, because of chronic unemployment, trade-union leaders refused to collaborate in any reorganization that would throw more people out of work. But today the production engineers who draw up the schemes are doing more business than ever before. Union leaders not only co-operate but often serve as chairmen of committees to examine the proposals and help to put them into operation. Recently a cotton factory in Lancashire was able to reduce its labor by 21 percent and its costs by 10 percent, and at the same time to increase its output per man-hour by 39 percent, its wages by 30 percent, and its total output by 15 percent. Improvements such as these have prompted Labor M.P.'s to taunt businessmen with the remark that "private enterprise works better under the Socialists than it did under the Tories."

What is perplexing about the business world is that although they freely admit that the greatest boon the government has brought them is good labor relations their greatest grievance is high taxation. And they do not see any connection between the two. At the present time the main bulk of the revenue from taxes is being spent on the social services, food subsidies, and housing, all of which have directly increased the well-being of the people in the lower income brackets. "What cuts would you like us to make?" is a question the Socialists frequently ask.

Most industrialists at once reply that food subsidies should come off. Although there would be a rise in the cost of food they claim that this would be offset by the reduction in income tax and the removal of purchase tax. However, since low-priced goods ranging from utility clothes to utility furniture do not carry purchase tax, this last would be of little benefit to the lower wage earners; and a reduction of income tax on a £6-a-week salary ($24) would probably cover only about 50 percent of the rise in food.

The question that very few industrialists have faced is this: Is high taxation the price they must pay for good labor relations? The Socialists say it is. They will not remove subsidies until the cost of food has dropped. "We certainly do not intend to follow a policy of cutting down the benefits to the workers of the country in order that better profits may be earned in industry," says Cripps sharply. But would the Conservatives do differently? In spite of all the agitation many people doubt it.

What are the men like who rule the Big Business world? First of all, they are not typical of the average businessman. It seems to be a maxim in Britain that the larger the business the more philosophic the chairman. The factory owner in the province is far more likely to deliver a diatribe against socialism than is the head of a giant corporation. The big men strike you as surprisingly mild-mannered and liberal-minded, with a marked lack of bitterness and an intense desire to get the country back on its feet again. Perhaps it is only in Britain that a capitalist businessman could work hand in hand with a socialist government; many of them are frequently called into consultation, sit on innumerable public committees, and impress you with a high sense of responsibility.

Geoffrey Heyworth, the chairman of Unilever's, is a quiet, determined, outspoken man with a Canadian accent which he picked up when he served with the Canadians during World War I. In 1944 he acted as chairman of the Gas Industry Committee which eventually recommended the nationalization of gas, and many of his business friends accused him of betraying private enterprise. "The facts were inescapable," said Heyworth brusquely. "Gas is a natural monopoly. There was nothing else to recommend."

Unilever's is one of the six largest companies in the world and one which, according to *Fortune*, "makes all U.S. enterprises look parochial." It operates more than five hundred companies placed in forty-three countries and produces a range of goods from soap and margarine to baby food, tooth paste, ice cream, and fertilizers. Heyworth joined the firm when he was eighteen. The story is that his mother, a widow with very little money, called at Lord Leverhulme's office to try and get her son a job. When she was told he could not see her, she waited on the pavement for several hours and caught him on his way home. "If he has your persistence," said Leverhulme, "send him along."

Today Heyworth describes himself as a "glorified sales manager." He is proud of the fact labor disputes are almost unknown in Unilever's, and believes a fundamental of good management is to keep his employees fully informed on the activities and aims of the corporation. Heyworth's opinions are listened to by the government. His repeated emphasis on the necessity of larger allowances for expenditure on new plant was thought to have prompted the concessions in Cripps's last budget.

Hanbury-Williams, the chairman of Courtauld's, and a former director of the Bank of England, is a tall, slim man with a charming smile. He is the son of an army general who during World War I headed the British Military Mission in Russia. He accompanied his father and in Moscow met the young Princess Cantacuzene, who is descended from two famous men— one, an emperor of Hungary in the fourteenth century and the other, tobacco-chewing Ulysses Grant. Some years later they met again in Washington and were married.

Hanbury-Williams was educated in the ways of business by wise old Samuel Courtauld, and is noted for his progressive views. He tells you he is not a Socialist, then adds: "But that doesn't mean that I think everything the Socialists have done is wrong." Like Heyworth, he has always enjoyed good relations with his staff, and since the war has set up Staff Advisory Councils on which the workers have the opportunity to discuss their ideas with the top managers. He is a friend and admirer of Cripps, and tells you sadly that if the coalition government had not forced Courtauld's to sell their American company, Viscose Ltd., when dollars were running out, just before Lend-Lease came into operation, they would now be earning the Treasury $18,000,000 a year.

Robert Sinclair, the chairman of the Imperial Tobacco Company, is a small white-haired man who joined the civil service after World War I, then resigned and went into business. As president of the Federated British Industries he devotes a large proportion of his time to public service. This organization represents over 80 percent of British industry and is the official organization from which men are drawn to represent the business world on a network of consultative and production committees. Sinclair worked closely with the Americans who came over to review British industry at Cripps's invitation and impressed them with his quick, forceful, common-sense approach.

When you visit Oliver Lyttelton in his office he roars at you: "Jolly brave of you to come into this capitalist den. Here's where we grind down the faces of the poor and make billions of pounds' profit every week." Lyttelton refuses to talk from an industrialist's point of view but branches off into the speech he gave the day before in the House of Commons or one he is likely to give the day after. Although most Socialists like to pick on him as "the typical capitalist," mainly because he is the most important businessman in the House of Commons, he reminds you good-naturedly: "I'm no capitalist. I don't even own one-thousandth of one percent of this company. I am a representative of the managerial class. I am for sale!"

Seventy-five-year-old Lord MacGowan is one of the few remaining pioneers of the business world. He built Imperial Chemicals into a £141,000,000 ($564,000,000) combine, which is one of the most powerful monopolies in Britain today, and for many years ruled it like a czar. Born in Scotland, he began as an office boy at 5 shillings a week; in the 1920's his salary of £55,000 ($220,000) a year was reputed to be the highest in the country. The *Observer* once wrote of him: "He makes no effort to play the democrat and only a rash subordinate would mistake his occasional felicitations as anything but the patronage of a confirmed autocrat."

Nevertheless in 1938 I.C.I. announced that "the dictatorial system is now to be modified and power to make decisions . . . vested in a reconstructed executive committee of the Board."

For some time the Socialists have been considering the nationalization of I.C.I. but MacGowan does not appear to be disconcerted. "We seem to be on the shelf—at least for the time being," he announces brightly. He has recently returned from South America, where he warned people not to underestimate the potential strength of Britain. "I told them the government was doing well," he says, "and coming from me," he grins, "they ought to listen."

If I have given the impression that the business world smiles on Socialism let me hastily correct it. At the next election the whole of its weight will be swung behind the Conservative party in one of the most hotly contested battles of the century. Businessmen are pressing not only for a reduction in taxation but for an end to "bulk buying" and above all for an end to nationalization.

Nevertheless, the fact remains that although they represent the right wing of British political thought many Americans would regard them as radicals. Conservatives as well as Socialists know that the days of pure individualism are over; and that, essentially, is the reason that industrialists, no matter how much they grumble and complain and castigate the government, continue to co-operate with it. And that is also the reason that Britain has preserved its national unity.

CHAPTER 22

Nationalization

The mere passage of an act of Parliament, the
mere transfer from private ownership to public
ownership is the beginning of the business; it is
not the end.

—HERBERT MORRISON

WHEN the Conservatives announced in their Industrial
Charter, published in 1947, that if they were returned
to power they would accept a large proportion of the Labor
government's nationalization program, many people both in
Britain and abroad were surprised and even indignant. New
York papers accused the Conservatives of turning pink and
added that the hue should be deepened by their blushes, while
businessmen asked plaintively: "If the Tories don't stand for
private enterprise what on earth do they stand for?"

Most Americans regard nationalization as the exclusive and
unpleasant hallmark of the left. Socialism means planned economy: planned economy means control of the basic industries:
control of the basic industries means nationalization: and nationalization means socialism. To those who insist upon their
issues being clear-cut and straightforward it is, in fact, the
transference of power from the hands of the many to the heavy
and single hand of the state.

This is undoubtedly what the answer ought to be but like
many things English it is not so simple. The truth is that in
almost every industry taken over by the government nationalization has at one time or other been recommended by Conservative politicians or non-Socialist businessmen. For instance,

274

Winston Churchill recommended the nationalization of the railways in 1918; Mr. Harold Macmillan, a member of the Conservative front bench, recommended the nationalization of coal in 1938; Sir Geoffrey Heyworth, the chairman of Unilever's, recommended the nationalization of gas in 1944. During the war the Dominions pressed for the nationalization of cables and wireless; before the war Lord Swinton, a Conservative Minister of Air, recommended the partial nationalization of civil aviation, and as far back as 1936 Lord MacGowan, the chairman of Imperial Chemicals, signed a report which stated that there were only two alternatives for electricity, one of them being: "Immediate and complete reorganisation on a regional basis under public control, by the setting up of Regional Boards which would buy out all existing undertakings."

The reason nationalization was suggested was because private enterprise had failed. The competing firms in almost all of these industries had never been able to co-ordinate their plans sufficiently to provide the community with an adequate service. For instance, in the electrical industry there were no standardized fixtures or charges even in the same districts; and the municipalities and companies who operated profitable urban businesses made no attempt to pool their resources and extend their services to the less economic country areas, with the result that more than half the farms in Britain had no electricity. This same lack of unification was also handicapping transport. The railways were being driven deeper into the red each year by the road haulers, who escaped the burden of paying for the upkeep of tracks and stations, and consequently were unable to raise the capital for re-equipment. And as for coal, the policy of short-term profits which had always been pursued by hundreds of coal owners brought the industry to such a perilous position, through both bad labor relations and a need for new capital, that the whole life of the nation was endangered.

All the industries taken over by the government in the last four years have figured in Labor party programs since 1918. But the argument for nationalization on grounds of efficiency alone has been so powerful it has overshadowed the argument for nationalization on grounds of Socialist theory. And as a result it has convinced many non-Socialists. This is why Quintin Hogg, a leading Tory M.P., is able to write: "No party can hope to succeed unless it produces a policy which creates secret doubts in the minds and hearts of the best of its opponents. . . . The resemblances are more significant than the differences in our political parties." And this is why Mr. Herbert Morrison states bluntly: "We shall only nationalize when it is good public business to do so."

Today Morrison's viewpoint is shared by many Socialists. It therefore came as a shock when the government announced its intention of going ahead with its plans to nationalize steel. Steel was efficiently run and output was rising. The case could not be argued on any other grounds except doctrine. This, people protested, was moving away from the Fabian conception of the "inevitability of gradualness." And the critics were not only Conservatives; a great many Socialists went around murmuring that it was a pity the government was in such a hurry. Although Labor members are bound to support the bill because it was an election promise, there is a marked lack of enthusiasm for it; and as a result the whole subject of nationalization is bound to become an issue between the two Socialist schools of thought.

In the meantime, the Socialists who believe in nationalization for the sake of efficiency are trying to perfect a model which will possess none of the faults of private enterprise but all of the virtues. Nationalized industries are not merely taken over by the government and run by civil servants. They are set up as public corporations and directed by boards of governors. The men on these boards receive salaries of £5,000 ($20,000) a year; and they are responsible both for administration and for policy so long as the latter conforms to the broad outline laid down by the minister in Parliament.

This pattern is not new. It is a variation of the design worked out and successfully introduced by previous Conservative administrations in three well-known institutions: the British Broadcasting Corporation, the Port of London Authority, and the London Passenger Transport Board. But since most of the present undertakings are on a far larger scale the framework requires skillful alteration; a greater degree of public control must be introduced but at the same time initiative must be preserved.

To most Americans this will probably seem a hopeless task, for the very phrase "public corporation" at once arouses suspicion. Public corporations mean salaried officials and in America salaried officials are viewed with disfavor. Because money is the undisputed yardstick of success the bureaucrat has always been slightly despised as someone lacking in real initiative; and as a result the business world usually attracts the ablest young men.

But in Britain it has always been the other way round. Public service is rewarded by honors and titles and acclaim, compared to which the attraction of merely making money has never had more than a secondary appeal to the truly ambitious. As Burke once remarked: "Passion for fame; a passion which is the instinct of all great souls."

One thing leads to another. Public service that is paid has managed to create a feeling for public service that is unpaid; and since unpaid public service must always be run on thoroughly democratic lines it has, in turn, produced a love and understanding for the committee which to the American mind is thoroughly incomprehensible.

No matter what government is in power, Britain is run by and through committees. Committees have built up the trade-union movement; they run local government; they run agriculture and industry and welfare and sport. Even the nation is run by a glorified committee: the cabinet.

But more perplexing than the love of committees is the fact that, somehow, these committees seem to work. Whereas American industry functions like thousands of small armies each with its general at the top, British industry operates through a network of consultation. This may be due to the national character, to which compromise is instinctive; or the national character may have been formed by committees. I would not venture to say. Whatever the answer, the fact that even under private enterprise the Englishman takes to the committee like a duck to water seems to indicate that if any country is capable of working nationalization it is Britain. And where others may fail Britain will probably succeed.

Coal was the first industry to be nationalized; it was taken over by the government in January, 1947. John Gunther once wrote that England was "an island of country houses built on a foundation of coal." Coal has always been the basis of Britain's prosperity as a nation. It has produced more individual wealth and more individual misery than any other industry. And the repercussions from it have rocked civilization. It transformed Britain from an island to the greatest empire in the world; it created fabulous fortunes; it formed dynasties; it built up the trade-union movement; it gave birth to the Labor party; and consequently it brought the Socialists into office. The history of coal is, in fact, the history of Britain.

Although King Henry III granted a license in 1239 "to the good men of Newcastle to dig coals," coal did not become an industry until the sixteenth century. When it first began to be used in London, Parliament complained to the King that it "infected the air with noxious vapours," and secured two proclamations prohibiting its further use and containing strict orders to inflict fines upon any delinquents. In spite of this order there is a record of a bill of 10 shillings for coal used at the coronation of Edward III.

The industry did not begin to prosper until the days of Queen Elizabeth. In 1568 English law decided that, with the exception of gold and silver, all minerals were the property of landowners—in other words that ownership was not confined to the surface of the earth but extended to the center. This was the beginning of a system of coal royalties that remained in force until 1938 and undoubtedly caused more bitterness than any other single phase of coal ownership. It meant that landowners leased their land to coal contractors with the provision that they be paid a set amount of money for every ton of coal mined. The contractors also had to make their profit, which meant that the miner saw himself a victim of what he termed "double exploitation." And the fact that this condition did not exist on the Continent, where minerals automatically belonged to the state, added to his grievances.

But the miners were not the only people who complained at the way the industry was run. At times consumers also felt badly used. As early as 1673 the first proposition for partial "nationalization" was put forward in the interest of housewives. It was outlined in a work called *The Grand Concern of England*, which suggested that the coal trade should be managed by commissioners empowered to supply all parts of the nation with coal at a uniform rate. "I need not declare," writes the author, "how the subjects are abused in the price of coal; how many poor have been starved for want of fewel by reason of the horrid prices put upon them, especially in time of war, either by the merchants or the woodmonger, or between them both."

The wages and long hours that the miners worked were probably no worse than those of other industries but the danger and the darkness made them worse. In a book written in 1873, a Northumberland miner, Richard Fynnes, describes the appalling conditions of an even earlier day:

For many years speculators and adventurers leased most of the mines; and seeking to make as much out of the investment as possible, ground down their workmen in a shocking and inhuman manner. Not only did they refuse to pay them a fair wage for their laborious and dangerous work— and the work was dangerous in a very high degree then—but they treated them as so many serfs who were utterly unworthy of any consideration whatsoever. Children of tender years were sent down into the pits to keep a trapdoor or to help-up, whilst they should have still been in the nursery; and owing to the long hours they were kept at work, it was impossible for them to see daylight except at the end of each week, or to catch a glimpse of it in the long days of summer. Females were also sent down into these dismal holes, and many continued to labour there until they became wives and mothers. They were even at this early period taunted with their barbarity and want of intelligence, when intelligence was not a very common commodity around them; but those who taunted them either forgot or wilfully refused to recollect that, situated as they were, it was almost impossible for them to acquire information. But notwithstanding these many drawbacks, the pitmen of Northumberland and Durham were by no means remarkable for their savagery, and if many of them exhibited a love for cock-fighting and other kindred sports then in vogue they were not singular in their tastes, but had both example and precept from many who assumed to be their superiors. Now and then, goaded by a sense of right and wrong, they would band themselves together for mischief and inflict grievous damage to life and property; but in their ordinary every day course of existence they were, as a whole, as intelligent and harmless as any community of men could be whose minds were as dark as their work.

During the nineteenth century the miners began to organize in trade unions and became the most politically-minded of all sections of the working population. In 1900 a miner, Keir Hardie, formed the Labor party and by the First World War the miners had more representatives in Parliament than any other union. Their anger against the unemployment and wage cuts of the twenties and thirties was far from passive; there were more strikes in the coal fields than in almost all the other industries put together.

The cause of the trouble was due basically to the fact that coal owners could not agree among themselves on a program of technical reorganization. Profits fell, wages were cut, and hours lengthened. Conditions of work were so bad only acute economic necessity kept the manpower force at the required level. Between 1927 and 1936 an average of one out of every four miners was out of work; short time was a source of constant anxiety; and in 1938 eighty other industries were paying higher weekly wages.

Added to this the miner had to combat both danger and disease. A census taken in 1938 revealed that one in every 1,350 miners contracted silicosis, that one in every 3 suffered some minor injury, and that one in every 960 was killed.

This increased the feeling of injustice and almost all miners' children who grew up between the wars shared a background of poverty and bitterness; and every miner discouraged his son from going into the pits. During the struggle against Hitler the only reason the mines were manned was because an Essential Work Order was in force.

Major Lloyd George, a Liberal politician who was Minister of Fuel in Churchill's coalition government, realized the problems that would face the industry when peace came, and in 1944 appointed a committee, headed by Sir Charles Reid, the leading mining engineer in the country, to investigate the position. The outcome was the famous Reid Report. This analysis revealed that Britain's efficiency, reckoned by output per man-shift, was below that of both the Ruhr and Holland, the two countries where conditions were similar enough to draw a comparison.

The root of the trouble, said the report, lay in the separate ownership of hundreds of small companies. Mining engineers had too little elbow room to lay out large, efficient mines, and small mining companies often could not afford to sink money in workings planned for long-term efficiency. Instead they aimed at starting output as soon as possible, and workings were developed piecemeal.

Separate ownership of many small mines also meant that it was difficult to merge neighboring mines, or to close down poor pits and concentrate on the more productive ones. And since most British mines earned small profits in the difficult years from 1924 to 1936, they could not afford to spend adequate sums on up-to-date equipment or on the surface.

There are [wrote the committee] mines on the point of exhausting their reserves, mines which should be closed down altogether and their reserves worked from adjoining collieries . . . mines between which valuable coal has been sterilised to form barriers. There are undertakings which have a lease of coal that could be worked to better advantage by another undertaking. . . . There are new sinkings required where the reserves which should be worked from them are leased to two or more undertakings. . . . It is evident to us that it is not possible to provide for the soundest and most efficient development and working of an area unless the conflicting interests of the individual colliery companies working the area are merged into one compact and unified command of manageable size. . . .

When coal was nationalized in 1947 the British public became the owners of 1,500 mines, 1,000 private companies, a million acres of agricultural land, 100,000 mineworkers' houses, and some 177,000 railway cars. It also became the owners of research, recruitment, training, manpower, distribution, and sales organizations.

The industry was at its lowest ebb. It had been steadily deteriorating for more than thirty years. In 1913 over a million men were employed in the pits; production was 287,000,000 tons, of which 94,000,000 were exported; in 1946 the manpower figure had declined to only 692,000, the lowest of the century; less than 170,000,000 tons were produced and only 9,000,-000 exported. The position was desperate for the output was barely sufficient to cover immediate needs at home, and all Britain's exports depended on coal.

The most urgent problem that faced the nationalized industry was how to check the drift away from the mines and raise production. Wages were lifted to their highest level; a five-day week was introduced; more paid holidays were guaranteed. It was arranged that miners should be allowed extra food rations, a chance to buy consumers' goods in short supply, and priority in housing. In the last two years nearly every colliery has introduced a medical service; training and educational facilities have been extended; and university scholarships in mining engineering have been offered to boys both inside and outside the industry. Altogether nearly five hundred short-term development and reorganization schemes have been completed.

These efforts have produced results. The drift has stopped. During the last two years the number of workers has slowly increased, and production has steadily risen. Today there are thirty thousand more men in the pits than there were before nationalization, and coal output has increased by twenty million tons. In a recent report issued by the European Economic Commission it was shown that British output per man-shift, calculated in relation to prewar figures, was now the highest in Europe.

The financial complications of taking over such a vast and diffuse industry were not the least of the government's worries.

An arbitration tribunal was set up to study the question of payments. After assessing the net reasonable maintainable revenue if the mines had not been nationalized it came to the conclusion that the owners should be awarded total compensation to the value of £164,600,000 ($658,400,000). It also had the task of assessing non-coal mining assets taken over from the colliery companies, such as brickworks, coke ovens and by-product plants. This figure has not yet been agreed upon but it is expected that it will be well over £100,000,000 ($400,000,000).

When the details are finally worked out the government will meet these sums by issuing government stock in line with other government securities. And the Coal Board will repay the money to the Treasury over a period of years. The Communists objected violently that the coal industry should have to "buy itself out." They preferred the method of straight confiscation. Whether or not the tribunal leaned the other way is open to argument. The *Times* described the terms as "fair and reasonable," an opinion which was evidently shared by many others for the day after the award was announced buyers scrambled for shares on a rising market.

Today the coal corporation is run by a national board composed of nine men appointed by the Minister of Fuel and Power. Under this board are eight divisional boards, and under the divisional boards, forty-nine areas. The areas are operated by coal technicians but the chairman of the divisions and the members of the national board are chosen for all-round administrative ability.

Today the Coal Board is headed by Lord Hyndley, a short, pink-cheeked, affable man, a former coal owner with a long record of public service. Hyndley's political acumen is beyond dispute for he was made a knight by the Lloyd George Liberals, a baronet by the Baldwin Conservatives, and a lord by the Ramsay MacDonald Socialists. His fellow members consist of another coal owner, two trade unionists, a chartered accountant, a scientist, a mining engineer, a barrister, and a civil servant, while the chairmen of the divisions consist of three businessmen, two trade unionists, a lawyer, a general, and an admiral.

All these men are highly respectable, and well known within their own spheres. The fact that the Minister took no chances on unknown and untried talent, preferring to seek established names outside the industry, has aroused a good deal of criticism. But he argued that the history of bad labor relations made it impossible to fill the jobs from the ranks of coal operators.

Other criticisms, even more emphatic, have been on the structure of the new corporation. Sir Charles Reid resigned from the Board in 1948, declaring that authority was too centralized to allow the industry to function efficiently. He claimed that divisions should be eliminated and all administrative power delegated to the area managers. Much attention was paid to these suggestions and it is believed that gradual changes may be made in the general direction he has indicated.

Besides the Coal Board's administrative difficulties it is faced with an immensely complicated human problem, the inevitable outcome of years of rancor. Although nationalization has succeeded in raising production it has not automatically infused the miners with the new spirit of sweet reasonableness that many people hoped. There are still too many restrictive practices, too many young men leaving the pits, too much absenteeism. And the miners are still grumbling. They regard the Coal Board as an improvement over the coal owners; nevertheless they review it with reserve, as though at any moment it might turn out to be a wolf in sheep's clothing.

In a recent survey taken by the Fabian Society typical miners' comments were: "Consultative Committees should have greater power. . . . The running of the industry is still left too much in the hands of the management and the miner's voice should be listened to with more attention. . . . The miner is made to feel that his opinion is not important. . . . There is a lack of consultation between miners and men. . . . The working miner has little influence over policy. . . . The status of the miner should

be raised. . . . There is lack of control from the bottom. . . . "
The Coal Board has the task not only of breaking down the
miner's psychology of "we" and "they" but of educating him
to the responsibility of ownership.

The Board's first act to remove long-standing grievances was
to shorten miners' hours and increase their wages. No one
doubts that this was absolutely necessary but it meant a loss of
£23,000,000 ($92,000,000) for the corporation in the first year.
And to cover the deficit for the second year, it was necessary to
raise the price of coal.

The only way costs can be reduced, aside from a further
increase per man, is by technical improvements. The Treasury
has advanced £150,000,000 ($600,000,000) for capital re-equip-
ment. However, most of the experts say that the benefits of
the schemes now being introduced will not be felt for many
years. For instance, the Bold Colliery in Lancashire is being entirely reconstructed; the work will take six years to carry out,
and five additional years may be required to bring the plan into
full operation. But by introducing more scientific methods it is
expected that instead of one man on the surface for only three
men underground the ratio will be one to every eight.

In the next few years there will be many changes in the structure of the corporation; heads will fall; criticism will be unre-
lenting. But if the industry achieves its target of raising output
25 percent by 1953, it will be producing 250,000,000 tons a
year, a figure which has not been reached since 1929. And once
again the nation will have a firm foundation.

The nationalization of transport involved an even greater
transfer of ownership than that of coal. The government took
over the railways, canals, and long-distance road haulage services.
It became the owners of 52,000 miles of railway, 20,000 locomo-
tives, 1,235,000 goods cars, 70 hotels, 100 steamships, and many
thousands of motor vehicles, valued at more than £1,000,000,-
000 ($4,000,000,000). Compensation was given in the form of
3 percent British Transport stock.

Nationalization of the railways had been urged by prominent

men ever since World War I. In an election speech in 1918 Winston Churchill said: "We cannot organize the great questions of land settlement, new industries and extension of production unless the State has control of the means of transportation." When Mr. Churchill was asked whether a national inquiry should precede nationalization he is reported as saying: "I cannot say, but I think it highly improbable that action on this vital matter can be delayed until a Royal Commission has wandered about. . . . "

Action, however, was delayed, and delayed indefinitely; and instead of prospering between the two wars the railways went deeper into debt. The basic cause was the lack of unity between the various forms of transport. Road competition undermined the railways; and the railways bought up the canals and put them into disuse to prevent them from being used as freight carriers. Wasteful overlapping and high overheads were ruining the four competing railway companies and costing the taxpayer a good deal of money.

Then came World War II. The transport system became the charge of a Minister of War Transport, and it was soon proved that under a unified control all three services were capable of handling an increased volume of traffic without loss to any one of them. Some of the more progressive industrialists, such as Samuel Courtauld, stated bluntly: "There is a good deal to be said for nationalising transport. The railways have been largely amalgamated in recent years, but there is still too much overlapping, and it might be better that a close net-work covering a small country like Britain should be under one ownership. Such a vital monopoly as this could only be entrusted to the government, and moreover railways have shown so few signs of progress and initiative for the last 60 years or so there seems to be little valuable of that kind to be killed."

Today nationalized transport is run by the British Transport Commission, composed of four members appointed by the Minister of Transport. The chairman, sixty-three-year-old Sir Cyril Hurcomb, is a man who has been a civil servant all his life. He is bluff, untidy, unsociable, and brilliantly quick; and the fact that he has managed to retain all his rough edges despite the polished atmosphere of the civil service speaks for his forceful personality.

At the present time Hurcomb's colleagues are a trade unionist, a former director of the Co-Operative Society, and a former railway director. These men only deal with questions of policy. Under them are four executives who are responsible for road, railways, canals, London transport, and hotels. When the Commission was originally set up it included General Slim, who commanded the Fourteenth Army in Burma, but since that time he has been recalled to the War Office and now holds Britain's top military job as Chief of the Imperial General Staff.

The railways have been advanced £250,000,000 ($1,000,000,-000) by the Treasury for capital equipment. Most of the money will be spent in replacing engines, cars, and tracks, which were worn out during the war. The Commission's first annual report has not yet been published but most people expect it to show a loss of £10,000,000 ($40,000,000). The directors believe that by the end of 1949 it will be paying its way.

The three other industries which have been nationalized* are civil aviation, gas, and electricity. Civil aviation was known to be a losing proposition which could only be kept going by large subsidies from the government. During the war Britain's aircraft consisted almost entirely of fighters and bombers. Consequently few modern transport planes will be ready before 1952 and in the meantime the country is operating uneconomical aircraft. Today there are two corporations, British Overseas Airways, and British European Airways, which are run by independent boards composed of industrialists and airmen appointed by the Minister of Civil Aviation. These boards hope that British aviation will be paying its way by 1954.

The other two industries, gas and electricity, have only been nationalized since April, 1948, and May, 1949. Both of them

* I have not included the Bank of England, which was a technical transfer and involved no organic change, or cables and wireless, which was taken over by the Post Office.

vest a good deal of authority in their area boards, which are set up in all parts of the country; and both of them have been told that their policy must be to develop supplies and keep down charges. Their first reports will not be published until a year or eighteen months after the date they were taken over.

Two of the three ministers in charge of nationalized industries are former University dons. Both are in their early forties, both went to Oxford, and both won first-class honors. They were in the same college and were friends. One is Hugh Gaitskell and the other is Lord Pakenham.

Gaitskell has the most difficult job for he is in control of three public corporations: coal, gas, and electricity. A man of charm and humor, he is one of the most popular of the younger ministers. For eleven years before the war he was head of the Department of Economics at University College, London. He has an outspoken and practical mind, not usually associated with the scholar, and has made a strong impression on the industrialists with whom he has had to deal. Gaitskell received a good deal of publicity in 1947 when he explained that electricity cuts would mean fewer baths. "Personally, I have never had a great many baths myself," he said cheerfully, "and I can assure those who are in the habit of having a great many that it does not make a great difference to their health if they have less. As for your appearance most of that is underneath and nobody sees it." Mr. Churchill solemnly quoted this surprising statement in the House and asked the Speaker whether the word "lousy" could now be permitted as a parliamentary expression.

The third minister of a nationalized industry is sixty-two-year-old Alfred Barnes, who rose from a working-class background to become the first president of the London Co-Operative Society. He is a thin man, with a wooden leg and a worn, kindly face, and is known for a shrewd business sense. He joined the Independent Labor party in 1908 and was one of the founders of the Co-Operative party; he has been in the House of Commons for twenty-three years, and will probably retire after the next election.

The most striking feature of the nationalized industries is the drive for efficiency. This is based on the government's insistence that public corporations must pay their way, and for many Labor supporters presents an entirely new attitude of mind. In the old days Socialists often argued that so long as a public undertaking provided a cheap service to the community it did not matter whether it was run at a profit or a loss; the government, they said, could easily foot the bill. Even Winston Churchill once held this view. "So long as the railways are in private hands," he said in 1918, "they may be used for immediate profit. In the hands of the State it might be a wiser expedient to run them at a loss if they developed industry, placed the trader in close contact with his market, and stimulated development."

Today this idea has gone by the board. And the reason is mainly due to the high rate of taxation. If a nationalized industry is not paying its way it has only two alternatives: either to increase its charges or to ask the government for a subsidy. And since subsidies mean even higher taxation the Chancellor of the Exchequer refuses to accept the burden.

Nationalized industries must therefore stand on their own feet. And if they fail to provide cheap goods and services they will face public disapproval that will lead to the dismissal of the men who run them. It is vital that the cost of essential services is kept low, not only for the sake of the consumer, but for the sake of the nation's export drive. A rise in the cost of coal or in the cost of freight charges at once sends up the price of all manufactured goods and makes it more difficult for Britain to compete abroad. The battle cry of efficiency is linked with the survival of the nation.

As an instrument of efficiency the structure of the public corporation is far from perfect. It is under constant criticism and is undergoing constant change; and all these changes have been in the direction of decentralization. When coal was nationalized, policy and administration were placed in the hands of a central board; when the railways were taken over, policy was in the hands of a central board but administration was delegated to executive branches which functioned beneath the board; when electricity was nationalized, a great deal of responsibility was vested in even smaller units, areas, and co-ordinated by a central authority; when gas was nationalized, the areas were entirely autonomous, the central body merely serving as a federal link. Judging from this the future pattern of nationalization will resemble the American political structure; branches of a public corporation will pay allegiance to a federal authority in the same sort of way that the American states are bound to the American government.

The decentralization of power at once raises certain questions. Because the emphasis is not on controlling nationalized industries more tightly, but on protecting them from outside interference, people ask: "How is Parliament to exert its authority?"

Some time ago the *Economist* wrote:

One by one the whole brood of National Boards and Corporations are hatching out and Parliament watches them with evident anxiety, wondering whether its offspring may prove to be cuckooes in the nest. How, it is asked, can Parliament ensure that the new Boards are neither stunted for lack of independence nor allowed to grow into wilful giants, a law unto themselves? How can Parliament and the public find out what they are really up to when they have become fully fledged? These are outstanding questions, yet, strange as it may seem, the problem of devising a means of controlling nationalised industries is quite new. It must be solved for it is one of the most important constitutional issues that have arisen in the United Kingdom for a long time.

The English have met this problem characteristically by leaving the situation vague. At the present time each nationalized industry must submit an annual report to Parliament. The report is debated and a general policy laid down by the minister responsible for the industry. The latter appoints the members of the national boards and sees that the policy is carried out. During the course of the year he will answer questions in Parliament dealing with broad issues; but he will not answer specific questions dealing with administration. His argument is that he has delegated his authority and is therefore not responsible for details. Herbert Morrison emphasized this attitude when he stated:

Boards have been set up to run socialised industries on business lines on behalf of the community, and Ministers are not responsible for their day to day administration. A large degree of independence for the Boards in matters of current administration is vital to their efficiency as commercial undertakings. A Minister is responsible to Parliament for action which may be taken in relation to a Board, or action coming within his statutory powers which he has not taken. . . . It would be contrary to this principle, and to the clearly expressed intention of Parliament in legislation, if Ministers were to give in Parliament or in letters information about day to day matters. . . .

Many people believe that eventually the minister may disappear altogether. The government, through Parliament, will continue to lay down the annual policy; a member of the government will answer questions about the industry in the House; and the corporation will be left to run itself without any close supervision. Parliament will have no more day-to-day control than it has over the B.B.C.

But if the nationalized industries are not subjected to continuous public prodding, who will protect the interests of the consumers? In private enterprise the spur of competition automatically sets in the customer's favor; but in a public monopoly it has to be artificially contrived. Since the English are experts at improvisation this has resulted in the invention of public organs known as "consumers' councils." These councils could probably not have come to life anywhere but in Britain for they are thorough expressions of the national character. First of all, they are composed of voluntary workers who receive no compensation other than their expenses, aside from the chairmen, who receive a small fee; and secondly, they involve a new network of committees. In each industry the consumers' councils represent the various interests which are particularly dependent on it. On the coal councils, for instance, factory owners and housewives sit side by side. Their job is to continually prod the national board into providing cheaper and better coal, to be consulted when the price is changed, to make suggestions for more efficient deliveries or, in other words, to protect the consumer. So far some of these councils have been extremely effective. If the Electricity Board finally agrees to install electricity on farms for only a nominal charge and allows the farmer to repay it over a long period, it will be the direct result of pressure from its consumer councils.

The teething troubles of nationalization are being dealt with as they arise by a nation which has always made a specialty of feeling its way. The *Economist* summed it up by saying: "If the new Boards are to combine the merits of both Civil Service and business units and to develop into distinctive organs of British Government, they are likely to do so gradually and almost imperceptibly as the result of hundreds of minor practical decisions. Parliament must be constantly ready to nurse and peck its young into shape."

So much for the school which believes in nationalization for practical purposes. When the government announced that it was going ahead with its plans to nationalize steel it was apparent that the other school had sprung to the fore. According to a report in the *Observer* of May, 1949, this is what happened:

Sir Andrew Duncan, Chairman of the Iron and Steel Federation, insisted up to the last minute that the Government would not nationalise steel. Waving a cigar as large as a walking stick, he said, over and over again, that everybody was wrong; there would, he agreed, be a bill on steel but not a nationalising bill. . . . Sir Andrew's confidence had some justification. It can now be said that he and Mr. Morrison came to a compromise which would have given the Government more control over the industry but would have stopped short of nationalisation. . . . There then followed a little comedy that had very serious results. Mr. Morrison went with his compromise to the T.U.C. in the hope of getting the Trade Unions on his side. By bad luck it happened that one or two of the steel experts on the General Council were abroad, and the lesser bretheren, knowing little about steel and caring less, could not at first decide what to do. However, loyalty won in the end. They decided, on insufficient evidence, that their absent experts would be in favour of nationalisation, and they therefore told Mr. Morrison that they could not support the compromise. Thus

Mr. Morrison was deprived of his strongest card—the support of the T.U.C. . . . Mr. Aneurin Bevan made himself the spokesman of the rebels in the Cabinet, and Ministers suddenly realised that the issue could disrupt the party. That was the end of any hope of a compromise bill.

Ever since this showdown the two schools of thought on nationalization, the practical and the theoretical, have been crystallizing. The Aneurin Bevan school is in the minority; and the fact that it was successful in pulling off its coup may easily act as a boomerang because it has forced Socialists to do a good deal of hard thinking. All Socialists agree on government control of the basic industries, and all Socialists agree on industrial democracy. But there is a growing and uneasy suspicion that perhaps control does not necessarily hinge on nationalization and perhaps nationalization does not necessarily produce industrial democracy. Other methods and ingredients may be more effective.

When the Fabians enlarged the idea of public ownership three-quarters of a century ago an enormous section of the population lived in great poverty submerged by sharp class distinctions. Nationalization presented the only clear picture of social and political advancement. But now that world is far behind. There has been not only a profound psychological change due to the development of democracy but a profound change due to the ruinous cost of fighting wars.

Today Conservatives as well as Socialists accept the principle of "government interference." They know Britain cannot recover from her financial straits without strong central direction. The budget which once upon a time concerned itself with collecting taxes is today recognized as the government's most important instrument of shaping policy; it redistributes wealth; it influences supply and demand; it largely determines savings and investment. And through these means it exerts great pressure on industry. "If the government can control industry by its ordinary powers why hurry to nationalize except on grounds of efficiency?" argue the Herbert Morrison Socialists.

Even on the subject of workers' control there has been a

good deal of rethinking. The Marxist theory of seizing power by
revolution and turning industry over to the workers was loudly
condemned by the Fabians. They accepted workers' control only
as a goal to be striven for by peaceful and democratic means,
and a goal that belonged to a distant and a more enlightened
age. Even so, their views were colored by the conditions of their
times, in which children only received a free education to the
age of twelve, and in which uneducated men had little chance of
rising to managerial positions. But today with a different background workers' control is being interpreted in a different light;
the emphasis is laid on the worker's right to sit on consultative
committees; on encouraging him to take advantage of educational facilities; on giving him the chance to work his way up.

The soul-searchings that were started with the steel bill were
accentuated when the Labor party announced its intention of
nationalizing sugar, cement, and industrial insurance. Both
sugar and cement are well-run, highly efficient monopolies, and
M.P.'s began to complain that it looked as though the party
were merely shopping around to forestall the theorists. One Labor member told me that he feared the Socialists were reaching
the end of the thinking the Fabians had done for them for the
last seventy years, and that the time had come when they must
re-examine their problems with imagination and independence.

To the practical Socialists imagination means not merely
transferring ownership on paper but making Socialism work.
In 1948 Herbert Morrison reflected this point of view when he
warned the Labor Party Conference: "Do not ignore the need
for allowing ministers adequate time to consolidate, to develop,
to make efficient or more efficient the industries which have
so been Socialised in the present Parliament."

The aim of the practical Socialist is two things: first, to nationalize only when it is common sense to do so, and second,
to perfect the public corporation so that social democracy
proves itself the most efficient method of enterprise. There
will undoubtedly be a struggle within the party but doctrinaire

Socialism has never appealed to the English people and the practical point of view is bound to triumph. As Robert Blatchford once wrote: "You can't chivvey or hustle a democracy, at least not a British democracy."

CHAPTER 23

Recovery

There does, indeed, still remain a serious and
baffling problem in our dollar balance.
—SIR STAFFORD CRIPPS, 1949

TODAY Britain's economic effort is geared to one objective: to be solvent when American aid ends in 1952. At the end of the war many people prophesied that Britain would have to undergo a severe transformation. Crippled by the financial sacrifices she had made, she would never again, they said, be able to produce the means of sustenance to feed her large population. They believed that her only hope lay in drastically reducing her numbers and becoming accustomed, like so many other once-great empires, to the role of a small secondary nation.

But the British took a different view. They were tired after six long years of fighting, but they were also proud; in their hour of victory it was unthinkable to accept defeat. They asked the Americans to extend them credit and give them a chance to prove their worth. Then they went to work. By 1948 they had made remarkable strides toward recovery. Instead of the im-

297

mense trade deficit they had been running with the rest of the world in the three previous years, their total exports and imports almost balanced.

But the dollar "gap" remained. Today, in 1949, Britain is still buying from the Western Hemisphere goods to the value of a thousand million dollars more than she is selling. Although this is a reduction by two-thirds of the deficit running in 1946, the figure is formidable. And the last third is bound to be the most difficult of all, for competition is rising. Can she do it? On the answer to this hangs not only the future of Britain but the future of western Europe.

Although Britain's balance of payment problem is due to the war, her difficulties began much earlier. For most of the nineteenth century she was the richest country in the world. In 1870, with only 2 percent of the world's population she produced one-third of the world's manufactures and provided two-fifths of the world's manufactured exports. During the nineteenth century she had been selling more goods and services than she bought, and lending money wherever she saw an opportunity for development. But in 1938, although she still had 2 percent of the world's population she made under one-tenth of the world's manufactures and shared only one-fifth of the world's manufactured export trade. From being the richest country in the world she had slowly reached the point where she was beginning to live on overseas capital.

The change had come about because other countries, particularly the United States and Germany, were making their own goods instead of buying them from Britain. The effect on British economy did not become noticeable until World War I during which she lost half her overseas investments and after which, for the first time, her accounts showed that she was in the red. For some years she managed to balance her books by "invisible" earnings from shipping, finance, and other services, but in the last three years before World War II even these were not adequate. In 1938 Britain's imports exceeded her exports, visible and invisible, by £70,000,000 ($280,000,000).

But though these facts were well known to economists, the British people as a whole had not grasped them. Industrialists, and the politicians who supported them, looked back at the old days and still dreamed of a revival. "Why, in my young days every man in Manchester had a gold watch and chain. That's what we must get back to" was a typical comment heard between the wars. Industrialists still thought in terms of limitless expansion and of founding family dynasties which should rival the wealth of the old aristocracy in stability and longevity, and although trade unionists and workers preached redistribution of wealth and common ownership through socialism, they scarcely questioned the fact that wealth would automatically continue to grow.

The Second World War struck Britain like a cyclone and increased her deficit in a way which was well-nigh catastrophic. Britain fought the war, as her Chancellor of the Exchequer, Sir John Anderson, said in presenting his budget in April, 1945, "without counting the cost." He went on to add: "The principles of good housekeeping scarcely apply when you are fighting for your lives over three continents." In five and a half years of war Britain had spent approximately $110,000,000,000. Against this, net Lend-Lease from the United States amounted to only $9,-179,000,000. Although far more people than ever before—twenty-two million men and women out of a population of forty-seven millions—had been at work, their standard of living had been drastically reduced. Imports had been cut by half and, in spite of Lend-Lease, consumption in some years fell by a quarter, and throughout the war by an average of 16 percent. Nearly three-quarters of everything Britain produced was devoted solely to the military effort. No new houses were built even though more than a million were damaged or destroyed; and every business, large or small, from the railways to the smallest grocer's shop, had struggled along with only sufficient repairs to prevent complete breakdown.

Even more serious, from the point of view of a small and thickly populated country which depended on trade for its existence, was the fact that exports had fallen by three-quarters;

and as if to make sure that nothing should be left undone to make Britain's recovery more difficult, a substantial part of her foreign investments, whose income had provided a large part of those "invisible" exports which had saved her between the wars, had been sold. They amounted to more than $4,000,000,-000. In addition she had incurred sterling debts to Commonwealth and other countries of nearly $12,000,000,000.

When, therefore, in August, 1945, Lend-Lease was suddenly canceled, Britain was faced with immediate bankruptcy. As Mr. Attlee, who had become Prime Minister, pointed out in the House of Commons, the very fact that the agreed division of war effort between the Allies had resulted in Britain's devoting three-quarters of her effort to military production, leaving her allies to provide her people with food and clothing, meant that when these supplies were cut off she was far worse equipped to rebuild her economy than those who had been helping her. "If the role assigned to us had been to expand our exports so as to provide a large margin over our current needs which we could furnish free of charge to our allies, we should, of course, be in an immeasurably stronger position than we are today."

As it was, excluding the cost of munitions and other military supplies under Mutual Aid, Britain was spending abroad at the end of 1945 $4,800,000,000 per annum more than she was earning. Not only were drastic economies in all dollar expenditure immediately necessary, but unless further help could be arranged, her people faced starvation.

It was in these circumstances that Lord Keynes was sent on a mission to the United States. One of the great intellects of his age, he was a man with a sardonic wit who did not suffer fools gladly. When he died in April, 1946, the *Times* wrote of him:

"By his death the country has lost a very great Englishman. He was a man of genius who as a political economist had a world-wide influence both on specialists and the general public, and he was also master of a variety of other subjects. . . . He was a man of action who intervened with critical effect in the great affairs of State."

Keynes was, in fact, one of those rare beings who could have been almost anything he wished to be, yet outwardly his life followed a typically English pattern. After winning scholarships at both Eton and Cambridge he entered the civil service. Having passed the examination near the top, he had a choice of the department in which he would like to serve, but instead of taking what was considered the "plum"—the Treasury—he chose the India Office. He had not been there long before he wrote a treatise on Indian currency which, although it was ignored by those responsible at the time, proved so correct that he was offered a fellowship at Cambridge. He resigned from the civil service and accepted it. Nevertheless in 1919 it was as a civil servant once more that he first became known to the outside world.

He went to the Paris Peace Conference as Chief Representative of the British Treasury, but disapproved of Allied policy over reparations so strongly that he again resigned and wrote a book called *The Economic Consequences of the Peace* in which he prophesied that these payments would have disastrous results. Once more events proved him right; and there is no doubt that the restraint which the western Allies have shown in the matter of reparations since the Second World War has been largely due to his influence.

As an economist Keynes's most famous and most controversial work was done in the 1930's when he wrote a book called *The General Theory of Investment, Interest and Money.* He began by stating in the introduction that he was going to contradict all the teaching he had done in the previous twenty years. He had come to the conclusion that to make a free economic system work to capacity—and so provide full employment—it would be necessary to have deliberate central control of the rate of interest and also, in certain cases, to stimulate capital investment. This was a revolutionary statement and, as the *Times* pointed out, "rested on a very subtle analysis of the working of the whole system." Today it continues to be debated wherever economics is seriously studied.

But Keynes was much more than an economist. A lover of

the arts, in 1925 he married Lydia Lopokova of the Imperial Russian ballet. For many years they formed the center of what was known in London as "Bloomsbury"—the artistic and intellectual set which included Lytton Strachey and Virginia Woolf. A brilliant conversationalist, he could be rude whenever he suspected pomposity or pretentiousness; yet he liked young people and was such a passionate lover of individual liberty that during the 1914-18 war, even though he was working late at night at the Treasury, he would get up fantastically early and travel long distances in order to defend young men who were facing tribunals on grounds of conscientious objection. Such was the man to whom Britain turned in her hour of financial need and who, as it turned out, wore himself to death in the negotiations.

When Lord Keynes went to America in 1945 to negotiate the loan, the British people faced starvation. Even so, the atmosphere was charged with suspicion and a certain amount of acrimony. Although British prestige was high and many Americans genuinely wished to see her recover her old position, others talked of the loan that had not been repaid after World War I, and felt that she ought to be grateful to the United States for having saved her from defeat, and this time to accept without complaint her new position as a secondary power. "Why doesn't Britain's population emigrate?" or "Why doesn't she sell her colonies?" were questions commonly asked. And in their hearts those who asked them felt that it was no bad thing if British pride had to take a fall in a century that so plainly belonged to the New World.

But the British knew that emigration was impossible on any large scale. Countries like Australia and South Africa which welcome British immigrants in theory have found it difficult to provide either houses or jobs for even 100,000 people a year. And as for selling the colonies, the natives who inhabited them were being given self-government as rapidly as possible; to barter away their future without their consent would have been a shameful act. At a conference held in Jamaica in 1947 the

West Indian delegates made it clear that under no circumstances would they agree to another rule, or, for that matter, even a transfer to the trusteeship of the United Nations.

Lord Keynes put the British case with all the brilliance and force at his command. He showed that because of Britain's geographical position she had carried a greater burden and suffered greater losses than the United States; the deterioration of her capital equipment was three times as heavy, the loss of her internal investments thirty-five times as heavy, and the sum total of her national debt 40 percent larger proportionately than America's. In addition, her shipping had been reduced by half whereas United States shipping had increased five times to over fifty million dead-weight tons.

Britain's war had been longer, he said, and the personal sacrifices of her people therefore greater. The British public had paid 53.3 percent of the cost of the war in taxation compared to 47.7 percent by the American people; 55 percent of Britain's total labor force was mobilized into the armed forces or war production by June, 1944, compared with 40 percent in the United States; and whereas American civilian consumption had increased 16 percent, British consumption had declined a similar amount. He also stated bluntly that while Lend-Lease aid to Britain equaled only 1 per cent of U.S. national production, British aid to the U.S. amounted to 15 percent of Britain's total production.*

The purpose of Lord Keynes's emphasis on these figures was to argue not that by her sacrifices Britain had a right to charity, but that if she was able to make such stupendous efforts in war she was equally able to make them in peace. As a financial investment alone, it would pay the United States to help her. And besides this, there were other reasons why Britain must be put on her feet. No one could deny that during the war she had shown herself the one stable democratic force in Europe. If

---

* The figures respectively were:

Total Lend-Lease from U.S. to U.K. $13,499,000,000
     "   "   "   "   U.K. to U.S. $ 4,320,000,000

Britain were to collapse, democracy in Europe could not survive, and America would have fought the war in vain.

These arguments, supported by the large body of Americans who genuinely desired to see Britain recover, triumphed, and the loan was negotiated. Nevertheless, its terms were in some respects so harsh to British eyes that Lord Keynes signed only with misgivings. The clause which insisted that sterling should become freely convertible into dollars within a year was particularly dangerous, and was resisted by the British for twelve weeks of negotiation. It was only accepted under protest, and in his speech recommending the loan for the House of Lords, Lord Keynes said:

"We ran here into difficulties . . . and we accepted in the end more cut and dried arrangements in some respects than we believed to be wise or beneficial."

But the loan was carried through both Congress and Parliament. In Britain there were protests and prophecies that its terms—and convertibility in particular—could never be fulfilled, but members of Parliament voted for it, as much in the belief that it was the beginning of a co-operation between Britain and the United States in peacetime which was essential if the peace was to be won as on its intrinsic merits. Events have shown them right. Convertibility did not prove possible for Britain, and the attempt to establish it brought her nearest to the point of collapse; yet the loan gave her time to show that she was capable of recovery, and also gave time for American opinion to understand the role that it must play in the postwar world. There are many people in Britain today who argue that without the loan there would have been no Marshall Aid, and without Marshall Aid Europe, and perhaps even Britain, would already be under Communist domination.

Today that fear is far behind. Britain's position has improved to an extent even greater than the greatest optimist expected. In 1947 the total deficit incurred by the sterling area with dollar countries was more than $4,000,000,000; by the end of 1948 this had been reduced by more than half to $1,700,000,000 and, instead of a deficit with the world as a whole, Britain's accounts were practically balanced. In addition, Britain had subscribed nearly $600,000,000 to U.N.R.R.A. and lent or given nearly $2,500,000,000 in sterling to other European countries in a joint effort for recovery. She has also lent sterling to the colonies for the development of their resources.

At the present time the dollar deficit is being met by gifts from the United States under the European Recovery Program and by loans from Canada. These facts have been emphasized so often by the British government that every family knows that without American help recovery would be impossible; and every family also knows that until Britain is standing on her own feet there will be no relief from the famous program of austerity. Sir Stafford Cripps in his 1949 budget emphasized Britain's position in an almost brutal way, forcing people to realize that their only hope lies in increased production. In spite of trade-union pressure for some concessions he insisted that wages and dividends must not rise until a greater output can be guaranteed.

The government's methods of achieving recovery are a matter of acute controversy both inside and outside Britain. Conservatives insist that it is being done not because of, but in spite of, their present leaders. They claim the credit goes to the 80 percent of industry still in private hands which is producing the desired results only by fighting its way through red tape. The Socialists, on the other hand, insist that only because of controls has it been possible to keep essential industries supplied in face of a shortage of basic materials; furthermore, unless a minimum standard of life had been maintained by food subsidies and a strict rationing of consumers' goods, it would have been impossible to get the co-operation and good will of the working people upon whom production ultimately rests.

In the meantime many Americans have watched the nationalization program with dislike; and when the government took over powers to direct labor, they were openly alarmed. Britain under a Socialist government, they said, was steadily emerging into just such a totalitarian state that America fought the war to prevent.

The truth is that whatever government had been in office many controls resulting in infringements of human liberty would have had to be imposed, for Britain is fighting a battle as decisive as the war itself. The government has been careful to use its powers cautiously, and out of the half a million people who passed through the labor exchanges in 1948 only three hundred were directed, and even these were given a free choice within the industry to which they were assigned. The fact that this policy is not a whim but a vital necessity is illustrated by the attitude of trade-union leaders, who give it their support in the belief that the loss of freedom is small compared to the loss which might result from unemployment if Britain failed to recover.

Today most British people, whatever their party loyalties, feel that the government has done well after a shaky start. During the first two years there was a lack rather than an excess of planning; and the fact that the Chancellor failed to deal in time with growing inflation and persisted too long in the attempt to carry out the convertibility obligation of the 1945 loan brought the country to a perilous position in 1947. But the advent of Sir Stafford Cripps as controller of the country's economic life, a sustained effort in almost every important industry, and a really able set of planners changed the situation.

In 1948, perhaps for the first time in history, a planned economy was seen to work brilliantly in a democratic country. Instead of compulsion, the weapon of totalitarian planners, constant and patient explanation by radio and newspaper, and above all in Parliament, where every major order and control was tirelessly debated, brought sufficient understanding to the majority of people for them to make the required effort. Production in 1948 was 15 percent higher than in 1938, and exports were nearly 50 percent higher.* Unemployment hardly existed. And by reducing her demands for dollar help by a quarter for the year

* Volume, not value.

1949-50 Britain showed, in the words of Thomas Finletter, that she was "moving in a straight line toward the objective of a dollar balance at the end of a four year period."

Nevertheless, Britain's battle is far from won. She is using the money America is giving her to buy grain, cotton, petrol, and heavy machinery on which her manufactures depend and which are vital to her recovery. The only way she can close the huge dollar "gap" which still faces her is by finding alternative sources of supply outside the dollar area and by selling more goods inside the dollar area. And neither of these things is easy to do.

The attempt to invade the North American market on a large scale is an entirely new venture for Britain. Before the war she sold the U.S. little over 15 percent of her total world export. There was scarcely a single British commodity of which America was the largest buyer; even Australia with 1/25 the population was a larger customer, and Eire was almost as great.

Although Britain bought between three and four times as much from the United States as she sold to her, in those days it did not matter. She secured all the dollars she needed from countries such as Malaya, India, and West Africa, who paid for the manufactured goods she sent them with the dollars they earned from raw materials. In addition, the Union of South Africa was able to offer new gold. But today all this has changed. Far from having dollars to spare, most of Britain's customers are in desperate need of them to buy commodities that once came from Germany and Japan. And Britain, therefore, must make strenuous efforts to elbow her way into the American market. These efforts are receiving every aid and encouragement from the British government. In the spring of 1949 Harold Wilson, the President of the Board of Trade, announced: "The task of expanding exports to North America is one of the greatest challenges in all our history to the merchant adventuring spirit of our traders." As a result a publicity drive has been launched to reorganize old-fashioned selling methods, and instead of concentrating mainly on quality goods for the eastern seaboard

and large towns, the British are aiming at markets in other parts
of the United States where lower-priced goods are needed. The
chief exports which she is trying to expand are: textiles, clothes,
motorcars, pottery, tin, and light metal goods. And efforts are
being made to increase such services as insurance, shipping,
and tourism.

The United States government expects Britain to balance
her payments as quickly as possible. It knows that the only way
she can do so is by penetrating the American market; yet at
the same time it has imposed certain conditions which make
British recovery more difficult and to many foreigners appear
to offer a baffling contradiction.

For example, shipping has always been one of the main industries of the U.K., and British costs are still lower than those
of the U.S. Even so, the American government, at the request
of its own shipping interests, insists that a half of the goods sent
to Europe under the Aid program shall be carried in American
ships. This, of course, reduces the total value of the Aid granted
and restricts British earning capacity in one of its strongest fields.

The same is true of rubber. The rubber industry in Malaya,
a British colony, earned more dollars in 1948 than all the U.K.
exports put together, yet these earnings would have been much
larger if the American synthetic rubber industry had been restricted to the statutory minimum of production required on
grounds of security. The British well understand that the
American synthetic rubber industry is essential in time of war;
but synthetic rubber is neither cheaper than nor superior to
natural rubber and if, instead of producing more than twice as
much as the law demands, Americans bought natural rubber,
they would go a long way, by this act alone, to bring the dollar
deficit of the sterling area to manageable proportions.

The need for Britain and other countries to cut their dollar
purchases has resulted in further complications. American trade
policy is based upon the principle of nondiscrimination. This
means that goods from all countries must compete on level
terms in every market. It was the policy pursued by Britain in
the nineteenth century when she was the main industrial coun-

try of the world. In theory it should please everyone because everyone likes to buy in the cheapest market, but in practice, when so many countries are short of dollars and when other countries are backward and require their infant industries to be fostered and protected, cheapness is not always the most important thing. For instance, the United States itself has departed from the principle in its relations with the Philippines, Puerto Rico, Hawaii, and Cuba; it discriminates against sugar from the rest of the world in favor of sugar from countries where its own nationals have large investments. All the European countries discriminate in the same way in favor of their own colonies, and Britain also grants preferences to some of the products from her Dominions. These are what are known as imperial preferences.

Although the policy of nondiscrimination is designed to break down these preferences and has been written into the trade agreements which have been signed by most of the nations of the world at Havana and Geneva, it is plain that it cannot be carried out in the world as it is today. In each of those agreements there are clauses which allow exceptions to be made and at the moment the exceptions are more common than the rule. Just as the United States is not prepared to forgo the preferences which it grants to the islands of the Pacific and Caribbean, neither Britain nor the other countries of western Europe can afford to forgo preferences which they grant to their colonial territories.

Even between the major countries of the world the attempt to enforce the policy is leading to many absurdities. When every country is short of dollars it is inevitable that dollar purchases should be cut; but if every time a country is forced to restrict dollar imports it is also forced to restrict imports from the rest of the world, the inevitable result is a reduction of world trade from which the United States and all other countries will suffer. For instance, recently Canada was buying more from America than she was selling to her and was forced, therefore, to cut down on three hundred articles of import from the United States. Among them were chocolate and jewelry. Applying the rule of nondiscrimination, the Canadians duly placed a ban on the import of chocolate and jewelry from Britain, although Britain had chocolate and jewelry to sell and the Canadians had more sterling than they knew what to do with.

Films are another example which have aroused great concern in Britain. British people love films and in 1947 more than thirty million went to the movies every week. Most of them prefer American films to British—or at least the average American film to the average British film. But the British government, with general approval from the public, decided that films were one of the luxuries which the British people would have to curtail because the dollars which had formerly been spent on American films were needed to buy essential raw materials such as cotton, which go into manufactured goods, and in turn buy bread. The British understood that this sacrifice was necessary and started to try and produce more films themselves. When, therefore, the American government, on behalf of the American film industry, protested that this was "discrimination" and demanded that more American films be imported into Britain, people were perplexed. "Surely," they argued, "if the Americans discovered we were spending the dollars they are giving us on going to the cinema rather than on material that will help us increase our exports they would be the first to object."

To this the Americans reply that by making films or buying goods from other countries at higher prices than those which reign in the U.S., the British are increasing the all-round cost of their production and therefore making it more difficult for themselves to compete in the American market. No doubt this is true, but the British point out that no man who is heavily in debt would try and meet his obligations by incurring even heavier debts with his chief creditor. Even if the value of the pound were reduced in terms of the dollar so that British exports became cheaper for Americans to buy, this would only mean that imports from the U.S. would become more expensive. As imports are likely to exceed exports for the next two or three years such a reduction would make matters worse.

The truth is that if the United States wishes the rest of the world to become independent of its aid by 1952 it must accept some discrimination against itself for the moment. It is only by buying as much as they can from each other in the immediate future that the other countries of the world can bridge the dollar gap and balance their payments. Once that has been done, and stability has been restored, then world trade as a whole should begin to increase, and the United States to reap the benefit of the aid it is now giving.

The British leaders do not underestimate the difficulties of the U.S. administration. The American government, with the general support of its people, has adopted a policy which is the hope of the world and which in the long run must be in the interests of the United States; but this policy undoubtedly means that some American businesses will not be able to expand as rapidly as they had hoped. The British themselves are in much the same position in regard to western Europe, for if western Europe is to unite and to plan its industries as a whole, some British concerns will have to make sacrifices in favor of former rivals on the Continent; and against this there will be considerable resistance. But just as the United States is bringing pressure to bear on the British government to overcome this resistance, so the British feel that they can ask in return that the same understanding and firmness be applied to American interests when, for the sake of world recovery, a sacrifice is demanded of them.

Looking ahead Britain has two other cards in her hand. One is the colonies and the other western union. Almost all the colonies of the world belong to the countries of western Europe and of these the largest proportion belongs to Britain. In the colonies are to be found many of the raw materials the world badly needs, such as copper, tin, gold, diamonds, uranium, bauxite, and timber. Other commodities such as vegetable oils, fats, fertilizers, cocoa, and fibers can be produced there, but much of this actual and potential wealth lies in regions which

are remote and where there is no skilled labor. Yet today the
demand is so urgent that what has been uneconomic may now
be worth while.

The difficulties of colonial development are far greater than
is generally imagined. The simple view that in Africa there are
large areas waiting to be exploited if only sufficient capital is
forthcoming is not borne out either by experience or by scientific
investigation. The soil of Africa is thin and over most of the
continent there is a dearth of water. In spite of considerable
research a rotation of crops has not yet been discovered which
will allow intensive cultivation. In a great portion of the country it is still necessary to give the soil back to the forest for
seven out of every eight years in order to restore fertility; and
although the British are making large-scale experiments in the
mechanized production of ground nuts in Tanganyika, and
attempting a rotation with sunflower and other tropical plants,
they are still only at the experimental stage.

Elsewhere in tropical countries extensive cultivation is only
possible if the land can be inundated to grow rice. In other
words, the dangers of soil erosion which Vogt has recently
emphasized on the American continent are far greater in almost
all the colonial territories which lie within the tropical zone.

Added to these difficulties, the majority of the people are
still extremely primitive. In parts of East Africa there are tribes
existing today who, in spite of a history of two thousand years,
have still learned no better than to till the ground with pointed
sticks. They have not even discovered the spade. There are
others whose wealth is still counted in camels or cattle and who
consistently overstock the territory they inhabit, with the result
that in many millions of square miles the soil has been exhausted and there is overcrowding and famine. A large part of
Africa is inhabited by people of the Mohammedan faith, but in
the center of the continent there are millions whose beliefs are
still pagan and who, in spite of Western rule, are still largely
under the influence of the witch doctor. Even in Nigeria, the
largest and one of the most advanced of the British colonies, it

is so difficult to hold a census that the best estimates cannot assess the population within a margin of five million.

The reasons for these primitive conditions are the same everywhere. Because of their ignorance of agriculture the people are underfed and as a result the majority of them are susceptible to disease. In some areas as much as 90 percent of the population is suffering from malaria and in others sleeping sickness and hookworm are almost as prevalent. The tendency to disease is strengthened by the climate, in which carriers such as the mosquito and tsetse fly flourish, and by native customs such as polygamy, which, contrary to expectation, has often resulted in a decrease rather than an increase in population because of the amount of disease spread. The people lack energy and by Western standards are inefficient. No matter how much capital equipment is provided, lasting progress can only come if these basic deficiencies are met.

The western European countries are more fully aware of these problems than the rest of the world. For many years research in tropical diseases and biology has been carried out on a large scale, and considerable development has been made. Critics are always more vociferous than constructors, but if an objective examination were made it would almost certainly be found that greater improvements in the standard of living have been made in territories dependent upon western European countries than in other tropical areas. As an example, the development of the plantations of the *Huileries Congo Belge* is as good a piece of pioneering as anything that has been seen since the opening up of the West of the North American continent; the Gezira scheme in the Sudan and the co-operative experiments on Mount Kilimanjaro under British guidance are equally impressive.

Since the Second World War a series of conferences has been held at which the countries of western Europe as well as South Africa have been represented. They have discussed a variety of subjects including labor relations, soil conservation, tourism, communications, and the combat of malaria and sleeping sickness; indeed co-operation in the field of colonial development is closer at this moment than co-operation in Europe itself.

The British contribution toward colonial development is the largest and takes two forms. They have demanded from each of their forty colonies a ten-year plan of development and welfare covering every aspect of the people's life. This is based on the realization that all progress in backward territories depends upon teaching the laws of good husbandry and hygiene. Toward these plans the British people are giving outright $480,000,000; to this sum money that the colonies themselves can raise by loan or taxation is added. In Nigeria, for example, which has five million inhabitants, the British contribution is $92,000,000 and another $88,000,000 has been added by the people of the colony. The money will be spent on agricultural development, education in the broadest sense, and small-scale industry; and there is no doubt that more depends upon the success of these individual plans than any others.

The second form of development is the founding of two great corporations to carry out schemes on a wide and spectacular scale. The Food Corporation finances undertakings in various parts of the world and has so far been responsible for the production of ground nuts in Tanganyika by mechanized cultivation, and for schemes in Australia to produce meat. The Colonial Development Corporation with an initial capital of $400,000,000 only operates in colonial territories and finances or undertakes anything from a scheme for the mass production of eggs in the Gambia, on the coast of West Africa, to the building of hotels in Jamaica for tourists from the United States. The difficulty facing both these corporations is a shortage of capital equipment and technicians; and if President Truman's offer to assist in the development of backward territories is to take practical shape there is no doubt that it is in this sphere that it can help most.

Nevertheless, however spectacular the experiments which these corporations may carry out, they are unlikely to achieve any lasting success unless they are closely linked to the basic development and welfare which each colony is planning for itself.

Progress itself brings its own problems. Large-scale development of either industry or agriculture concentrates the African in new communities, breaks up his tribal life, and leaves him without tradition or security. In the Western Hemisphere we are so accustomed to the earning of wages that it is hard for us to understand how such a step can be a revolution, but in most African communities wages are not earned and each man does his work as part of a family in a tribe in which everyone has obligations and rights. It is a feudal system. When this system is broken down and men find themselves in communities which have no customs, and no obligations beyond those for which they are paid, they are apt to degenerate. The truth of this can be seen throughout the whole of South Africa and was well exemplified in the riots which took place in Durban at the beginning of 1949. Western methods of organization through trade unions are not easily understood by those who have no industrial background; and the creation of social life in a brand-new community for people, many of whom are pagan and whose only experience has been tribal life, is difficult in the extreme. The witch doctor is some check on men's predatory instincts and when he is removed and there is no religion or code of ethics to take his place it is not surprising that people find it hard to understand why honesty is important.

These reasons, combined with the most formidable obstacle of all—the fact that in most of the continent white settlement is either forbidden or impractical—means that development in Africa is bound to be slow, and can offer no short-term solution to Europe's problems. Since the war both the tsetse fly and malaria have been conquered in small areas, and, if these experiments can be applied on a large scale, not only will the health of the African improve but the population will greatly increase. In that case all the food the continent can produce will be needed by its own people, who already number more than 150 million; but provided the food is there, efficiency and enterprise

should increase as well, and world trade should expand. This is
the hope that underlies the efforts that Britain and the European
powers are making.

Because of the slowness of colonial development it is often
argued that the countries of western Europe have more immediate advantages to gain from union among themselves. In
western Europe there is a productive capacity second only to
that of the United States and a traditional skill which, if properly
mobilized, would put European goods on the market at competitive prices. To Americans, with the history of their own
federation behind them, the conclusions to be drawn from this
seem obvious; the countries of Europe should abolish the trade
barriers which divide them, federate, and plan their production
as a whole.

To Europeans the solution is not quite so easy. They can see
that, if it were possible to organize their 270 million people as
a single community, all would benefit in the long run; but they
also know that the process might demand such sacrifices from
sections of each country that it would be impossible to carry it
through except under a dictatorship or during a war. The
British in particular, therefore, who have achieved a remarkable
degree of stability since the war, are cautious in their approach,
but in the European Council which began its existence in 1949
they hope to find means of increasing production and trade
without causing dislocation which would present opportunities
for the Communists to exploit.

But both the colonies and western union are long-term policies, and Britain's immediate future depends on whether she
can close the dollar "gap" by 1952. The fact that America is
subsidizing Britain to the tune of 6 shillings a week per family
is well known to the British people. And this generosity is not
taken for granted. British people feel deeply indebted to
America, and instead of disliking their creditor, a practice which
is usually regarded as inevitable, friendship for the United
States has never been firmer, or gratitude more genuine. Win-

ston Churchill described Lend-Lease as "the most unsordid act in history." And most British people think of Marshall Aid in the same light. Recently I overheard a conversation between two men on a train.

"And what's more," one of them was saying, "they're careful of our feelings. The Americans I know act as though it was perfectly natural to help us. . . ."

His companion nodded solemnly. "They're real gentlemen," he said. And this from the English is a tribute indeed.

CHAPTER 24

Western Union

I represent a party which does not yet exist:
civilisation. This party will make the 20th century. There will issue from it, first, the United
States of Europe, and then the United States of
the World.

—VICTOR HUGO

BURKE once said that when bad men combine good men associate. Under the threat of Soviet arms and the menace of Soviet communism the free countries of Europe are taking their first, uncertain, and historic steps toward federation. The course of civilization depends on their success, and their success depends on the moral leadership of Britain.

Britain goes to the Council of Europe as the most disciplined, the most unified, the most respected, and the most experienced of all the democracies. She understands the art of association. Not only is she the head of a great Commonwealth of Nations which represents the most remarkable collaboration of modern times, but her very life as a European power has been built on the principle of uniting in time of danger. Five times during the last four and a half centuries she has fought to prevent the Continent from coming under the grip of any single state; and she has triumphed each time by gathering the smaller countries of Europe into a grand alliance which, in the last thirty-five years, has been joined twice by the United States.

In 1940 she went farther. When France was on the threshold of capitulation Mr. Churchill held out an offer of common citizenship with Britain. Although this proposal was not accepted, it gave birth to the idea of western union.

Today a real working union has become a necessity, for the old system of alliances is no longer practicable. The countries of Europe are too impoverished to build up adequate defenses on independent lines. Their only hope lies in pooling their military resources and planning a common strategy under a single command.

Mr. Churchill drew the attention of the world to the urgent necessity for military union in his speech at Fulton, Missouri, in 1946, which drew such bitter criticism but now is regarded as prophetic. However, some time before the address was delivered Ernest Bevin had already begun to seek agreement in Europe for a common defense plan. These negotiations were successful and resulted in the Brussels Pact, which was signed in 1948 by the Foreign Ministers of the United Kingdom, France, Holland, Belgium, and Luxembourg.

This was a momentous step. For the first time in history countries at peace bound themselves to collective military planning. They set up a committee of Defence Ministers and under that a joint committee composed of Chiefs of Staffs to plan strategy, and another joint committee to co-ordinate the production of armaments and supplies. And they agreed to fight under a single command. At present their leaders are Field Marshal Montgomery and Air Marshal Robb.

But the Brussels Pact was only a beginning. No one supposed that these nations were strong enough to stop the Red Army from overrunning the Continent. The signing of the Atlantic Pact, therefore, was hailed as the second great step in the process of unification, for Europeans believe that it means the United States not only will support them if Russia attacks but will join in their plans to prevent an attack from taking place.

However, there is little point in nations concentrating on their frontiers if the enemy is at their back. When the war ended Europe was exhausted, impoverished, and cynical, and the Communists were increasing so rapidly that in France and Italy they composed the largest single party in the state. In an effort to stop the rot America extended Marshall Aid, which is the foundation on which all reconstruction is now taking place. But

America cannot go on carrying the burden indefinitely. Her financial assistance comes to an end in 1952, by which time Europe must be ready to stand on her own feet. Can she do it? Can she ever again build an economy which will provide her people with an adequate standard of living? Can she ever again give them a faith which will seem worth while defending, with all the sacrifices that defense demands?

Many people believe that her only hope lies in tightening the economic and political ties between her nations. This they call "western union." The term, however, is vague and elastic; although it contains many ideas it has not yet assumed a definite form and, consequently, it means different things to different people. Its shape and its growth rest with the British, for Britain is the pivot around which Europe revolves, and without her collaboration the whole structure would soon fall to the ground.

Today there are two opposing schools of thought in England based, fundamentally, on conflicting opinions concerning the national recovery. The advocates of one school believe that Britain will never again be able to balance her trade alone. They point out that the world trade in manufactured goods has been falling for a generation and yet Britain is trying to capture even more trade than she had before the United States became a serious competitor. They predict that this will fail and claim, therefore, that the whole basis of Britain's economy must be radically altered.

Britain needs larger home markets which, they say, only Europe can provide. If the 270,000,000 people of western Europe, with all their ingenuity and productive skill, were combined in one economic unit, wasteful competition would disappear and they would be able to sell in world markets on equal terms with the United States.

This argument has always appealed to Americans. Averell Harriman voiced the views of many of his countrymen when he said recently that "high living standards in the United States . . . had been possible only because the United States has an open, continent-wide trading area" and that "improved productivity of European labour is similarly dependent on the establishment of larger open markets that permit industrial specialization on a geographical basis."

Americans, however, are apt to oversimplify the picture. They often point to the federation of their own thirteen states as an example and ask why Europe cannot do the same. But this is a misleading comparison. First of all, the American states were unified by generations of British rule; they shared common customs, a common language, and a common law. And aside from this, a large and unexplored continent lay at their feet. The people of Europe not only have differences in culture and outlook which have been ingrained by several thousand years of history, but live in thickly populated areas whose resources have long ago been fully developed.

Even those Englishmen who believe that economic federation must come are conscious of the immense difficulties. If tariffs were abolished there is little doubt that the Belgian textile industry would expand at Britain's expense for the Belgians have a lower standard of living; the same is true of German steel, which would undercut both the French and the British; and many continental countries would be able to produce vegetables at a price that would severely damage British horticulture.

In the beginning this would mean rising unemployment for the British, and for other countries whose established industries were hit in the same way. If labor could move about freely, as it can in the United States, the situation would not be so serious, for Frenchmen, Englishmen, or Germans could find work in other countries. But the language barrier is a formidable obstacle that will take many years to remove. And at the present time Europe is still desperately short of houses.

However, assume for the moment that these difficulties are overcome, and labor has full mobility. At once fresh problems arise. The British have the most highly developed system of social security in the world, which, of course, is financed by the British taxpayer. No other European country has a similar system because the people will not agree to the high taxation necessary to support it. Are the English to give the foreigners who flow into Britain the advantage of their social services, and yet when they go abroad to receive nothing in return? Recently I heard a Frenchman and an Englishman arguing on this subject. The Frenchman was a fervent advocate of western union but when the Englishman insisted that economic federation could only take place if the French would mend their ways and pay their taxes he grew indignant: "We fought the war for freedom," he said, "and we're not going to have a lot of income tax inspectors snooping around. As far as taxation is concerned you'll have to mind your own business."

Unfortunately in a joint economy taxation becomes a joint responsibility. The British balance their budget; if the pound sterling were merged into a common currency it would mean that the exchange value of that currency would be at the mercy of an inflation caused by the French or the Italians. It would almost certainly have to be devalued in terms of dollars. And as a result everything that Europe buys from the United States would become more expensive.

The advocates of economic union believe that eventually all these obstacles can be overcome. But even so, they know that a joint European economy can still only succeed on one condition: that the United States will allow imports to compete freely in the American market. For no matter how much Europe expands its trade it must buy cotton, petrol, wheat, and tobacco from the North American continent; and it therefore must earn the dollars with which to do it.

This means that if America wishes to see complete European fusion she herself must eventually pull down her tariffs. When Governor Dewey visited the British Parliament in May, 1949, and was asked whether he thought American businessmen understood this he replied in the negative. He said quite frankly that if imported European goods undercut American goods there would be an immediate outcry. Yet in the same speech he urged the British to make the sacrifices on behalf of western union which he said Americans were not ready to make on behalf of the world.

For all these reasons most of the Englishmen who believe in union know that it can only come gradually. The merging of interests must be done in such a way that new industries are built up to replace old ones that are forced to close shop. Each country is living on such a narrow margin that serious dislocations would cause grave industrial unrest which might give the Communists the very ascendancy that western union is designed to prevent.

In spite of these fears, there are a handful of people in Britain who believe in immediate political federation. They are known as "The Federalists." They argue that because the difficulties are so great, union will never come unless national sovereignty is surrendered at once; a European government must be elected to force nations to make the necessary adjustments. Although this view was shared by a good many Europeans at the end of the war, in the last few years enthusiasm for it has waned. Continental statesmen, as well as British, realize that the people they represent are not ready to put their future into the hands of a Parliament in which a majority of foreigners would have the power to decide their fate. Even though decisions are taken for the common good the medicine might be so strong it would kill rather than cure.

But these two views, one moderate and one extreme, are only variations of the same belief. There is a second school of thought which, although it supports western union, opposes economic federation in the full sense. Its followers begin by insisting that Britain is not dependent on Europe for her recovery. They point out that since Britain and the Continent are both manufacturing areas neither one is complementary to the other, for no matter how many tariff barriers are pulled down they will still be short of raw materials. It is more sensible, therefore, for Britain to concentrate, as she is now doing, on developing her colonies; to try and expand her sales in the dollar countries which can supply her with raw materials; and to increase her trade with the east of Europe. Russia has the wheat and timber that Britain wants and needs the manufactures Britain can supply in return.

Above all, they argue, Britain must not loosen her ties with the Dominions. Since the war she has received a loan of $1,250,-000,000 from Canada, as well as long-term wheat agreements which have enabled her to buy below the world price; she has received an outright gift of £30,000,000 ($120,000,000) in gold from Australia and £80,000,000 ($320,000,000) from South Africa; and South Africa, Australia, and New Zealand are concentrating on growing the foodstuffs which she needs so that she will not have to spend dollars in Canada, to which Canada has given her full consent. Such loyalty and friendship are unique and nothing should be done to prejudice them.

This, however, does not mean that Britain must remain aloof from Europe. Although economic fusion is undesirable, collaboration is essential. The sensible thing, they claim, is to co-ordinate production between the various countries of Europe so that overlapping can be eliminated. For example, both Britain and France are trying to expand their export of engineering goods. Although Britain can supply France with all the tractors she needs, the latter is planning to raise production by fifty thousand a year. The same applies to agricultural output. Although supplies from Britain's Dominions and colonies are increasing, almost all the countries on the Continent are trying to compete in the English market.

If these expansion programs could be co-ordinated each country would have more of a guarantee that their exports would find a buyer. The way that this could be achieved has already been demonstrated by the Four-Year Plan, which was drawn up jointly by the seventeen countries who asked for Marshall Aid. Each country outlined its industrial targets and submitted them to a committee for comparison and criticism. When it was found that some countries were expecting to sell far more to their neighbors than their neighbors had any intention of buying, negotiations took place and adjustments were made. The committee was purely advisory and each national government retained the right to disagree. Nevertheless, the very fact that for the first time in history countries gave one another the fullest possible information about what they intended to do was of enormous benefit: it prevented overproduction of the wrong goods at a time when materials were short and when financial losses might have had far-reaching and serious results.

This sort of planning, of course, is not union but co-operation. And as a theory it appeals to the majority of British people far more strongly than does allowing their future to be decided by continental nations who have neither the same rigorous code of ethics nor the same experience of government. This last point was brought home forcibly when America asked the countries of Europe to draw up their plans; many of them lacked the machinery and the experts to do it and consequently went to the British for help.

Whatever happens, this school goes on to argue, Britain's political stability must not be jeopardized for it is the only sheet anchor in Europe. If a country is paralyzed by strikes, unable to pay its civil servants because the people will not pay their taxes, or constantly preoccupied by changes in its constitution, it cannot prosper. These troubles have beset France and Italy since the war and are likely to upset Germany as well. Nothing would be more fatal for western Europe than that the British should be so closely tied to their neighbors that they would be at the mercy of these disorders. Besides her moral leadership Britain has made postwar financial contributions to the recovery of western Europe which are second only to those of the United States. For all these reasons, Englishmen argue that federation must be designed so that Britain has the right to retain its national sovereignty, even though it voluntarily agrees to adapt its program to the common good.

This conception of union as association rather than federation is supported by the Treasury and the Board of Trade, and cuts across all political parties. In the years immediately following the war Mr. Churchill favored a fuller merging of interests. The broad historical perspective through which he views the affairs of the world inspired him with a vision of what Europe might become, but this early enthusiasm passed, and lately he has been noticeably cautious in his utterances. On April 22, 1949, addressing the Economic Conference of the European movement he emphasized that the British had maintained their lives "by supplies of wheat, meat and other foodstuffs from the great dominions of the Empire. This trade has been built up with mutual advantage and neither we nor they can afford to relinquish the system." He went on to say that he was certain that Britain could draw far closer to Europe and enter far more forcibly into European life without abandoning the ties with the Dominions. "But I believe it would be a mistake to search for an immediate and clear cut solution. Step by step is a good principle."

These themes will be reflected in the Council of Europe. But transcending all practical considerations is an instinct in the Englishman's heart that Britain is standing on the threshold of a great moment; that the genius which has brought her safely through so many centuries must now be put to the service of others, for only by infusing Europe with her own great moral strength can she save it. "Europe is a spiritual conception," wrote Gordon Sewell. "But if men cease to hold that conception in their minds, cease to feel its worth in their hearts, it will die."

Step by step may lead from association to partnership, and from partnership to the federation of which men have dreamed so long. If this comes about, Britain's struggle to develop democratic socialism may be judged one of the great contributions of the age. For Europeans of all parties know that a merging of interests, no matter how gradual, cannot take place under a system of *laissez faire*. It can only be brought about by a common plan, a common resolve, a common vision, and a common and abiding faith.

INDEX